Unrequited Toil

Written as a narrative history of slavery within the United States, *Unrequited Toil* details how an institution that seemed to be disappearing at the end of the American Revolution rose to become the most contested and valuable economic interest in the nation by 1850. Calvin Schermerhorn charts changes in the family lives of enslaved Americans, exploring the broader processes of nation-building in the United States, the growth and intensification of national and international markets, the institutionalization of chattel slavery, and the growing relevance of race in the politics and society of the republic. In chapters organized chronologically, Schermerhorn argues that American economic development relied upon African Americans' social reproduction while simultaneously destroying their intergenerational cultural continuity. He explores the personal narratives of enslaved people and develops themes such as politics, economics, labor, literature, rebellion, and social conditions.

Calvin Schermerhorn is a professor in the School of Historical, Philosophical, and Religious Studies at Arizona State University. He is author of *The Business of Slavery and the Rise of American Capitalism, 1815–1860* (2015), coeditor of Henry Goings's *Rambles of a Runaway from Southern Slavery* (2012), and author of *Money over Mastery, Family over Freedom: Slavery in the Antebellum Upper South* (2011).

Cambridge Essential Histories

Cambridge Essential Histories is devoted to introducing critical events, periods, or individuals in history to students. Volumes in this series emphasize narrative as a means of familiarizing students with historical analysis. In this series, leading scholars focus on topics in European, American, Asian, Latin American, Middle Eastern, African, and World History through thesis-driven, concise volumes designed for survey and upper-division undergraduate history courses. The books contain an introduction that acquaints readers with the historical event and reveals the book's thesis; narrative chapters that cover the chronology of the event or problem; and a concluding summary that provides the historical interpretation and analysis.

General Editor

Donald T. Critchlow, Arizona State University

Other Books in the Series

Michael G. Kort, *The Vietnam War Reexamined*

Maura Jane Farrelly, *Anti-Catholicism in America, 1620–1860*

David M. Wrobel, *America's West: A History, 1890–1950*

Mark E. Neely Jr., *Lincoln and the Democrats: The Politics of Opposition in the Civil War*

Howard Brick and Christopher Phelps, *Radicals in America: The U.S. Left since the Second World War*

W. J. Rorabaugh, *American Hippies*

Sean P. Cunningham, *American Politics in the Postwar Sunbelt*

Jason Scott Smith, *A Concise History of the New Deal*

Stanley G. Payne, *The Spanish Civil War*

J. C. A. Stagg, *The War of 1812*

Ian Dowbiggin, *The Quest for Mental Health: A Tale of Science, Medicine, Scandal, Sorrow, and Mass Society*

Wilson D. Miscamble, *The Most Controversial Decision: Truman, the Atomic Bombs, and the Defeat of Japan*

Edward D. Berkowitz, *Mass Appeal: The Formative Age of the Movies, Radio, and TV*

Charles H. Parker, *Global Interactions in the Early Modern Age, 1400–1800*

John Lauritz Larson, *The Market Revolution in America: Liberty, Ambition, and the Eclipse of the Common Good*

James H. Hutson, *Church and State in America: The First Two Centuries*

Maury Klein, *The Genesis of Industrial America, 1870–1920*

John Earl Haynes and Harvey Klehr, *Early Cold War Spies: The Espionage Trials That Shaped American Politics*

Unrequited Toil

A History of United States Slavery

CALVIN SCHERMERHORN

Arizona State University

CAMBRIDGE
UNIVERSITY PRESS

CAMBRIDGE
UNIVERSITY PRESS

University Printing House, Cambridge CB2 8BS, United Kingdom

One Liberty Plaza, 20th Floor, New York, NY 10006, USA

477 Williamstown Road, Port Melbourne, VIC 3207, Australia

314–321, 3rd Floor, Plot 3, Splendor Forum, Jasola District Centre,
New Delhi – 110025, India

79 Anson Road, #06–04/06, Singapore 079906

Cambridge University Press is part of the University of Cambridge.

It furthers the University's mission by disseminating knowledge in the pursuit of
education, learning, and research at the highest international levels of excellence.

www.cambridge.org
Information on this title: www.cambridge.org/9781107027664
DOI: 10.1017/9781139226585

First published 2018
Reprinted 2019

Printed in the United Kingdom by TJ International Ltd. Padstow Cornwall

A catalogue record for this publication is available from the British Library.

Library of Congress Cataloging-in-Publication Data
Names: Schermerhorn, Calvin, 1975– author.
Title: Unrequited toil : a history of United States slavery / Calvin Schermerhorn,
Arizona State University
Other titles: History of United States slavery
Description: Cambridge ; New York, NY : Cambridge University Press, [2018] | Series:
Cambridge essential histories | Includes bibliographical references and index.
Identifiers: LCCN 2018011065 | ISBN 9781107027664 (alk. paper)
Subjects: LCSH: Slavery – United States – History. | Slavery – Economic aspects –
United States. | Cotton trade – United States – History.
Classification: LCC E441 .S34 2018 | DDC 306.3/620973–dc23
LC record available at https://lccn.loc.gov/2018011065

ISBN 978-1-107-02766-4 Hardback
ISBN 978-1-107-60858-0 Paperback

For Eva and Marion

Contents

Acknowledgments

This book was made possible by a fellowship at the Virginia Foundation for the Humanities in Charlottesville, the generosity of its then-president Robert C. Vaughan III, and the enthusiastic support of William W. Freehling, along with the input and suggestions of my fellow fellows in 2013–14. Since graduate school, Joseph C. Miller has shaped my understandings of slavery as history, and I'm also indebted for the input and guidance of scholars including Edward L. Ayers, Edward E. Baptist, Sven Beckert, Richard James Bell, Daina Ramey Berry, Christopher Bonner, Kathryn Boodry, Paul Finkelman, Alexandra Finley, Alan Gallay, Jerome S. Handler, Kelly M. Kennington, John Majewski, W. Caleb McDaniel, Maurie J. McInnis, Keri Leigh Merritt, Susan Eva O'Donovan, Damian Alan Pargas, Heather Cox Richardson, Seth Rockman, Caitlin Rosenthal, and Joshua D. Rothman. I'm grateful to John Ulrich at Harvard Student Resources for his assistance and to Leslie C. Doyle at Arizona State University for her fantastic work. Donald T. Critchlow and Steven Deyle provided deft editorial guidance, and thanks also to Kristina Deusch and Deborah Gershenowitz at Cambridge University Press. Arizona State University supported this book in many ways, and I wish to thank Matthew F. Delmont and Matthew J. Garcia especially. Google Books and the University of North Carolina's Documenting the American South project made so many hard-to-find volumes accessible. Thanks to Nick Brandt for supporting a preview of this work, to Clint and Eileen Merritt for lively conversations, and to Ronnie Broadfoot and Nell Carlson for warm hospitality while I worked at the Harvard Business School's Baker Library. This book would not have been possible without the loving and patient support of my wife, Margaret, and I reserve a special note of gratitude to Marion and Eva for tirelessly asking, *Daddy, tell us what you're writing about.*

Introduction

The essence of US slavery was forced labor. Enslaved people's unrequited toil built a significant portion of the nation's wealth. They labored in many farming, mining, construction, transport, and factory settings. But by the 1830s most worked in cotton fields in the Deep South in the most important sector of the American economy. The cotton bales they made streamed into factories in New and old England, spun into yarn and woven into fabric that clothed people across the globe. Cotton shipped abroad each year increased from just a few thousand bales in 1790 to 4 million by 1860. It rose as a proportion of US exports nearly fivefold from 1800 to 1820. By 1840, cotton made up half the value of the nation's exports, reaching above 57 percent in 1860. And the population of enslaved people grew rapidly too. Nearly 1.2 million bondspersons counted in 1810 became ancestors of nearly 4 million in 1860. They toiled over a landscape several times as large and were fourfold more productive in cotton yielded per enslaved worker. Slavery remade the landscape, shaping the contours of significant parts of the country.

Enslaved people became the largest share of property other than the land itself. As property they were worth correspondingly more over time. Between 1770 and 1810, slaves as capital were worth between two and a half and three years of national – not just Southern – income. The value of slaves was roughly double the national value of housing, and in the South, "slave capital largely supplanted and surpassed landed capital."[1] In 1830, aggregated slave property was worth $577 million or 15 percent

[1] Thomas Piketty, *Capital in the Twenty-First Century*, trans. Arthur Goldhammer (Cambridge, MA: Harvard University Press, 2014), 160–61 (quote, 161).

of the national wealth. By 1860, the figure reached more than $3 billion or nearly 19 percent of the total US wealth (the equivalent of $12.7 trillion as a share of 2016 gross domestic product).[2] By then slave property was worth more than all the investments in factories and railroads combined.

Cotton growth guided seemingly everything, even in parts of the country where cotton did not flourish. A slave market spanned the distance of 1,000 miles from the top of the Chesapeake Bay in Maryland to the Brazos River bottom in Texas. To get all those bondspersons into the cotton fields, enslavers broke up African American families in old neighborhoods in the Seaboard South. Those were the descendants of enslaved people brought into colonies since the early seventeenth century. And when enslavers set out to make a fortune, they took the able-bodied with them, constructing slave labor camps or what they called plantations.

And slavery affected nearly every American, in the cotton shirts, ships' sails, and banknotes made of cotton fiber. Americans tasted slavery in pies or cookies sweetened with cane sugar, chewed twists of tobacco, enjoyed a bowl of rice, or ate bread baked with Virginia wheat flour. All those commodities were slave-made. Those who savored Texas beef steaks or Southern barbecue ate products of slave labor too. And collateral industries thrived on it even where slavery was outlawed. Some New England factories made coarse woolens designed to clothe bondspersons. Northern bankers furnished capital to buy cotton acreage and slaves. Some banks even sold bonds derived from slave assets, becoming virtual slave dealers. Other city merchants from Boston, Philadelphia, and New York took commissions and shipped cotton.

At the base of those supply chains, slavery was much more personal. It was violent social control over African-descended people. Slavery in colonial British North America became closely associated with African heritage. As it developed, slavery and race became fused to such a degree that noticeable markers of African descent became disqualifications from civil rights. Over time, African-descended people had to demonstrate that they were not slaves. And for black people in most states, slavery was the basic assumption in American law. By the same token, European descent became closely associated with citizenship and a rough political equality

---

[2] Edward E. Baptist, *The Half Has Never Been Told: Slavery and the Making of American Capitalism* (New York, NY: Basic Books, 2014), 246; Samuel H. Williamson, "Seven Ways to Compute the Relative Value of a U.S. Dollar Amount, 1774 to Present," *MeasuringWorth*, online: www.measuringworth.com/uscompare/, accessed: April 10, 2017.

in the early United States, so much so that by the 1840s, a recent male European immigrant could virtually step off the ship and go to the polls to vote while an African American man whose ancestors had been in the country for several generations could not.

African-descended Americans bore the social costs of slavery. They paid several times over, in fact. They paid at the point of sale when children were stolen by strangers, when parents were snatched up by slave traders, or when spouses were separated at sheriffs' auctions following owners' deaths or business failures. Enslaved people forfeited social capital when separations prevented ancestors' wisdom and knowledge from being passed to the next generation. They paid with ruined health. Their bodies were bruised, broken, or raped through machine-tooled violence in the fields and under their roofs, tears of anguish and humiliation running down the generations. They paid for the pernicious myth that dark skin was inferior to light – that African ancestry was lower than European. And they paid with the generations-deep theft of wages, stolen inventions, and unrepaid investments in mastering the skills that produced millions of bales of cotton and other goods and commodities. Yet enslaved people did not simply struggle along with the forlorn hope of a better day.

They unfastened chains as solitary fugitives and as armed rebels. Some stood up to individual owners and overseers. Others joined invading forces. In each generation, handfuls picked up books and took up pens, using hard-won literacy to publicize African Americans' protests and visions of liberation. They worked to undermine slavery's laws and political support. In quiet places of worship, they developed new theologies, new ways of knowing, and new ways of narrating their world. African-descended artists set about creating literature, music, and poetry, fundamentals of American culture. The shared experience of forced labor bound many together, but the unruly strategies of enslavers tended to pull bonds-people relentlessly apart. Slavery was never one thing, and enslaved people were never homogenous. There was no stagnation or sleepy plantation. There was precious little community. And never before did slavery transform in such a short time and within one political nation as in the United States of America.

Cotton capitalism stood at the center of US slavery, but it was one among many variations over space and time. There was never one Slave South but "many Souths," each with differing kinds of slavery.[3] Work

---

[3] William W. Freehling, *The Road to Disunion*, vol. 1: *Secessionists at Bay, 1776–1854* (New York, NY: Oxford University Press, 1990), 35.

varied by region and social situation. Some bondspersons labored in city factories or urban dwellings. Others grew grain, sawed timber, smithed iron, milled flour, or caulked ships' hulls. Some cultivated rice in the swampy Lowcountry while others staffed Louisiana canebrakes. Bondspersons served plates of food or drove wagons, and worked on steamboats or in railroad gangs. Some were forced to perform sex work. The young pulled weeds and tended cattle. The aged cradled babies and groomed horses. And their toils changed over time. Cotton slavery, along with nineteenth-century African American language, folklore, and religious persuasions, would have been unrecognizable to the first African arrivals in British North America in the early seventeenth century. Instead of cotton slavery being normative, it should be thought of as the product of a certain time and place, distinctive in the Americas and indeed the globe, a highly commercialized outcome of a centuries-long process.

Slavery in British North America began when castoffs of a broader Atlantic slave trade arrived in distant outposts of empire. The engine of the transatlantic slave trade of the seventeenth and eighteenth centuries was sugar and, secondarily, gold and silver. But what became the Eastern United States grew no sugar, and its gold had not yet been discovered. One historian terms the first generations of enslaved people "Atlantic creoles."[4] They arrived in New England, New York, the Virginia and Maryland Chesapeake, and the Carolina Lowcountry. Atlantic creoles were often multilingual, Muslim, Catholic, or adherents of African traditional religions.[5] They generally understood the geography over which they were scattered.

On arrival in the colonies, few Atlantic creoles considered themselves African, let alone African American. Those identities took time to develop. Many seventeenth-century arrivals in New Amsterdam were from southwestern Africa and arrived speaking Kongo or Mbundu as well as Portuguese or Dutch. Some arrived from Madagascar. Others were already creolized, re-exported from the Caribbean or Brazil. The English conquered New Amsterdam in 1664, and New York became the biggest slave colony in English North America in the seventeenth century. Until 1700 more African-descended people lived in New York than in Virginia or South Carolina. In New York, African-descended

---

[4] Ira Berlin, *Many Thousands Gone: The First Two Centuries of Slavery in North America* (Cambridge, MA: Harvard University Press, 1998), 29.

[5] Stephanie Smallwood, *Saltwater Slavery: A Middle Passage from Africa to American Diaspora* (Cambridge, MA: Harvard University Press, 2008).

bondspersons tended to work on small farms or in trades and transportation. Things were different farther south.

Virginia's earliest African arrivals were also from southwestern Africa, and a few worked their way out of slavery to become small landowners. Many toiled side by side with unfree indentured servants, poor Englishmen and women in tobacco fields with whom some made common cause. But in seventeenth-century South Carolina, most enslaved people were not even African-descended. They were captured Indians, taken from confederacies reaching as far west as present-day Arkansas, exported from Charles Town to destinations like Boston and Barbados. In the seventeenth century, the English North American colonies were societies with slaves as opposed to West Indian slave societies, the difference being that societies with slaves were places in which slavery was marginal to economic activity and political institutions. Laws and customs tended to keep enslaved people in chains, but they had some degree of mobility and did not seem a grave threat to domestic security. During the eighteenth century, patterns changed.

The Chesapeake and Carolina Lowcountry emerged as slave societies in the decades after 1700. South Carolina enslavers shifted from exporting captive Indians to exporting rice. To do that they began buying Kongo and Senegambian captives (embarked from present-day Angola, Senegal, and Gambia) to toil in rice fields. As soon as the colony began importing Africans, South Carolina passed laws giving enslavers private authority to maim and kill in the name of discipline and security.

In the eighteenth century, Chesapeake tobacco planters replaced English indentured servants with imported Africans, this time from the Bight of Biafra in present-day southern Nigeria and Cameroon. Perhaps four in five were Igbo. Unlike Atlantic creoles, these bondspersons were captured from the forested interior. Captives did not arrive speaking English or other European languages, but they did carve out distinctive cultural spaces on plantations. And by the time George Washington was born in 1732, Virginia was a slave society exporting tobacco. Like the Carolina Lowcountry, Tidewater Virginia relied on its black majority as the labor backbone of the staple crop.

In slave societies, owners and managers intensified violence to boost productivity, mitigate rebelliousness, and prevent uprisings. Virginia passed laws permitting enslavers to inflict disfiguring punishments on bondspersons while requiring poor whites to perform militia service, policing the colony's growing slave population. At the same time, New York and the mid-Atlantic colonies north of Delaware relied less on slave labor. Their slave laws relaxed or fell into disuse, yet racial designations did not. Anti-black racism followed slavery's development but did not unfollow its decline. As Virginia and South Carolina became slave societies, they drew a rigid color line. Any person of African descent was presumed to be enslaved. From the Lowcountry to New England, as one historian puts it, "racial exploitation and racial conflict have been part of the DNA of American culture."[6] And as they invented racial slavery, Americans were quickly commercializing it. That made it distinctive in both North America and the Atlantic world.

Slavery was not generally commercialized in North America before the eighteenth century. In Native American contexts, captives were often incorporated – on the lowest rungs of a society – in place of lost members. They had spiritual and social worth rather than commercial value. Most captives were children and females, some traded and others captured, who were easier to incorporate than adult males. And captivity was not necessarily *better* in African or Native American contexts than in US slavery so far as material conditions or physical treatment were concerned. In the North American interior, Iroquois captives, for instance, were subject to arbitrary and intensive personal violence long after capture.[7] Comparing circumstances of personal violence versus contexts misses the point. Differing global slaveries were not qualitatively better or worse; rather they had different defining characteristics and values structures.

In precolonial West Africa, being enslaved meant *not belonging* to a lineage. Captives had political value, and enslavement did not imply chattel slavery or commercial ownership. Captives were outsiders. Lineages or kinship networks – rather than individuals – were the building blocks of polities, states, and kingdoms. Bondspersons tended to be kidnap victims, human debt payments, or war captives. Some had been condemned for witchcraft. By definition they were outside of a lineage in places in which status and citizenship were determined by membership. Slaves streaming in from tributary states or captives of foreign wars were different ethnicities than captors, but African slavery was not a function of race.

The charge that black people enslaved – and sold – other black people would not have made sense to African people whose identity was Akan,

---

[6] David Brion Davis, *Inhuman Bondage: The Rise and Fall of Slavery in the New World* (New York, NY: Oxford University Press, 2006), 226.

[7] Andrés Reséndez, *The Other Slavery: The Uncovered Story of Indian Enslavement in America* (New York, NY: Houghton Mifflin Harcourt, 2016).

Yoruba, or Bambara. To Europeans unfamiliar with the intricacies of African political economies, captives looked black or African and could be lumped together. John Pory, colonial Virginia's first elected speaker in its assembly, popularized the myth that Africans were biblically "descended from Ham the cursed son of Noah."[8] The Hamitic myth legitimating enslavement ignored historical context and difference. Some enslavers noticed differences but attributed stereotypes to them. "Igbos," writes one historian, were thought "prone to suicide and must be watched; Coromantees [Akan from present-day Ghana] were rebellious and must be chained; Angolas were passive and need not be chained." But such superficial observations mask the incredible complexity of African political, social, and linguistic diversity, along with the fact that participating in the slave trade was often a defensive strategy. Some polities, such as Dahomey in present-day Benin, were highly stratified kingdoms while others, such as the Balanta of present-day Guinea-Bissau, were acephalous (headless). Dahomey consolidated and took captives to protect its own citizens from slavery while the Balanta took refuge in places enslavers found hard to penetrate. There were other critical differences. Among African polities, linguistic differences could be as pronounced as those between English and Chinese. Some were Muslim like the states of the Sokoto Caliphate in present-day northern Nigeria; others were Christian, like the kingdom of Kongo centered in what is now northern Angola, while many were devoted both to a world-historical religion such as Islam and also the gods of their ancestors.[9] In that context, enslaved people were those without a social identity other than that of their captors. Even so, slavery within West African polities was characterized by toil and degradation.

Most enslaved people in Africa worked in food production, which was usually female gendered. Environmental conditions in forests and most savannas prevented agricultural methods using draft animals. Human power was essential. And most African slaves were female. Ironically, not belonging to a lineage could in some circumstances make slaves fit for civil service since it implied no family loyalties. And some polities fielded slave armies loyal to the government rather than to a lineage or

[8] Ibram X. Kendi, *Stamped from the Beginning: The Definitive History of Racist Ideas in America* (New York, NY: Nation Books, 2016), 34.

[9] Marcus Rediker, *The Slave Ship: A Human History* (New York, NY: Viking, 2007), 212–13 (quotations); John K. Thornton, *Africa and Africans in the Making of the New World*, 2nd edn. (New York, NY: Cambridge University Press, 1998).

faction within it. Until the nineteenth century, there were few polities in West Africa in which enslaved people labored on commercial plantations.

West African captives lived so close to the bone that few women were able to reproduce. And in response to European demand at the coast, the "way of death" usually associated with the transatlantic Middle Passage started deep inland, along a slaving frontier.[10] Some 25 million African captives were taken in the four centuries of the transatlantic slave trade, males being sold and females retained by a one-to-two ratio. For males, captivity meant the likelihood of death, if not humiliation, violence, and transport to the coast, often through middlemen, followed by incarceration and sale to European enslavers based on ships. That was no free market. On the West African coast, the one-way trade in captives to maritime buyers was overlaid with a complex web of taxes and gratuities to the local and regional authorities. In Luanda, in present-day Angola, Europeans had to pay for the privilege of buying captives, and local authorities tightly controlled trade. So too in Ouidah in present-day Benin, where the captive trade supported the Dahomey monarchy.

Sale at the coast was the torturous beginning of the transatlantic crossing. Some 12 million – mostly males – crossed the Atlantic under those circumstances over four centuries; survivors were resold and enslaved in the Americas.[11] By 1776, of all of those who sailed to the Americas, 80 percent of those who had crossed the Atlantic were African. Of the millions who crossed the Atlantic, however, about 560,000 arrived in British North America and the United States, or about 4.7 percent of the total. By comparison, 21 percent went to Spanish America; 4 percent went to the Dutch colonies; about 22 percent went to the British West Indies, including Barbados and Jamaica; more than 14 percent went to the French West Indies, including St. Domingue (Haiti), Guadaloupe, and Martinique; and 34 percent (a third) went to Brazil.[12] For many, the path was indirect, and transport among colonies was part of a terrifying ordeal.[13] That Middle Passage across the Atlantic Ocean was a journey into a new kind of slavery. It began in sugar fields where captives grew

[10] Joseph C. Miller, *Way of Death: Merchant Capitalism and the Angolan Slave Trade, 1730–1830* (Madison, WI: University of Wisconsin Press, 1988).

[11] Sowande' M. Mustakeem, *Slavery at Sea: Terror, Sex, and Sickness in the Middle Passage* (Urbana, IL: University of Illinois Press, 2016).

[12] Enrico Dal Lago, *American Slavery, Atlantic Slavery, and Beyond: The U.S. "Peculiar Institution" in International Perspective* (New York, NY: Routledge, 2016), 22.

[13] Gregory E. O'Malley, *Final Passages: The Intercolonial Slave Trade of British America, 1619–1807* (Chapel Hill, NC: University of North Carolina Press, 2016).

crops for export and intensified over hundreds of years. Slave ships arrived legally in the United States until 1808, when Congress banned the landing of foreign captives.

As it developed in the nineteenth century, US slavery became closely associated with chattel slavery. As formerly enslaved James W. C. Pennington put it, "[t]he being of slavery, its soul and body, lives and moves in the chattel principle, the property principle, the bill of sale principle."[14] Chattel slavery was the ability to sell a human being privately. It implied a market value and a cash equivalent. American enslavers bought captives with cash and credit and took out equity mortgages on slaves just as they did on real estate, the body of the enslaved person performing the function of collateral. Scholars call that commodification. In the early US republic, some states imposed restrictions on chattel slavery, such as outlawing the sale of a bondsperson under a deed of manumission (an act of freeing an individual). But even states that outlawed slavery did not convert chattel slaves to non-slaves simply because they crossed a border into free territory. Courts made that clear repeatedly. Instead, enslaved people were treated as moveable assets.

In fact, US slavery between 1815 and 1865 was a "radically commercialized" extension of slavery in the Atlantic world.[15] In that antebellum moment, argues one historian, "[s]lave property was mobile, self-supporting, more liquid than any store of value short of sterling bills, and perhaps the most attractive kind of collateral in the entire Western world."[16] Enslaved people could be converted into cash readily. Their market value was equity enslavers could leverage to raise capital. But the process did not happen immediately. The commercialization of American slavery closely followed a transition from colonial slavery to cotton slavery. The old British system of merchant capitalism supported the growth of rice, sugar, tobacco, and collateral commodities markets. It was capitalistic but organized within an imperial framework. After 1783, the American economy changed dramatically, reorienting to a new birth of capitalism. Cotton – native to Mexico but scarcely planted before the Revolution – suddenly became vitally important. And the political economy of slavery shifted.

[14] James W. C. Pennington, *The Fugitive Blacksmith; or, Events in the History of James W. C. Pennington, Pastor of a Presbyterian Church, New York, Formerly a Slave in the State of Maryland, United States* (London: Charles Gilpin, 1849), iv.

[15] Joseph C. Miller, *The Problem of Slavery as History: A Global Approach* (New Haven, CT: Yale University Press, 2012), 120.

[16] Baptist, *The Half Has Never Been Told*, 297.

That seismic transition was part of a world-historical event known as
the Industrial Revolution. Between 1780 and 1810, Britain generated
more wealth in a shorter time than any society in global history, and at
the center of that divergence from the other empires of the world was the
manufacture of cotton yarn and fabric and the money and credit that
financed it. English factory owners imported technologies from traditional centers of spinning and weaving in South Asia and China, incrementally mechanizing production while bringing divisions of labor
together under factory roofs. Water and then steam power from abundant
coal boosted efficiencies that gave northwest England a global comparative advantage in the booming textile business. London and Liverpool
merchants financed the process. And British imperial might opened markets for cheap cottons, which disrupted old patterns of trade, labor, and
consumption. In factories, workers were brought under the supervision of
owners who regimented their working days and, increasingly, policed
their behavior. Owners paid workers for their output, whether measured
in pieces or in hours spent working.

The key to American slavery was forcing work with violence and small
incentives, and wages enslaved people earned were confiscated by owners.
William Wells Brown called that "unrequited toil," which was a protest
against the dignity of fairly paid labor.[17] Even without paying bondspersons,
enslavers created factories in the fields. Enslavers strictly regimented time,
policed workers' lives, and demanded ever higher productivity. Their work
regime was fully incorporated into an emerging capitalist modernity.[18]

The process spurred cotton cultivation in many places, including the
Caribbean or West Indies, but the American South – within the newly
independent United States – had a critical advantage. "What distinguished
the United States from virtually every other cotton-growing area in the
world was planters' command of nearly unlimited supplies of land, labor,
and capital, and their unparalleled political power."[19] Ironically,
American independence gave unprecedented political representation to
enslavers. All that was needed was a strategy.

The confluence of a newly independent United States and a growth in
demand for cotton led to a vision of a continental empire. When enslavers

[17] William Wells Brown, *Narrative of William W. Brown, A Fugitive Slave, Written by Himself* (Boston, MA: The Anti-Slavery Office, 1847), 14.
[18] Mark M. Smith, *Mastered by the Clock: Time, Slavery, and Freedom in the American South* (Chapel Hill, NC: University of North Carolina Press, 1997).
[19] Sven Beckert, *Empire of Cotton: A Global History* (New York, NY: Vintage, 2014), 105.

in South Carolina and Georgia – where cotton grew well – looked to the west (lands straddling the Mississippi River), they saw forests beneath which cotton plantations could be constructed. The sovereignties of Native Americans did not seem to count much against the shimmering possibilities of a cotton paradise worked by bound laborers. When Virginia and Maryland enslavers looked to that same southwest, they viewed an outlet for their seeming surplus of bondspersons, the descendants of Igbos and Kongo captives now farming grain, cutting shingles, and transporting bushels. And when New Yorkers and other East Coast city merchants cast an eye on the distant river bottoms draining into the Mississippi River meandering toward New Orleans, they glimpsed the potential market for credit and consumer goods in the southern interior.

And those interests in cotton, slavery, and credit coalesced in the federal government. The new US republic committed itself to westward expansion, a euphemism for conquering a continental empire. What it called the Old Southwest – the lands that became Alabama, Arkansas, Mississippi, Louisiana, Tennessee, and Texas – held the key to prosperity and power. And in a generation, American exports were reoriented to this global commodity, manufactured in England, and sold seemingly everywhere from New York to Luanda to Dhaka, in present-day Bangladesh. Even New England factory owners – upstarts in the new industrial bonanza – took a friendly interest in the expansion of cotton slavery. But as slavery expansion became entrenched in the political institutions of the federal republic, slavery sowed divisions.

Enslavers were too aggressively expansionist for many fellow citizens. Beginning in the 1810s, the movement of so many bondspersons across the South and into the West created suspicion among non-enslavers. Citizens in states like Ohio and Illinois, where slavery had been prohibited by the 1787 Northwest Ordinance and outlawed in state constitutions, looked west and saw enslavers as a threat to democracy. By the same token, enslavers considered barriers to slavery a threat to their rights. Citizens taking bondspersons from Virginia to Missouri held fast to their constitutionally protected property in people. Out of that conflict grew political disagreement that fell into crisis after 1845 when the United States annexed the enslavers' republic of Texas. Historians have viewed the resulting US war against Mexico as the catalyst of the American Civil War of 1861–65, which brought chattel slavery to an end.[20]

---

[20] Michael F. Holt, *The Fate of Their Country: Politicians, Slavery Extension, and the Coming of the Civil War* (New York, NY: Hill and Wang, 2004).

I

Counterrevolutionaries

Patriots insisted that the War of American Independence (1775–82) was a struggle against British political slavery. In 1774, Thomas Jefferson, a slave owner and newly elected member of the Virginia General Assembly, voiced the widespread view that the imperial crisis was a "deliberate, systematical plan of reducing us to slavery."[1] But it was also a war to preserve and extend chattel slavery in the Chesapeake south to the Georgia Lowcountry. The seeming paradox of American freedom and American slavery is resolved by the fact that a rough political equality for whites was conditioned by if not premised on black–white inequality. Fighting for principles of political equality against a distant colonial authority, American Patriots struggled to preserve their own rights to property in people. African-descended Americans experienced the crush of those two opposing forces.[2] Boston King was one. Enslaved near Charles Town (now Charleston), South Carolina, he escaped to the British, becoming a Loyalist and – as a consequence – a man without a country. He fled to New York with the British forces. And when the war ended, he fled again, becoming an expatriate in Nova Scotia, England, and finally Sierra Leone in West Africa. Like most bondspersons, he was faced with a series of narrow, even choiceless choices, and responded the best he could to contingent circumstances.

---

[1] Thomas Jefferson cited in Peter A. Dorsey, *Common Bondage: Slavery as Metaphor in Revolutionary America* (Knoxville, TN: University of Tennessee Press, 2009), 114.

[2] Edmund S. Morgan, *American Slavery, American Freedom: The Ordeal of Colonial Virginia* (New York, NY: W. W. Norton, 1975); Gerald Home, *The Counter-Revolution of 1776: Slave Resistance and the Origins of the United States of America* (New York, NY: New York University Press, 2014).

King was born in North America to a father who had survived the Middle Passage from Africa, most likely embarked on a slave ship sailing from Luanda in present-day Angola. "My father was stolen away from Africa when he was young," he testified in 1798.[3] Between 1730 and 1744, nearly three-quarters of South Carolina's slaves had suffered capture and sale in the Kongo-Angola region. They were overwhelmingly male, and many captives were prisoners of war like the leaders of the 1739 Stono Rebellion. When Spanish authorities in Saint Augustine welcomed enslaved refugees fleeing down the coast from Carolina owners, they found that they were welcoming fellow Catholics. King's father was a devoutly religious Anglican, although a law passed at mid-century outlawed missionary work to slaves. After 1750, most captives came from West Africa. King said nothing of the origins of his mother, but she was a seamstress and a healer adept at herbal remedies learned from local Indians. South Carolina has been termed a "Colony of a Colony" because in the eighteenth century, it produced rice and other foodstuffs for the British sugar islands along with export commodities like indigo.[4] Rice-growing South Carolina used slave labor to grow food that other enslaved people would consume.

By the time Boston King was born in 1760, South Carolina was majority black, and majority enslaved. He was spared fieldwork. When he was six, he performed household chores, and at nine he was tasked with tending cattle. King became a groom's assistant, taking care of horses for a master who enjoyed the popular sport of horse racing. He fell in with chums who taught him to curse and swear. At twelve years old, he had a dreamlike vision of the Apocalypse including a glimpse of damned souls. King became a Christian. He quit cursing and keeping bad company, yet he could not advance in his faith through learning or public worship. But faith did not keep him from hardship. For losing or misplacing a tool, "my master beat me severely, striking me upon the head, or any other part without mercy." The beatings came so hard that he could not work for weeks at a time.[5] The War of Independence became King's path out of slavery.

---

[3] Boston King, "Memoirs of the Life of Boston King, a Black Preacher: Written by Himself, during His Residence at Kingswood School," *The Methodist Magazine* (March–June 1798), 105 (quotation), online: http://antislavery.eserver.org/narratives/boston_king/, accessed: July 29, 2016.

[4] Alan Gallay, *The Indian Slave Trade: The Rise of the English Empire in the American South, 1670–1717* (New Haven, CT: Yale University Press, 2002); Peter H. Wood, *Black Majority: Negroes in Colonial South Carolina from 1670 through the Stono Rebellion* (New York, NY: Random House, 1974), 13–34 (quotations).

[5] King, "Memoirs of the Life of Boston King," 107.

It was a perilous road. British forces drove a wedge between Patriot enslavers and bondspersons like King. In 1779, General Sir Henry Clinton had issued a proclamation promising slaves freedom in exchange for service. It was patterned on a similar proclamation given by Virginia governor Lord Dunmore in 1775, which summoned black Loyalists by the hundreds. In South Carolina, thousands of enslaved people fled to the British. The British took Charleston in May 1780, but King initially hesitated. His parents were still in the area, and fleeing to the British meant possibly losing contact. But one day he was accused of stealing a horse and, faced with severe punishment, King recalled, "I determined to go to Charles-Town, and throw myself into the hands of the English." It was a desperate move. "They received me readily," he sighed, "and I began to feel the happiness of liberty, of which I knew nothing before." Liberty was tenuous and solitary. "I was much grieved at first," he recalled, "to be obliged to leave my friends, and reside among strangers."[6] Liberty nearly killed him. King contracted smallpox and, near death, was aided by an English soldier. King's loyalty followed from his duty to the man. He worked as a nurse and as a manservant. And when the British lost South Carolina, King departed Charleston on a British warship. He wasn't alone.

Throughout the colonies, African-descended Loyalists aided a counterinsurgency against Patriot rebels. While Patriots were creating clandestine committees of correspondence to organize resistance against British authorities, they became alarmed when African-descended people formed similar communications networks. A Georgian worried to John Adams in 1775 that "[t]he negroes have a wonderful art of communicating intelligence among themselves; it will run several hundreds of miles in a week or fortnight."[7] Patriots insisted that they were fighting against political enslavement by Britain. But facing a counterrevolution of black freedom, they were careful to distinguish political slavery for whites from chattel slavery for blacks.

So many Africans had landed recently in the colonies that Patriot officials became panicked over possible slave rebellions. Virginia attempted to impose a prohibitive tax on slave imports, but Parliament overruled it. Both North Carolina and Georgia suspended slave imports. As disagreements between the colonies and Britain mounted in 1774,

---

[6] King, "Memoirs of the Life of Boston King," 108.
[7] Sylviane A. Diouf, *Slavery's Exiles: The Story of the American Maroons* (New York, NY: New York University Press, 2014), 117.

Massachusetts, Connecticut, and Rhode Island banned the slave trade, citing its immorality. Whatever the reasons, the colonies suspended the importation of captives susceptible to the contagion of liberty that Patriots themselves were carrying up and down the Eastern Seaboard.[8]

African-descended Americans seized the ideas of the Revolution and claimed them as theirs. Patriots' rhetoric of political liberty inspired protests from the enslaved, and so did a British legal case, *Somerset v. Stewart.* In 1772, word reached America of a British court's granting freedom for an enslaved man, James Somerset. Somerset was enslaved by a Boston customs official. While in England, Somerset fled from his owner after suffering injuries and abuse. When Somerset was recaptured, his owner consigned him to a ship bound for Jamaica. The court intervened and found that it was illegal for any bondsperson to be transported from England for the purpose of sale. Although ambiguous, the *Somerset* decision contributed to a rising tide of antislavery activism.

African-descended colonists seized on the case to argue that they too were free. In early 1773, African-descended Bostonians led by Felix Holbrook petitioned the governor and legislature for slavery's abolition. The legislature debated the petition, but opinion was divided. Radicals like merchant John Hancock considered it hypocritical to press for political liberty from Britain while holding slaves. But savvy political leaders like John Adams demurred. While sympathetic, he contended that it would be difficult to endorse African-descended people's calls for liberty while making common cause with Virginians and New Yorkers who owned bondspersons.[9]

Like Patriot committees of correspondence, word of the petitions from Holbrook and others traveled up and down the colonies, on the lips of black sailors and from the mouths of wagoners and travelers. It inspired similar black activism in other locales. African-descended residents of Salem, Stratford, and Fairfield, Connecticut petitioned against slavery, contending that "the Cause of Liberty" was inconsistent with holding slaves.[10] A group of black residents petitioned the New Hampshire government for freedom. Protests inspired by the *Somerset* decision erupted in New Jersey and other colonies, and in a third petition submitted to

---

[8] Edward Countryman, *Enjoy the Same Liberty: Black Americans and the Revolutionary Era* (Lanham, MD: Rowman & Littlefield Publishers, 2011).

[9] George William Van Cleve, *A Slaveholders' Union: Slavery, Politics, and the Constitution in the Early American Republic* (Chicago, IL: University of Chicago Press, 2010), chap. 1.

[10] Douglas R. Egerton, *Death or Liberty: African Americans and Revolutionary America* (New York, NY: Oxford University Press, 2009), 60.

Massachusetts authorities, enslaved people joined Holbrook and demanded liberties based on natural rights. Again, the petitioners received no official response.

In the revolutionary ferment of ideas, Lemuel Haynes gave one of the most urgent antislavery appeals building on the emerging black Patriot rhetoric. Haynes was the ideological brother of Thomas Paine, author of the radical pro-Patriot tract *Common Sense*. Haynes joined a Massachusetts militia in 1774 and a Connecticut regiment of the Continental Army during the war. He went on to become a preacher and theologian. "Liberty is [e]qually as pre[c]ious to a [b]lack man," he argued in 1776, "as it is to a white one, and [b]ondage [e]qually as intollarable [*sic*] to the one as it is to the other."[11]

Liberty has a powerful and widespread appeal, but one of the ironies of the American Revolution was that liberty for some was construed as their right to hold others in bondage. It was not merely that talk of liberty prompted a discussion of slavery, but that slavery framed discussions of liberty. When Virginia leaders like Thomas Jefferson, Patrick Henry, or George Washington raised protests to imperial authority, they did not have to look farther than their own fields to imagine the effects of political oppression. Virginians would not be made slaves of a distant, unrepresentative British government and warned Britons that a Parliament that taxed subjects without proper representation was a looming tyranny. Loyalists rejected that position and held that Parliament represented all subjects. In his 1775 pamphlet on the justice of imperial taxation, British essayist Samuel Johnson bitingly wrote: "If slavery be thus fatally contagious, how is it that we hear the loudest yelps for liberty among the drivers of negroes?"[12] After Lord Dunmore's proclamation, hundreds, if not thousands, of black Virginians fled to the British.

During the Revolution, some 100,000 bondspersons unfastened their chains. While most were later re-enslaved, many like Boston King made good their escape. But King left behind everything, including family, evacuating Charleston with the British forces for New York City, which had been under British control since the fall of 1776.

---

[11] Joanne Pope Melish, *Disowning Slavery: Gradual Emancipation and "Race" in New England, 1780–1860* (Ithaca, NY: Cornell University Press, 1998), 171.

[12] Samuel Johnson, *Taxation no Tyranny: An Answer to the Resolutions and Addresses of the American Congress* (London: T. Cadell, 1775), 89; David Waldstreicher, *Runaway America: Benjamin Franklin, Slavery, and the American Revolution* (New York, NY: Hill and Wang, 2004).

There King found himself some 750 miles away from slavery in South Carolina, but scarcely free. He attempted to ply his carpentry trade, but lacked carpentry tools and was forced to work as a domestic servant and manual laborer. After failing to earn enough in carpentry to clothe himself, he consented to serve a master who worked him for four months without pay. But life brightened on the war-torn landscape. As King scouted for work and scrounged for food, he met a fellow refugee, Violet. The thirty-two-year-old had fled an owner in Wilmington, North Carolina, about 170 miles up the coast from Charleston. The two shared a familiar accent and the experience of war.

Their courtship was brief. Boston and Violet married in 1780. Behind British lines, King was also able to worship with black Methodists, including refugees from the Virginia Tidewater. But that first year of marriage was turbulent. King came down with an illness that incapacitated him for five weeks. Scraping by, King risked re-enslavement by working aboard boats in New Jersey, attending a school at night, and learning to read the Bible. But northern New Jersey was scarcely stable. Irregular militias on both sides were taking property, harassing, and murdering one another. In late 1775, a twenty-one-year-old enslaved man named Titus had ditched his farm implements and set off for Williamsburg, Virginia, after word of Dunmore's proclamation reached Monmouth County. Two years later, the six-foot-tall "Colonel Tye" reappeared at the Battle of Monmouth. Afterward, Tye led a Loyalist guerilla band that captured supplies and killed and arrested Patriots. Operating from Refugeetown on Sandy Hook, Colonel Tye's multiracial militia enacted the Patriot nightmare of armed former slaves taking vengeance on whites.[13]

Tye's campaigns were part of the social disruptions loosed by war, which nearly swept up Boston King. British authorities in New York City received Tye's captives and paid him handsomely for much-needed supplies of livestock. But his command was short-lived. Tye died of wounds suffered in a raid in September 1780. Fleeing re-enslavement in New Jersey, Boston King escaped across the Arthur Kill River near Amboy at low tide. He crossed Staten Island and commandeered a boat that he rowed to Manhattan, where British authorities readmitted him to the city. He soon returned to Violet. "When I arrived at New York," King sighed, "my friends rejoiced to see me once more restored to liberty, and joined me in praising the Lord for his mercy and goodness."[14]

[13] Egerton, *Death or Liberty*, chap. 3.
[14] King, "Memoirs of the Life of Boston King," 158.

And while black Loyalists found freedom among the British, Patriots promised freedom to African-descended soldiers who fought for the cause of independence. Both the US Continental Army and state militias enrolled African-descended soldiers, enslaved or free, and some of the former served in place of their owners. Whatever the wishes of commanders, units tended to be integrated. Some African-descended soldiers rose to noncommissioned officer, but none was commissioned an officer. African-descended enlistees tended to serve longer than their white counterparts and made up 10 percent of the Continental Army, or about 5,000 soldiers.[15] Despite Patriot commitments to slavery's continuation, African-descended soldiers helped win the War for Independence.

By 1781, Patriots were winning the war. French military and financial assistance turned what looked like an impending American defeat in 1780 into an opening for peace negotiations. British forces invaded Virginia and from Yorktown and Portsmouth harassed the Patriots. Thousands more African-descended refugees fled to them, and British forces under Banastre Tarleton raided as far west as Thomas Jefferson's Albemarle County. Sixteen enslaved people fled George Washington's Mount Vernon on the Potomac River, and in all British General George Cornwallis's forces attracted 4,500 former slaves.[16]

Then French forces landed 3,000 soldiers and imposed a naval blockade of the Chesapeake. The British invasion of Virginia was halted. Disease ravaged British soldiers and black Loyalists alike. Epidemics of typhus and smallpox broke out in camps, killing hundreds of the British troops under General George Cornwallis. African-descended fugitives from slavery were forced into the deadly camps and perished along with British soldiers. Many who fled from their erstwhile liberators were captured by forces under Washington, who led a force from New York in response to the invasion. Cornwallis was under siege at Yorktown, and hundreds of refugees starved and perished from disease in between the beleaguered British and the Franco-American forces. Cornwallis surrendered at Yorktown, Virginia, in October 1781. As had been the case on Gwynn

---

[15] John Wood Sweet, "Venture Smith and the Law of Slavery," in *Venture Smith and the Business of Slavery and Freedom*, ed. James Brewer Stewart (Amherst, MA: University of Massachusetts Press, 2010), 83–128.

[16] Gary B. Nash, *The Unknown American Revolution: The Unruly Birth of Democracy and the Struggle to Create America* (New York, NY: Penguin, 2005), chap. 7; Andrew O'Shaughnessy, *The Men Who Lost America: British Command during the Revolutionary War and the Preservation of the Empire* (New Haven, CT: Yale University Press, 2013), chap. 7.

Island some twenty miles up the Chesapeake Bay, black refugees were in deplorable conditions as disease compounded famine. Virginia Patriot St. George Tucker observed that "[a]n immense number of Negroes have died in the most miserable Manner in York[town]."[17] The survivors would be re-enslaved. As French ships sailed back to the Caribbean, word of Cornwallis's surrender was on its way to London. The War of Independence was over.

Despite the importance of enslaved people in the Revolution, peace negotiations between British and American diplomats ignored the plight of African-descended Loyalists. Their strategic importance had disappeared. In defeat, many British officers like Banastre Tarleton betrayed little sympathy for the plight of African-descended Americans. Following the war, he would become perhaps the most energetic supporter of the transatlantic slave trade as a Member of Parliament representing Liverpool.[18] The Treaty of Paris in 1783 recognized American independence, but British negotiators consented to American demands to recover their slaves. That threatened to shatter refugee communities in New York City.

British forces evacuated New York in 1783 after news of the Treaty of Paris arrived. Enslavers arrived to claim some 6,000 African-descended refugees. King recalled seeing "our masters coming from Virginia, North-Carolina, and other parts, and seizing upon their slaves in the streets of New-York, or even dragging them out of their beds." Dread of re-enslavement terrorized many of King's friends and fellow worshippers. "For some days," he recalled, "we lost our appetite for food, and sleep departed from our eyes." But one British commander stood up for the black Loyalists who had risked so much. Disregarding terms of the peace treaty, British commander Sir Guy Carleton refused to return Boston King and thousands of others to slavery.

But that meant leaving for good. At the end of April 1783, British officials recorded 3,000 African-descended refugees in what officials called a "Book of Negroes" as part of an evacuation of Loyalists to Nova Scotia. Many were given General Birch Certificates, so called after Brigadier-General Samuel Birch who issued them. Boston and Violet King were among them. He was listed as a twenty-three-year-old "stout fellow"

---

[17] Michael A. McDonnell, *The Politics of War: Race, Class, and Conflict in Revolutionary Virginia* (Chapel Hill, NC: University of North Carolina Press, 2007), 476.

[18] Paula A. Dumas, *Proslavery Britain: Fighting for Slavery in an Era of Abolition* (London: Palgrave McMillan, 2016), chap. 1.

and she a thirty-five-year-old "stout wench," stout meaning sturdy or robust. They stepped onto dry land in early August in Birchtown, Nova Scotia, among 400 refugees who started a settlement. Birchtown was an enclave and several miles from Shelburne near the southeast tip of the island.

Life was difficult for black Loyalist refugees. Besides poor prospects in farming, the King family faced hostility from white Nova Scotia residents. In 1784, white former soldiers attacked Birchtown. Boston and Violet King went through periods of famine and hardship, working a variety of jobs. Boston became a Methodist minister at Preston, near Halifax.[19] But when the opportunity came to leave Nova Scotia with other refugees for a colony in West Africa, they took it. British abolitionists helped found Freetown, Sierra Leone, which promised to be a haven for African-descended people, including former slaves despite its close proximity to Bance Island, a hub of the transatlantic slave trade. Thomas Peters, who had fled from slavery in Wilmington, North Carolina, in 1776, led some 1,196 African-descended Canadians to Freetown after securing sponsorship in England. But the refugee colony foundered because of poor preparation, fights among the leadership, hostility from locals, and above all a disease environment that claimed the lives of most of the settlers. Colonists were forced to seek help from neighboring slave traders. Violet and Boston King emigrated in 1792 and sojourned in England in 1794. Boston taught briefly near Bristol. The Kings returned to Sierra Leone in 1796 and continued to preach their Methodist faith. But black Americans were not going *back* to Africa so much as being cast ashore in a foreign, hostile place, thousands of miles from where King's father had been embarked as a child. That odyssey ended for Boston King in 1802 when he, like Violet, succumbed to malaria on a West African landscape that was never quite home.[20]

The American Revolution decided the question of independence, but it did not decide whether slavery was a residue of the colonial past or a force shaping the future United States. Enslaved people had proved a powerful undercurrent that showed the inconsistencies in Patriots' rhetoric and Patriots' reluctance to include African-descended people in their vision of freedom and self-government.

---

[19] James W. St. G. Walker, *The Black Loyalists: The Search for a Promised Land in Nova Scotia and Sierra Leone, 1783–1870* (Toronto: University of Toronto Press, 1993 [reprint; 1976]), chap. 4.
[20] Egerton, *Death or Liberty*, chap. 8.

2

Slow Death for Slavery?

In the newly independent United States, slavery seemed to be on the road to marginality, even extinction. Britain punished the new nation for revolution by closing its West Indian markets to Chesapeake tobacco and Carolina rice, which left enslavers with surplus bound laborers working at a losing economic game. And after the tumultuous seven-year war, enslaved Americans faced a conflict of rootedness versus rootlessness, knitting ties against the constant unraveling done by enslavers. But victorious Patriots hedged against freeing bondspersons too soon. They scrambled to patch up the slave societies in the Chesapeake, Carolinas, and Georgia, while mid-Atlantic enslavers reasserted their control over African-descended people.

It is often asked why the republican principles of liberty and self-government did not apply to enslaved people. One answer has to do with the economic geography of slavery. After 1776, states with small or marginal slave populations began to abolish slavery gradually. But freedom did not equal citizenship. In the flush of Revolutionary fervor, the sole state that outlawed slavery immediately was Vermont, which had the smallest slave population. The rest of New England, along with New York, Pennsylvania, and New Jersey, refused to emancipate enslaved people, instead setting a course for gradual abolition or else leaving it to courts and African-descended people to challenge their enslavement. States dependent on slave labor did not consider abolition. But some permitted manumission or freeing bondspersons individually. Virginia, Maryland, and other states to the south (except North Carolina) liberalized manumission laws. They left in place property rights in people, and few enslaved people succeeded in bargaining their way out of bondage.

Despite British closures of West Indies rice markets, South Carolina and Georgia planters resumed importing captive Africans. Noticing such a demand, enslavers in the Chesapeake began selling bondspersons in an interstate trade. And even in states where slavery was marginal, enslavers held on to the bondspersons who had market value in other states.

States north of Delaware gradually abolished slavery, but a long colonial history of associating African descent with servitude worked against full equality even where slavery was marginal or disappearing. That perception disadvantaged free African-descended people. As colonial hierarchies crumbled, those at the bottom of the old structures of patronage often found themselves at the mercy of wage and labor markets that even in the best of times permitted workers to scrape by. The new United States was a fragile confederation of independent states that acted like small republics. When Britain formally recognized an independent United States, the federal constitution would not be drafted for four years, and like their colonial predecessors, the new states formulated individual laws regarding slavery. Between 1777 and 1804, all states north of Maryland adopted measures that set slavery on the road to abolition, most doing so gradually. During the upheavals of war, Revolutionary state governments created new state constitutions – some more than one – that experimented with republican government. Abolition appeals by black activists such as Lemuel Haynes and Felix Holbrook were part of the language of liberties and rights, and in the course of fighting a revolution for those ideals, many state legislators stood on principle when attempting to write abolition measures into law. But appeals to abandon slavery found more purchase in areas where slavery remained marginal.

Like so many other questions state constitutional conventions tackled, measures concerning slavery were subject to compromise based on competing interests. Vermont took a bold early step in its 1777 constitution, abolishing slavery and servitude for males over twenty-one and females over eighteen. The constitution established religious liberty and enfranchised nearly all adult males regardless of race or previous condition of servitude. But colorblind measures were uncontroversial in a state with a handful of enslavers and a miniscule population of black people. Not counting Native Americans, Vermont was 0.3 percent nonwhite in 1790. In neighboring New Hampshire, the language of its 1783 constitution was just as stridently pro-individual rights, but slavery was left ill-defined. The slave population fell from 633 to 158 people between 1767 and 1790 and would be counted in single digits in nineteenth-century censuses. Neighboring Massachusetts adopted similar language. The first article of the Massachusetts constitution of 1780 reads, "[a]ll men are born free and equal, and have certain natural, essential, and unalienable rights," which was essentially what Felix Holbrook had argued in 1773 and black activists like minister Lemuel Haynes and poet Phillis Wheatley articulated during the Revolution.[1] But Massachusetts omitted a clear statement of slavery's illegality.

The challenge to slavery in Massachusetts came not from freedom-seeking statesmen but from a former slave. Whether Quok Walker had the Massachusetts constitution in mind when he fled the farm of his Worcester County owner in the spring of 1781 is unclear. But the twenty-eight-year-old clearly thought himself a free man at twenty-five. He refused to return, and the enraged owner and some hired men caught up with him at the farm of his younger brother and beat him with the handle of a whip. They locked him in a barn. Walker escaped and hired a lawyer to sue not for his freedom, but for the assault.

Walker sought a legal remedy while the War of Independence was still raging in the southern part of the country. It was an exceptional move that illustrates how far Revolutionary rhetoric had penetrated the popular understanding. Walker wagered that a court would uphold the republican principles for which Massachusetts Patriots were fighting. The case, *Walker v. Jennison*, ended in the Supreme Judicial Court's 1783 ruling that "the idea of slavery is inconsistent with our own conduct and Constitution."[2] In the meantime, favorable rulings by lower courts had already freed Massachusetts resident Mum Bett, who emerged from slavery as Elizabeth Freeman.[3]

But even in freedom, women were not citizens. Married women's legal identities were still considered parts of their husbands' under laws of coverture. "I desire you would [r]emember the [l]adies," Abigail Adams wrote her husband, John Adams, in March 1776, "[r]emember all [m]en would be tyrants if they could."[4] Founders ignored such prayers. And black women like Elizabeth Freeman were doubly disenfranchised.

---

[1] Emily Blanck, *Tyrannicide: Forging an American Law of Slavery in Revolutionary South Carolina and Massachusetts* (Athens, GA: University of Georgia Press, 2014), 119 (quotation), "Slavery in New Hampshire," Slavery in the North, online: http://slavenorth.com/newhampshire.htm, accessed: July 29, 2016.

[2] *Commonwealth of Massachusetts v. Nathaniel Jennison* (1783), in *A Necessary Evil? Slavery and the Debate over the Constitution*, ed. John P. Kaminski (Madison, WI: Madison House, 1995), 18.

[3] Ben Z. Rose, *Mother of Freedom: Mum Bett and the Roots of Abolition* (Waverly, MA: TreeLine Press, 2009).

[4] Abigail Adams to John Adams, March 31, 1776, cited in Lynne Withey, *Dearest Friend: A Life of Abigail Adams* (New York, NY: Simon and Schuster, 2001), 81.

The Walker decision did not free any other slaves, but it decided that Massachusetts law did not protect slave property. The legal ambiguity worked in favor of Walker and abolition, but it also meant that any other bondsperson would have to sue for freedom. Some owners were enraged at the decision. One attempted to sell his bondspeople to Barbados. But public opinion was squarely on the side of the high court. Slavery was marginal in Massachusetts, as it was elsewhere in New England, even though New Englanders had enslaved Africans and Indians since the seventeenth century.[5] When New York and Pennsylvania confronted the issue, they also confronted financial interests in slavery.

New York made a false start in abolishing slavery. While fugitives from Virginia and elsewhere were fleeing to British-occupied New York City in 1777, the state passed a constitution that protected property, including slave property. The 1777 constitution permitted freeholders – owners of real property – to vote regardless of race. Delegate and congressman Gouverneur Morris proposed that "every being who breathes the air of this State shall enjoy the privileges of a freeman," but fellow delegates received his statement as so much bluster.[6] Several years later, future governor and chief justice of the US Supreme Court John Jay wrote to Morris and Robert R. Livingston, "I should also have been for a clause against the continuation of domestic slavery," but New York enslavers made up a considerable financial interest.[7] Black New Yorkers pressed for their freedom, and Jay led the New York Manumission Society.

Unlike elsewhere, military service was one avenue to freedom in New York. While Boston King was in New York City in 1781, the state government manumitted any enslaved person who served the Patriot cause in the state militia or in George Washington's Continental Army. The state was also willing to punish Loyalists by stripping them of slave property. Following the British evacuation, the legislature declared that known supporters of the Crown forfeited their slave property. In 1786, there were nearly 19,000 African-descended people in New York. Federal census-

---

[5] Wendy Warren, *New England Bound: Slavery and Colonization in Early America* (New York, NY: Liveright, 2016).

[6] Douglas R. Egerton, *Death or Liberty: African Americans and Revolutionary America* (New York, NY: Oxford University Press, 2009), 111.

[7] Patrick Rael, *Eighty-Eight Years: The Long Death of Slavery in the United States, 1777–1865* (Athens, GA: University of Georgia Press, 2015), chaps. 1–2; John Jay to R. R. Livingston and Gouverneur Morris, April 29, 1785, in *America's Founding Charters: Primary Documents of Colonial and Revolutionary Era Governance*, vol. 3, ed. Jon L. Wakelyn (Westport, CT: Greenwood Press, 2006), 802 (quotation).

takers would count 21,324 slaves in New York in 1790, more than half of all those held in bondage north of Maryland. The state would not pass an emancipation law until 1799, and even that measure trapped members of families in slavery until the second quarter of the nineteenth century.[8]

Pennsylvania struggled with the issue of human liberty versus property rights in its 1780 constitution. Philadelphia was the largest American city, home to the national Congress convened under the Articles of Confederation, and in many Americans' minds the epicenter of liberty. The Declaration of Independence had been drafted and adopted there. Pennsylvania was also the geographic center of Quakerism, and the Society of Friends was a vocal opponent of slavery. African-descended reformers petitioned the government to live up to the Revolution's republican ideals and restore "the common blessings" of liberty to which all Americans were entitled.[9] Besides that, Pennsylvania's population was just 3 percent black, and enslavers were distributed through a small proportion of the population. In 1780, about 400 Philadelphia residents owned 539 bondspersons, and in neighboring Chester County about 200 owners held 493 people in slavery.[10] Yet despite such a marginal interest in slavery, the state refused to end it.

After a flood of petitions and Quaker organizing, Pennsylvania passed an abolition act that failed to free any slaves. The 1780 abolition act held that any child born of a slave mother after March 1, 1780 would have to serve twenty-eight years of bondage. Any child born to an enslaved mother would still be enslaved. The measure made it possible for an owner to hold in slavery two more generations of descendants. One pair of historians contends that under Pennsylvania law, an enslaved female born in late February 1780 could give birth at age forty to a child who would not be freed by the law until 1848, nearly seventy years after the act was passed. Pennsylvania ended up abolishing slavery in 1847, but in practical terms the abolition act was a life sentence to slavery made in the name of liberty.[11] Some Pennsylvania enslavers exploited a loophole, taking pregnant bondswomen out of state so that babies would not be born under the abolition act, and the legislature had to close the loophole in 1788. Lower New England states took their cue from Pennsylvania.

---

[8] Leslie M. Harris, *In the Shadow of Slavery: African Americans in New York City, 1626–1863* (Chicago, IL: University of Chicago Press, 2003), chap. 1.
[9] Egerton, *Death or Liberty*, 98.
[10] Gary B. Nash and Jean R. Soderlund, *Freedom by Degrees: Emancipation in Pennsylvania and Its Aftermath* (New York, NY: Oxford University Press, 1991), 138.
[11] Nash and Soderlund, *Freedom by Degrees*, 111.

Rhode Island passed an abolition law in 1784, but it was also a half-measure that freed no slaves immediately. As in Pennsylvania, the Society of Friends agitated for black freedom. With the help of Quaker businessman Moses Brown (brother of slave trader John Brown), Rhode Island passed a gradual abolition measure that freed all slaves born after March 1, 1784, females at eighteen and males at twenty-one.[12] But while the measure freed Rhode Island bondspersons, shippers and merchants remained active in the transatlantic slave trade, just as they had before the Revolution. Between 1751 and 1775, Rhode Island slavers embarked 41,581 captives and sold the survivors in the Americas. In the next quarter century – even after state abolition – Rhode Island shippers embarked nearly 25,000 more captives on the Middle Passage. Following the Revolution, half of the captives embarked on Rhode Island ships were sold to Cuba, a Spanish colony. Thirty percent went to South Carolina and more than 8 percent went to neighboring Georgia. Rhode Islanders would continue to embark tens of thousands more in the nineteenth century. And yet fewer than 400 enslaved people were counted in Rhode Island in 1800, subject to its gradual abolition act.[13]

Other so-called free states were reluctant to extinguish citizens' property in people. Connecticut, home to fewer than 3,000 enslaved people, passed the Gradual Abolition Act of 1784, which freed no bondsperson then in slavery but only those born after March 1, 1784, and only after twenty-five. Life expectancy at birth was not much above thirty. It took until 1804 for New Jersey to pass a gradual abolition measure that freed all enslaved children born after the Fourth of July but also bound them to service for twenty-one years if female and twenty-five if male. Liberty ultimately fell on the shoulders of enslaved people and loved ones.[14] Enslavers' property rights was one of a constellation of impediments to African-descended people's rise from slavery. But there was a widespread expectation that slavery would be confined to a narrow patch of land on which it might be extinguished.

---

[12] Joanne Pope Melish, *Disowning Slavery: Gradual Emancipation and "Race" in New England, 1780–1860* (Ithaca, NY: Cornell University Press, 1998), chaps. 2–3.

[13] Christy Clark-Pujara, *Dark Work: The Business of Slavery in Rhode Island* (New York, NY: New York University Press, 2016), chap. 1; Gregory E. O'Malley, *Final Passages: The Intercolonial Slave Trade of British America, 1619–1807* (Chapel Hill, NC: University of North Carolina Press, 2014).

[14] James J. Gigantino II, *The Ragged Road to Abolition: Slavery and Freedom in New Jersey, 1775–1865* (Philadelphia, PA: University of Pennsylvania Press, 2015).

Early national attempts to regulate the spread of slavery were ambivalent. Congress under the Articles of Confederation prohibited slavery in the territory north of the Ohio River and west of Pennsylvania to the Mississippi River. The Northwest Ordinance of 1787 – passed while the Constitutional Convention was meeting – provided that "there shall be neither slavery nor involuntary servitude" in the territory. States carved out of it, including Ohio, Indiana, Illinois, Michigan, and Wisconsin, abolished it.[15] Some of those states, like Ohio, adopted antislavery constitutions, but others, like Indiana and Illinois, treated African Americans as second- or third-class citizens, imposing requirements that black residents post bonds, carry identification attesting to their free status, and become subject to fines or even slavery for a term should they fail to comply.[16] In 1790, the first US Congress responded to pressure from enslavers to safeguard slave property south of Virginia. It passed the Southwest Ordinance covering what became Tennessee, and providing "that no regulations made or to be made by Congress, shall tend to emancipate slaves."[17] South of Tennessee no one expected Congress to restrict slavery. And when the Thomas Jefferson administration made the Compact of 1802 with Georgia, in which that state ceded lands west of its present border to the federal government, federal authorities promised to remove Indian nations that stood in the way of slavery's expansion. So even before the rise of the cotton economy the federal government encouraged slavery's expansion into the Old Southwest and restricted it north of the Ohio River.

At the same time Americans were theorizing race and racial difference. Prejudice against African-descended people had existed at least since the early days of the slave trade from Africa, but it was not until the eighteenth century that Europeans developed an idea of white exceptionalism. Early in the century, Swedish biologist Carl Linnaeus classified human beings as a primate species and then divided humans into subspecies including Europeans, Native Americans, Asians, and Africans. While disparaging their physical features, Linnaeus contended that African-descended people were "[c]rafty, indolent, negligent ... Governed by caprice."[18]

[15] John Craig Hammond, *Slavery, Freedom, and Expansion in the Early American West* (Charlottesville, VA: University of Virginia Press, 2007), 9.

[16] Matthew Salafia, *Slavery's Borderland: Freedom and Bondage along the Ohio River* (Philadelphia, PA: University of Pennsylvania Press, 2013).

[17] Jeffrey Allen Zemler, *James Madison, the South, and the Trans-Appalachian West, 1783–1803* (Lanham, MD: Lexington Books, 2014), 129.

[18] Andrew S. Curran, *The Anatomy of Blackness: Science and Slavery in an Age of Enlightenment* (Baltimore, MD: Johns Hopkins University Press, 2011), 158.

Europeans, by contrast, were "acute, inventive," and ruled by law.[19] Such thinking appeased Europeans' conceptions of superiority, emphasizing inherent characteristics rather than religion or achievement. Some European scholars like Johann Friedrich Blumenbach disputed such hierarchies, but he was in a minority. In 1780, classically educated Virginia governor Thomas Jefferson penned an elegant blueprint for his newly independent state, *Notes on the State of Virginia*. At a historical moment with so many open possibilities, he argued against African American citizenship on the assumption that "that the blacks, whether originally a distinct race, or made distinct by time and circumstances, are inferior to the whites in the endowments both of body and mind."[20]

Slavery ought to be removed, he contended, but so should African-descended people. Their historical memories of wrongs posed a gathering threat to European-descended Americans. Jefferson contemplated a gradual abolition measure that freed females at eighteen and males at twenty-one, but that freedom would be coupled with expatriation. They must be sent away from America. Racial attributes closed the possibility of citizenship. Black men were more sexually aggressive, he argued, "but love seems with them to be more an eager desire, than a tender delicate mixture of sentiment and emotion."[21] Blacks' memories "are equal to the whites[']; in reason much inferior," he argued; "in imagination they are dull, tasteless, and anomalous." He made some allowances for the fact that African-descended people had been put to agricultural labor, but did not let that excuse their apparent lack of intellectual and moral advancement. "They astonish you with strokes of the most sublime oratory; such as prove their reason and sentiment strong, their imagination glowing and elevated," he conceded. "But never yet could I find that a black had uttered a thought above the level of plain narration; never see even an elementary trait of painting or sculpture." Positioning himself as a proponent of racism and a critic of African-descended authors' literature, Jefferson deprecated Phillis Wheatley's poetry and Ignatius Sancho's writings. "Their griefs are transient," he argued, as if to excuse the litany of charges used to

---

[19] George M. Fredrickson, *Racism: A Short History* (Princeton, NJ: Princeton University Press, 2015), 56.

[20] Thomas Jefferson, *Notes on the State of Virginia* (1787), online: http://avalon.law.yale.edu/18th_century/jeffvir.asp, accessed: July 29, 2016.

[21] Jefferson, *Notes on the State of Virginia*.

distance African-descended Americans from inclusion in the Revolutionary experiment.[22]

Yet at the time of the Revolution, slave owners in the Chesapeake remained deeply ambivalent. Virginia and Maryland passed liberalized manumission statutes between 1782 and 1796. Until then it took an act of the legislature to manumit slaves. Some Quakers had already taken the lead. Mary Pleasants of Goochland County, Virginia, manumitted five slaves, for instance, on the Fourth of July, 1781. From religious and moral "conviction" and "being fully persuaded that freedom is the Natural Right of all mankind, and that no law, moral or divine, has given me a right to, or property in the persons of any of my fellow creatures," Pleasants freed sixty-year-old Cato, fifty-six-year-old Will, fifty-five-year-old Dick, sixty-year-old Judy, and sixty-six-year-old Biddy.[23] All were among a tiny proportion of the slave population that lived past forty. But freedom came without back wages or health care.

Yet even at the slow pace of gradual abolition and individual manumissions, African Americans seemed to be moving in the direction of freedom. In 1776, free people of African descent accounted for just 5 percent of the black population. But by 1790, they were 8 percent; by 1800, 11 percent. The number of free black people in Virginia rose by half between the start of the Revolution and 1790. More than half of Delaware's black population was free in 1800 and a fifth of African Americans in Maryland was as well. North of the Mason-Dixon Line all of the states passed either immediate or gradual abolition laws by 1804. Yet even in this ferment of freedom, countervailing forces began to pull the process back toward slavery. Most bondspersons were young, and manumission represented a financial loss that enslavers were unwilling to take. Among them was George Washington, who favored a gradual emancipation law for Virginia in the 1780s, but opposed Quaker antislavery activism. His ambivalence played havoc with his bondspersons.

In death, Washington granted freedom for some but left others to be sold. When Washington died in 1799, 316 bondspeople lived at his Mount Vernon plantation home. Some were hired, some were his, and some were held jointly with other relatives. Washington's will directed 123 slaves to

---

[22] Jefferson, *Notes on the State of Virginia* (quotations); Henry Louis Gates Jr., *The Trials of Phillis Wheatley: America's First Black Poet and Her Encounters with the Founding Fathers* (New York, NY: Civitas, 2003).

[23] Manumissions July 4, 1781, Folder Three, Pleasants Family Papers, Mss BR 12–15, Robert Alonzo Brock Collection, Huntington Library, San Marino, California.

be manumitted, but only after Martha Washington died. Washington also provided resources from the estate to care for the elderly and ordered that orphans and those too poor to support themselves be bound out to service. But that still left some members of families enslaved and subject to the whims of a new owner or owners. One hundred fifty-three bondspersons were the property of Martha Washington as part of inheritance she owned jointly with relatives. The Washingtons had attempted to raise money for their freedom by selling lands, but those plans failed. Martha ordered the manumissions take place before her death, and those named in Washington's will received freedom in 1801. Meanwhile some escaped, and when nephew Bushrod Washington inherited Mount Vernon, he took over an estate that was burdened with debt. Bushrod was an associate justice of the US Supreme Court and also a founder of the American Colonization Society, which encouraged black emigration as an eventual solution to slavery. But encouraging African-descended residents of Mount Vernon to emigrate from their homeland did not pay the estate's debts, and in 1821, Washington sold fifty-four to Louisiana enslavers. Washington's legacy was an irony verging on tragedy when the chattel principle undermined a dying attempt at justice.

Spanning the political distances among the states and their regions, the federal Constitution safeguarded enslavers' property rights in people but set limits on the political representation of enslaved people's owners. To enslavers, the Constitution was a half-measure. And given the strength of slavery in the broader Atlantic world in the 1780s – the height of the transatlantic slave trade – it is surprising that enslavers did not insist on more secure constitutional protections for their slave property. The reason was that enslavers were bargaining from a position of relative weakness in 1787. The old slave economies of tobacco and rice were threatened by the Revolution. In gaining independence, Virginia and Maryland enslavers lost the British tobacco market. Exiting the British Empire, South Carolina and Georgia rice growers lost their Caribbean market for grain. It was just four years since the end of the American Revolution and four years before the outbreak of the Haitian Revolution, and in that lull the future of North American slavery was unclear. In 1787, Hispaniola (the western third of which was St. Domingue, the future Haiti) and other Caribbean islands supplied much of Britain's cotton. In 1791, Britain imported four times as much cotton from its West Indies colonies as in 1781. Cotton growers in the French Caribbean, Brazil, Suriname, and Demerara quickly followed suit. No one knew that St. Domingue would erupt in rebellion – or that cotton would be America's great contribution to the British industrial revolution. But instead of the absolute protections for slave property, the Southern delegates received half-loaves at the 1787 Constitutional Convention.

The Constitution protected slave property but limited enslavers' representation in the national legislature to three-fifths of the numbers of their bondspersons plus the number of free residents (excluding Indians). The Constitution's 1808 Clause prohibited Congress from banning the imports of foreign captives for twenty years, which covered the expected career lives of merchants and growers who agreed to the prohibition. The constitution empowered the government to return fugitive slave property. Delegates from states where slavery was marginal argued that the Constitution was a framework that slowly constricted a political evil. In 1787, delegate James Wilson told his fellow Pennsylvanians that "I consider [the 1808 Clause] as laying the foundation for banishing slavery out of this country."[24] Wilson could hope for gradual abolition on the Pennsylvania model.

But farsighted observers like James Madison of Virginia glimpsed the possibility that cotton was key to America's future prosperity and with it slavery's expansion. Two years after the Constitutional Convention George Washington wrote fellow Virginian Thomas Jefferson that "the increase of that new material (cotton) ... must be of almost infinite consequence to the prosperity of the United States."[25] Both understood that cotton meant slavery.

And where cotton grew, slavery expanded. Until Congress abolished slavery in 1808, the port of Charleston, South Carolina, was a regional destination for ships carrying the transatlantic slave trade. Of the 133 slaving voyages that arrived in the United States in 1807 alone – carrying more than 20,000 African-descended captives – 126 ships landed in South Carolina, six in Louisiana (one after landing first in Charleston), and one at Savannah. The *Union* of Newport, Rhode Island, arrived in Charleston in January 1807, with 168 of 188 surviving captives bought off the Gold Coast. The *Fourth of July* followed in February with 44 of 59 slaves surviving the journey from the Rio Pongo on the Windward Coast. The crew of the Philadelphia-based brigantine *Washington* put down a slave uprising en route to Charleston from Senegambia and arrived

[24] Paul Finkelman, *An Imperfect Union: Slavery, Federalism, and Comity* (Chapel Hill, NC: University of North Carolina Press, 1981), 25.
[25] George Washington to Thomas Jefferson, quoted in Sven Beckert, *Empire of Cotton: A Global History* (New York, NY: Vintage, 2014), 100.

with 32 of the 38 human beings purchased there. Captives were sold as individuals or in small lots on the docks.[26] The *Cleopatra* of Liverpool embarked 402 captives in the Congo River region before setting sail across the Atlantic. Forty Africans died along the way. Besides the trip itself being a living hell for the human cargo, the ship's master, supercargo, and boatswain killed three crew members and starved, tortured, and maimed several others. Captain John Butman's successful defense was that his brutality served the legitimate ends of the trade. During the *Cleopatra*'s voyage, the British Parliament banned its subjects from participating in the slave trade. So after selling 362 Africans in Charleston, Butman reflagged the *Cleopatra* as an American ship and sailed straight back to Africa to buy another cargo of captives. He raced against time since the US Congress had passed an act barring the slave trade to America starting in 1808. After hauling down the British flag and flying an American one, the *Cleopatra* departed Charleston in April, less than two months after Congress had passed the act prohibiting the importation of foreign captives after January 1, 1808. It sailed directly to the African coast. Then Butman pushed the ship back to Charleston, arriving in December with 218 of 290 captives loaded in the Congo River region. The hasty voyage resulted in an unusually high death rate of 25 percent. Twelve Angolans and Congolese captives escaped confinement in South Carolina. The rest languished on the ship until March of the following year, after the 1808 ban on imported slaves fell. The survivors were treated like warehoused commodities, sold when market scarcity drove up prices.[27]

A revolution commencing with the idea that all men are created equal culminated in an enslavers' republic. There were radical elements to the American Revolution. It flattened colonial hierarchies of class and overthrew British rule. Patriots developed a grammar of political freedom, framed in ringing terms, uniting citizens from Massachusetts to Georgia. It also inspired African Americans who used that language of liberty to argue for their inclusion in the project of American freedom. But Patriots who banded together to fight British redcoats also fought British-allied

---

[26] Voyages: The Trans-Atlantic Slave Trade Database, Voyage Identification Numbers: 25478 (*Fourth of July*); 36863 (*Union*); 25392 (*Washington*), online: www.slavevoyages.org/voyage/search, accessed: April 10, 2017; Ira Berlin, *The Making of African America: The Four Great Migrations* (New York, NY: Pantheon, 2010), 76–98.

[27] Voyages: The Trans-Atlantic Slave Trade Database, Voyage Identification Numbers: 25511, 80854 (*Cleopatra*), www.slavevoyages.org/voyage/search, accessed: April 10, 2017; Emma Christopher, *Slave Ship Sailors and Their Captive Cargoes, 1730–1807* (New York, NY: Cambridge University Press, 2006).

Indians and African-descended loyalists. In creating a nation they also created racial categories that infused the project. Indians and African-descended people had no rightful place in that vision.[28] The American Revolution was profoundly transformative for citizens, but their gains were accented by the Revolution's shortcomings for women and people of African descent. In a republic of white male citizens, black disqualification would be predicated on perceived inferiority. As the old aristocracy was replaced by a new one in which white men were citizens, 20 percent of the Patriot army – who were nonwhite – became a forgotten fifth. And as the old slave economies of tobacco and rice gave way to a growing empire of cotton, profound changes reshaped US slavery.

[28] Robert G. Parkinson, *The Common Cause: Creating Race and Nation in the American Revolution* (Chapel Hill, NC: University of North Carolina Press, 2016).

3

Cotton Empire

The defining feature of the early nineteenth-century American South was the violent expropriation of land and coercion of labor to produce cotton. Called war capitalism, it was an interlocking geopolitical and economic strategy to bring ever more land under cultivation of cotton using slave labor. Choctaws, Chickasaws, Muscogee-Creeks, Cherokees, and Seminoles, among other Native American peoples, were forcibly removed from the lands of the Deep South. And Euroamerican settlers moved in, buying lands and forcing African-descended laborers to cut forests for timber, clear land for fields, and grow cotton and other staples. War capitalism was less a betrayal of Revolutionary republicanism than a strategic response to Britain's industrial revolution, which gave American planters an interest in producing cotton bales for market. And it became the desolation of African American families moved into places from which Native Americans were removed.

At the end of the American Revolution, cotton was marginal to the US economy. At the time, the luxurious long-staple cotton species, grown in the coastal lowlands of Georgia and South Carolina, competed with fiber grown in Brazil and the Caribbean. Long-staple cotton was a niche market. In 1790, cotton production in the United States was just 3,135 bales. Then a slave uprising in the French West Indies made American cotton more competitive.

The revolution in Saint-Domingue (renamed Haiti), beginning in 1791, cut exports of cotton from the island sharply. The French slave colony accounted for 24 percent of Britain's cotton imports in 1790. That fell to 4.5 percent by 1795. Haiti's cotton exports to France fell precipitously as well. North American cotton filled the void, and during the Haitian

Revolution, American merchants were abuzz with predictions that American wealth would be built on it. Technological advances helped realize such hopes.

The invention of an engine or gin that removed seeds improved worker productivity and made slave-grown cotton profitable. To be useable, the sticky seeds of upcountry cotton needed to be removed from cotton lint, and it took a worker ten hours to separate seeds from a pound of cotton by hand. In 1793, Yale graduate Eli Whitney patented a saw gin, which mechanically separated the fibers of upcountry or short-staple cotton from the seeds. A worker could seed or gin about fifty-five pounds of cotton in the same ten-hour day, one worker doing the job of more than fifty. Whitney did not invent the cotton gin. Roller gins had long been in use removing seeds from long-staple cotton. But Whitney's improved machine – along with many others – came on the market at the precise time that Americans were ramping up short-staple cotton production for export and doing it with slave labor. And that fiber held a number of advantages.

Short-staple or upcountry cotton (*Gossypium hirsutum*) was cheaper than flax, silk, or wool. It was easier to grow, dye, spin, and weave than any other fiber. And English textile mills turned bales of it into popular yarns and fabrics. Fashion supported slavery when consumers bought cheap cotton printed dresses, stockings, vests, and shirts. And as American growers struggled to meet demand, the development of upcountry cotton began to ripple back into old African American neighborhoods in the Chesapeake. Short-staple cotton was hardier than its coastal cousin. Cotton was not native to British North America, but *G. hirsutum* grew well in the temperate climate south of Virginia and especially in the river bottoms and alluvial plains of what became the Deep South. Cotton and slavery moved together, and by 1860, American bondspersons would make more than 1,430 times as much cotton as in 1790.[1]

In South Carolina and Georgia, enslavers pushed upriver and drove bondspersons to plant cotton along the Santee, Congaree, Broad, and Saluda Rivers. South Carolinians built the Santee Canal to the Cooper River, which was one of the first canals of its kind. Canals and rivers became arteries of slavery and of cotton as the Carolina upcountry cotton frontier developed. Georgians planted short-staple cotton in the region stretching from Augusta to Columbus, Georgia's Black Belt. And as

[1] Lewis Cecil Gray, *History of Agriculture in the Southern United States to 1860*, vol. 2 (Washington, DC: The Carnegie Institution of Washington, 1933), 1026, 1033.

plantations grew along the Savannah River, the Ogeechee, the Oconee, the Flint, and the Coosa, Georgians assembled enslaved people from the coast and from the Chesapeake, pushing out Creek Indians as they carved up river bottoms into cotton fields.

American cotton development worked hand in glove with English industrial growth. Factory owners in northwest England demanded upcountry cotton for mid-grade fabrics, then growing in popularity. In 1792, the United States exported 138,328 pounds of cotton lint (twice the output of 1790), which could take 1.38 million hours of work to seed. That was about the same production as the Dutch colony of Demerara (today part of Guyana). The year after Whitney's gin, Americans exported 1,601,000 pounds. And cotton production surged. The United States produced twenty-three times as much cotton in 1800 as in 1790. In 1810, it produced two and a half times the 1800 total, and the 1820 total was nearly double the 1810 total, or more than 106 times the 1790 crop.[2] Predictions of an easy fortune in cotton seemed to be coming true for enslavers, merchants, and shippers of cotton.[3]

The growth of cotton marched in lockstep with the geopolitics of slavery, and both were part of an aggressive US expansion policy. In the 1783 Treaty of Paris ending the Revolutionary War, Britain recognized US land claims all the way to the Mississippi River, with Spain claiming land south and west of Georgia at about 32 degrees of northern latitude, or where the Tombigbee joins the Alabama River. Spain also claimed Florida. Despite American and European claims, however, lands west of the Appalachians were still governed by Native American nations and confederations such as the Muscogee-Creek, Cherokee, Choctaw, and Chickasaw. The Jefferson administration began pressuring southeastern Indians to vacate lands sought by American citizens. In the meantime, the biggest obstacle to US growth west of the Appalachian Mountains was the port of New Orleans on the Mississippi River.

New Orleans was the key to the western regions of what became the cotton kingdom. And it was controlled by a hostile European power. "There is on the globe one single spot, the possessor of which is our natural and habitual enemy," Thomas Jefferson wrote, contemplating

---

[2] Gray, *History of Agriculture in the Southern United States to 1860*, 1026; Hugh Thomas, *The Slave Trade: The Story of the Atlantic Slave Trade: 1440–1870* (New York, NY: Simon and Schuster, 1999), 571.

[3] Angela Lakwete, *Inventing the Cotton Gin: Machine and Myth in Antebellum America* (Baltimore, MD: Johns Hopkins University Press, 2003).

an alliance with the British against the French to whom Spain ceded the port. The exports of states bordering the Ohio and Tennessee Rivers as well as the Mississippi River ran though New Orleans. Spain took control of Louisiana in 1763, including New Orleans, and in 1795, the United States negotiated free passage on the Mississippi River. In 1800, Spain ceded Louisiana to France in the secret Treaty of San Ildefonso and with it control of the vital port. Before France took it over, Spanish officials closed the port to US trade in October 1802, while American diplomats in Paris were trying to buy New Orleans. As with the cotton business, however, the revolution in Haiti played havoc with French colonial plans.[4]

The Haitian Revolution was the largest slave rebellion in modern history, and by 1802, it had become an independence struggle after French First Consul Napoleon Bonaparte attempted to reestablish slavery there. Napoleon sent a massive force to conquer Haiti. But in the summer and fall of 1802, French troops fell to yellow fever and the uncompromising strategy of nationalist leaders like Jean-Jacques Dessalines. Dessalines fought against slavery and white rule. Atrocities were rampant on all sides. But the Haitian rout of the French convinced Napoleon to sell not just New Orleans but all French Louisiana and, if possible, to use the proceeds to salvage his imperial project in Europe and elsewhere in the Caribbean.

To the Thomas Jefferson administration, this meant additional cotton lands. "I know that cotton is the most profitable production of the US. and that the Missisipi [*sic*] territory is well adapted to it," Thomas Jefferson wrote in March 1802.[5] Not waiting for Congress to act, Jefferson ramped up negotiations with Napoleon's ministers to secure New Orleans and as much of Spanish Florida as could be had (Jefferson believing at the time that Spain had ceded Florida to France). He was surprised by the turn in negotiations in the spring of 1803 in which France agreed to sell all of the Louisiana territory to the United States. After French officials agreed on a price, American officials financed the purchase with a cash outlay and $11.25 million in US government bonds. British banking firm Baring Brothers and Company handled the deal, mortgaging Louisiana to the

---

[4] Jefferson quoted in Robert D. Bush, *The Louisiana Purchase: A Global Context* (New York, NY: Routledge, 2014), 148.

[5] Thomas Jefferson to Thomas Mann Randolph, March 12, 1802, Founders Online, National Archives and Records Administration, online: http://founders.archives.gov/documents/Jefferson/01-37-02-0042, accessed: June 3, 2017.

United States in part through a Dutch affiliate. The acquisition doubled US territory, including the lands of future Missouri and Kansas, flashpoints of conflict over slavery's expansion.

In the fall of 1803, Americans took control of New Orleans, boosted trade, and started carving up plantation lands up the Mississippi and the Red River in Louisiana. The result soon became clear: New Orleans quickly became a hub of America's cotton empire and its biggest slave market. Cotton and sugar planters turned Jefferson's empire of liberty into an empire of slavery in the lower Mississippi Valley after Haiti secured independence in 1804.

In founding the Haitian republic, the second independent republic in the Americas, Haiti's leaders repudiated slavery and the very calculations that framed US expansion in the lower Mississippi Valley. One irony of slavery's geopolitics in the United States is that the American slave country grew in response to the determined emancipationist struggles led by rebel leader Toussaint L'Overture and President Dessalines. Declining Caribbean cotton production gave the United States advantages, while plummeting sugar production in the midst of the rebellion provided an opening to Louisiana growers whose fortunes would rise in the 1820s. Despite the Haitian commitment to liberty and ending racial inequalities, however, the Jefferson administration worked to isolate Haiti. Enslavers feared its contagion of liberty would spread to bondspersons in North America at precisely the time they were growing in economic importance.[6] About the time of the Louisiana Purchase, Charles Ball followed many black Marylanders on an African American trail of tears to cotton country. His ordeal traces the process of cotton's rise.

Charles Ball opened his eyes on a landscape in upheaval. Born in Maryland in 1781, he grew up farming tobacco and corn in southern Maryland. Like so many, his family fractured after his mother's owner died in debt. "We were all sold on the same day to different purchasers," Ball recalled. "Our new masters took us away, and I never saw my mother, nor any of my brothers and sisters afterwards." He witnessed Georgia and Carolina slave traders spirit off the children, while a new owner kept him in the region. Ball's father "never recovered from the effects of the shock which this sudden and overwhelming ruin of his family gave him."[7] Ball's

---

[6] Laurent Dubois, *Avengers of the New World: The Story of the Haitian Revolution* (Cambridge, MA: Harvard University Press, 2004).

[7] Charles Ball, *Slavery in the United States: A Narrative of the Life and Adventures of Charles Ball, a Black Man, Who Lived Forty Years in Maryland, South Carolina and*

siblings were sold to make cotton. He would follow, cotton exercising what seems like a gravitational pull on bondspersons.

Ball was about twenty when he was sold and shackled with fifty-one others and force-marched away from his wife, Judah, and their children. In chains, he walked south by southwest, crossing one big river after another, the Potomac, the Roanoke, the Catawba, and so on, viewing the ominous signs of what was to come. "I had now no hope of ever again seeing my wife and children," he mourned, "or of revisiting the scenes of my youth." Despair led to thoughts of suicide.[8]

But he was resilient and determined to remember the geography he crossed and those whom he encountered. Ball reached the Congaree River in South Carolina where enslavers were importing bondspersons like himself, plucked from American families and Africans newly disembarked from the Middle Passage, so great was the demand. "I became intimately acquainted with some of these men," Ball recalled, among whom were Muslims. "There was one man on this plantation, who prayed five times every day, always turning his face to the east, when in the performance of his devotion."[9] Ball memorized the story of one West African captive he met in South Carolina. "More than one-third of us died on the passage," across the Atlantic, the man told Ball, "and when we arrived at Charleston, I was not able to stand. It was more than a week after I left the ship, before I could straighten my limbs. I was bought by a trader, with several others; brought up the country, and sold to our present master. I have been here five years."[10] He joined African Americans like Ball in the cotton fields.

Every African-descended person, it seemed, was making cotton. "The labour usually performed by slaves, on a cotton plantation, does not require great bodily strength," Ball observed, "but rather superior agility, and wakefulness."[11] Enslavers demanded bondspersons' attentiveness and nimbleness, and under coercion cotton pickers performed a melancholy dance through the long furrows, collecting the white lint from sharp bolls, the cotton plants' natural defenses competing against the skill and dexterity of the pickers. Child labor was prized because it was cheap and pliable, but all worked alongside one another in a cotton gang.

Georgia, as a Slave under Various Masters, and Was One Year in the Navy with Commodore Barney, during the Late War (New York, NY: John S. Taylor, 1837), 16–21; Damian Alan Pargas, *Slavery and Forced Migration in the Antebellum South* (New York, NY: Cambridge University Press, 2015).
[8] Ball, *Slavery in the United States*, 69.   [9] Ball, *Slavery in the United States*, 164.
[10] Ball, *Slavery in the United States*, 186.   [11] Ball, *Slavery in the United States*, 210.

And Ball soon discovered the secret to cotton's profitability: the violence of the pushing system. "Flogging – though often severe and excruciating in Maryland, is not practised with the order, regularity, and system, to which it is reduced in the south," he argued.[12] Enslavers made whipping into a science, fashioning long whips counterweighted at the handle, often with lead. This high-technology "whipping-machine" was simultaneously an instrument of torture and a strategy for raising worker productivity. With the cotton gin already saving labor, enslaved cotton productivity rose fourfold between 1800 and 1860, about the same as the productivity of cotton spinners in Manchester cotton mills between 1819 and 1860. The crucial difference was human- versus power-driven equipment. While American enslavers developed whipping technology, Manchester mills were fitted with increasingly complex machines.[13] Augmenting torture was improved crop science, including cotton varieties of *G. hirsutum*, which yielded more lint per boll and hardier plants.[14] But enslavers calculated that the greatest returns could be had by regimenting violence.

Overseers implemented a quota system with carrots and with sticks, dividing ostensible gang labor into individual production targets. On his first day in the field, Ball picked thirty-eight pounds as an inexperienced hand, younger workers picking twice as much. But he learned quickly under the whip. "I looked forward to something still more painful than loss of character which I must sustain," he recalled, "for I knew that the lash of the overseer would soon become familiar with my back, if I did not perform as much work as any of the other young men." He picked forty-six pounds the next day and fifty-two after that. And taking stock of how much the best workers were able to average, "the overseer told us, that he fixed the day[']s work at fifty pounds; and that all those who picked more than that, would be paid a cent a pound, for the overplus." Anything short of that would earn a whipping, administered while the worker was spread chest-down on the ground, females exposed to sexual humiliation as well as torture. "Twenty-five pounds was assigned as the daily task of the old people," Ball recalled, "as well as a number of boys and girls, whilst some of the women, who had children, were required to pick forty pounds, and

---

[12] Ball, *Slavery in the United States*, 59.

[13] Edward E. Baptist, *The Half Has Never Been Told: Slavery and the Making of American Capitalism* (New York, NY: Basic Books, 2014), 141 (quotation); chap. 4.

[14] Alan L. Olmstead and Paul W. Rhode, *Creating Abundance: Biological Innovation and American Agricultural Development* (New York, NY: Cambridge University Press, 2008), chap. 4.

several children had ten pounds each as their task."[15] Under such a system, if a mother helped her child, she would be whipped for not meeting her quota. And when bondspersons met those quotas, owners and overseers tended to raise them.

The regime was relentless, and new arrivals like Ball faced severe hardships acclimating. Depending on the climate, cotton-picking could start in August and continue into the next year. Cotton ripened in stages, and plants that furnished cotton in late summer could be picked again in early fall and then in late fall or early winter according to the variety and climate. Enslavers prized cream-colored lint that was not discolored by parasite or environmental damage and had been ginned to keep the fibers intact and with only a minimum of dirt and debris. They tasked overseers with stern discipline in the fields, at the cotton gins, and in the warehouses.

The pushing system in the fields was a ruthless part of cotton supply chain management. Southern planters took great financial risks on cotton. Upfront costs were high, including land and labor. Unlike free labor employers, slave owners paid labor costs before the work was done when they purchased a bondsperson. Enslavers were often debt-burdened to start with, and they assumed additional financial risks, including insurance and shipping costs. They owned cotton bales all the way to market in far-off cities. Cotton merchants called factors typically advanced a planter 70 percent of the expected sale price when it was delivered, but if the bales were damaged or lost, or if the cotton market took a tumble, the planter could end up owing back part of that advance, much of which paid mortgages on lands and slaves anyway. Planters talked a game of gentility and paternalism, but their calculations of profit and advantage fell hard on African Americans whom they pushed to plant, tend, pick, gin, and bale cotton. Any planter who did not implement the pushing system risked a competitive disadvantage against one who did. Torture became part of cotton's business model. And if the planter failed or the market crashed, bondspersons were in danger of being sold.

Ball worked under the pushing system for several years, slowly integrating into the new social environment. He held on to hope of reuniting with his family in Maryland, but escape was not simple. Owners and overseers were like human barbed wire. Plantations were part of an incarceration regime, a carceral landscape as mean as any prison. Overseers were the guards and sometimes the executioners. But there

[15] Ball, *Slavery in the United States* (quotations); Baptist, *The Half Has Never Been Told*, chap. 4.

were invisible barriers to leaving as well. Bondspersons formed families, rebuilding social capital, and if they escaped, they lost their relatives, their networks, and large portions of their selfhood. Yet there were many factors pushing Ball to escape. Besides toiling under a whip, Ball was constantly hungry, poorly clothed and sheltered, and subject to pests like hornets, mosquitoes, poisonous snakes, and hazards like thickets of razor-edged saw grass that plagued the fields.

The work regime was one of constant disruption. Ball was transferred from slave labor camp to slave labor camp, working on the plantation of one of his owner's daughters before the owner died and he decided he'd had enough of slavery in South Carolina. It was 1809, a year after the United States prohibited the foreign slave trade to domestic shores. Fearing betrayal, Ball told no one he planned to escape. He fled one night, walking back to Maryland, keeping to the woods, crossing the rivers, eating corn ripening in the fields. After rejoining a wife who scarcely remembered him and children who greeted him as a stranger, Ball tried to rebuild his life in Maryland. But it was a turbulent time in the nation's history. Soon the United States was again at war with Great Britain.

When British warships arrived in the Chesapeake, Charles Ball joined what some have called a second war for American independence in the War of 1812. And like the struggles of the Jefferson administration to expand the cotton and slave country, the principal outcomes of the war in the South was a victory for enslavers and the conquest of land from southeastern Indians. This was not the full intent of Congress when it declared war in 1812 over the issue of British navy impressment of American sailors and the capture of US ships and cargo by both the British and the French. But when American forces under General Andrew Jackson moved south from Tennessee, they marched into a civil war between two Creek factions.

Cotton land taken from Creeks was a major outcome of the War of 1812. The flashpoint for American involvement in the Creek civil war was the Fort Mims Massacre. On August 30, 1813, Red Sticks – the traditionalist faction among the Muscogee-Creek Confederation – attacked a hastily constructed stockade on a plantation in the Mississippi Territory (present-day south Alabama). The force of 700 overwhelmed the local militia, killing 250 of the fort's defenders and then another 100 or so civilians. Reports of the massacre became a rallying cry for Americans, some of whom saw inter-Indian alliances as part of a larger alliance with the British. Andrew Jackson suspected that this internal enemy was allied with an external one. Using that pretext, his forces moved against the Red Sticks, culminating in the Battle of Horseshoe Bend in March 1814. Jackson's forces won, and he demanded the Creeks cede some 23 million acres in Alabama to the United States. The context was cotton. And the Treaty of Fort Jackson was a major American victory for enslavers who were already pressuring Indians to vacate lands on which short-staple cotton grew well.

American victory in the War of 1812 reestablished enslavers' supremacy. Jackson led Tennessee and Kentucky riflemen, former Haitian bondsmen fighting as free men, New Orleans militiamen, and even Creole pirates against the British Army in January 1815. Together they won the Battle of New Orleans. Then news arrived that the United States and Britain had already agreed to peace in December 1814. Nevertheless, Jackson rose in the estimation of his countrymen, and the message was clear to both Indians and Europeans that Americans of Jackson's stripe would ruthlessly defend the gains secured in the war. Enslavers clamped down on bondspersons, many of whom had fled to the British. And under the pretext of pursuing British dead-enders and fugitive slaves, Jackson stayed in the saddle, pursuing fugitives from slavery.

The victory against the British at New Orleans was also a victory for trade with the British. Before the War of 1812, the Thomas Jefferson and James Madison administrations tried to maintain American neutrality by banning US exports, first with the Embargo Act of 1807. But such restrictions hurt domestic merchants, shippers, and enslavers. The federal government briefly hampered the cotton trade. But the Jefferson and Madison embargoes made many exporters into smugglers. Following passage of the Non-Intercourse Act of 1809, for instance, some 270 US vessels set sail, illegally unloading 65,000 bales of cotton in Liverpool, England, between early June and late August, representing about 41 percent of the 1808 US crop.[16] Intermittent smuggling followed, even during wartime. After the war ended, American ships sailed for England with more cotton than ever before. And Americans bought cheap British textiles, salt, and coal. They were soon importing credit too.

Britain became a most favored nation trading partner. To regulate and encourage trade, the United States and Britain agreed to give free access to

---

[16] Sydney G. Checkland, "American Versus West Indian Traders in Liverpool, 1793–1815," *Journal of Economic History* 18.2 (June 1958): 155; James L. Watkins, *King Cotton: A Historical and Statistical Review, 1790 to 1908* (New York, NY: James L. Watkins and Sons, 1908), 29.

American vessels in British ports. And debt-burdened British merchants dumped manufactured goods on American markets, undercutting domestic producers and selling at impossibly cheap prices. From then on American consumers demanded cheap yarns and fabrics, and English mills made possible a fast fashion industry using slave-produced cotton. By 1817, Americans were running a trade deficit with Great Britain, importing finished goods and credit while exporting raw cotton and foodstuffs. Cotton overtook foodstuffs in the 1820s to become America's chief export.

A transatlantic "cotton triangle" formed linking Liverpool, New York, and Southern ports.[17] New York became the premier financial city of the United States and was also the main import-export center. Southern cotton was shipped out of ports like New Orleans and Charleston, but often made its way through New York City on its way to Liverpool en route to textile factories. Packet lines – sailing ships departing on schedule – were attractive to merchants who wanted the latest market information. And cotton merchants specialized as the market matured. Between 1820 and 1839, the number of Liverpool merchants dealing in cotton declined by more than 40 percent. But remaining merchants gobbled up a larger market share. As time went on, a smaller pool of importers consolidated a dominant share of the cotton trade for themselves. Big firms specializing in cotton extended credit to American merchants and sold to English manufacturers. Cotton merchants owned packet lines, and an interest in cotton that blossomed on Southern plantations ran through Northern cities as well.[18] And up that chain British credit bought more slaves.

Americans produced more and more cotton demanding more and more acreage, and the cotton frontier swept westward, filling in the Creek cession of 1814 and moving beyond it. The 1825 cotton crop was more than two and a half times larger than the 1815 crop. Cotton production more than doubled between 1820 and 1830. In 1791, Georgia and South Carolina produced all of the nation's cotton. By 1826, Georgia and the Carolinas produced just half, and by 1859, just 20 percent. In 1826, Alabama, Louisiana, Mississippi, and Tennessee produced about 40 percent of the cotton crop. By 1859, Arkansas, Louisiana, Mississippi, and Texas – the

[17] Gene Dattel, *Cotton and Race in the Making of America: The Human Costs of Economic Power* (Chicago, IL: Ivan R. Dee, 2009), 61 (quotation); Scott Reynolds Nelson, *A Nation of Deadbeats: An Uncommon History of America's Financial Disasters* (New York, NY: Knopf, 2012), chaps. 5–6.

[18] David M. Williams, "Liverpool Merchants and the Cotton Trade, 1820–1850," in *Liverpool and Merseyside: Essays in the Economic and Social History of the Port and Its Hinterland*, ed. John R. Harris (London: Cass, 1969), 189.

westernmost cotton states – produced more than half the crop. And after the closure of the foreign slave trade planters on the cotton frontier demanded African-descended workers like Charles Ball. The cycle of family disarticulation of which he was a part in 1785 and again fifteen years later was repeated and amplified. About one in ten enslaved people in the United States was forced across state lines in the 1820s, a figure that rose to one in seven in the 1830s.[19] And as the geographic center of cotton blew to the west, so did the geographic center of slavery, reaching the western border of Georgia by 1860, 600 miles from Petersburg, Virginia, where it had been in 1800. It is difficult to see that as anything but intentional.

To clear new land for cotton, the Andrew Jackson administration made Indian removal a top priority. It did so by inducing Native Americans to sign treaties ceding land to the United States. In 1830, Choctaws – inhabiting the Mississippi Black Belt from the east bank of the Mississippi River southeast to the headwaters of the Big Black River to the Alabama state line – were forced to sign the Treaty of Dancing Rabbit Creek, bringing their lands under US authority but granting Choctaws allotments, which they could sell to pay for their own removal or occupy subject to US and state law. It was not a removal treaty, but it nevertheless became a pretext for Choctaw removal. Government agents refused to register many legitimate Choctaw claims while eagerly entering lands bought by speculators and other white buyers. Between 1833 and 1846, the lands ceded in the Treaty of Dancing Rabbit Creek were resold to agriculturalists. And when they refused to abide by fraudulent claims, army personnel and contractors removed the Choctaw people, a fifth of whom died from starvation, exposure, and diseases such as cholera, smallpox, and whooping cough. Chickasaws followed.[20]

Pressure on Native American nations was immense. The Indian Removal Act of 1830 sped the process, authorizing the United States to move Indians west of the Mississippi River, granting lands there. The 1832 Treaty of Pontotoc reads in part: "The Chickasaw Nation find themselves oppressed in their present situation by being made subject to the laws of the States in which they reside." Under such pressure, the

---

[19] Sven Beckert, *Empire of Cotton: A Global History* (New York, NY: Vintage, 2014), 104; Steven Deyle, *Carry Me Back: The Domestic Slave Trade in American Life* (New York, NY: Oxford University Press, 2005), Appendix A.

[20] Francis Paul Prucha, *The Great Father: The United States Government and the American Indians*, vol. 1 (Lincoln, NE: University of Nebraska Press, 1984); Katherine M. B. Osburn, *Choctaw Resurgence in Mississippi: Race, Class, and Nation Building, 1830–1977* (Lincoln, NE: University of Nebraska Press, 2014), chap. 1.

Chickasaw nation agreed to turn over lands to the United States in exchange for allotments or the ability to sell that land and "seek a home in the west, where they may live and be governed by their own laws." Creek lands were taken under the Third Treaty of Washington in 1832. Cherokees – who had been allies against the Red Sticks in the 1814 campaign that led to the Treaty of Fort Jackson – were harassed by white Georgians. The Treaty of New Echota in 1835 was the pretext for the Cherokee Trail of Tears in 1838.

The Trail of Tears has traditionally been represented as a military action overseen by the War Department, but it was the most visible type of war capitalism. Land companies like the New York and Mississippi Land Company and the Boston and New-York Chickasaw Land Company sold shares in speculations on tracts of Indian territory, often bankrolling fraudulent claims made on Chickasaw lands. The government contracted out removal, paying steamboat captains, removal agents, food vendors, and blanket suppliers to do the dirty work of forcing Indians from their homelands. The Alabama Emigrating Company formed out of another land company to profit from the Creek Trail of Tears. As Native Americans were forced out, African Americans were forced in.

The key to that process was the political strength of US enslavers. State power was key to expropriating lands and sanctioning private violence that supported the pushing system. The United States enforced treaties on Native Americans, and wars and removals cost much more than tariffs protecting domestic industries. The United States supported war capitalism by expropriating Indians lands, promoting trade with Great Britain, and refusing to regulate the overland interstate slave trade while enforcing federal fugitive slave laws. States secured property rights in lands and enslaved people, courts enforced contracts, and within that political economy plantations paid high returns on investments. By the 1830s, "American cotton farmers had succeeded in turning themselves into the world's most important growers of the industrial age's most important commodity."[21] War capitalism showered its riches on enslavers and landowners. As a group, enslavers were the wealthiest class of citizens, even as their proportion of Southern white families declined from a third in 1830 to a quarter in 1860. Meanwhile, the cotton crop's value grew from about $12.5 million in 1810 to nearly $250 million in 1860. Yet for all enslavers' power, they faced an array of determined adversaries in the people they claimed to own.

---

[21] Beckert, *Empire of Cotton*, 119.

4

Black Insurgency

Gabriel tore off the veil of a republic founded on liberty and civil rights in a planned rebellion involving up to 1,000 participants. He was born in slavery in 1776 in Henrico County, Virginia, on Thomas Prosser's tobacco estate. As a child he learned to read and write, and along with an older brother, Solomon, he trained as a blacksmith, probably at the urging of his enslaved parents. Gabriel had an imposing physical presence, a "bony face well made," but he was missing teeth and had "two or three scars on his head," the visible marks of fights and punishments. His face was long, his hair was short, and he had charisma. Between six feet two and three inches tall, Gabriel was reportedly "a fellow of courage and intellect above his rank in life."[1] And in his early twenties, he planned a radical sequel to the American Revolution.

When individual bondswomen and men ran off, they eroded slavery, but when enslaved leaders like Gabriel led a rebellion in 1800 Richmond, Virginia, they threatened to crack it apart. Uprisings brought home the high risks and terrible costs of American slavery. Enslaved people became the republic's great "internal enemy who longed for freedom," in one historian's phrasing.[2] Rebellions were political uprisings showing – and in turn forcing authorities to admit – that the republican language of liberty and equality on which the United States was built referred to citizen

---

[1] Douglas R. Egerton, *Rebels, Reformers, and Revolutionaries: Collected Essays and Second Thoughts* (New York, NY: Routledge, 2013), 27.

[2] Alan Taylor, *The Internal Enemy: Slavery and War in Virginia, 1772–1832* (New York, NY: W. W. Norton, 2013), 8.

property owners rather than the people at large. And insurgents exposed
slavery as forced labor and plunder. The Revolution was not complete,
they contended, without freedom for the enslaved.

Gabriel's path to rebel leader began in Richmond, Virginia's capital city and a hive of political discontent. Prosser died in 1798 and
Gabriel fell to Thomas Henry Prosser, the first owner's son. He was
Gabriel's age, but known for his cruelty and ambition. Prosser hired
Gabriel and Solomon out in Richmond, collecting their blacksmiths'
wages. But the city of some 5,700 residents – half African-descended
and one-fifth free black – was fertile ground for enslaved networks.
African Americans were seizing hold of a revolutionary set of ideas
with which to subvert and destroy slavery. Gabriel was also stealing
pigs and was punished in 1799 for an incident that started as hog
theft and went bad when Gabriel bit part of the ear off a white man,
for which he was branded and whipped. By the following year, he
was gathering allies in Richmond.

Sam Byrd, Jack Bowler (also known as Jack Ditcher), and Ben
Woolfolk joined Gabriel in what amounted to a revolutionary club.
Byrd was free, he could read and write, and he kept a list of recruits.
Woolfolk was from the Prosser plantation, and he recalled Gabriel's intent
to "purchase a piece of silk for a flag on which they would have written
'death or liberty,'" which was his group's motto. Virginians still recalled
a time when Lord Dunmore promised freedom should they fight against
Patriot owners. Patrick Henry's valiant defense of American independence and his 1775 speech demanding "give me liberty or give me
death!" still resonated. As Thomas Jefferson aspired to the presidency in
1800, Virginia citizens talked of their liberty and the republican institutions they created in the ferment of the American Revolution. Indeed,
Jefferson and his Democratic-Republican followers had initially
embraced the radicalism of the French Revolution.[3]

But they showed their limited embrace of liberty, fraternity, and equality when opposing black revolutionaries in Haiti. Black Virginians were
also well aware of the seeming contradictions between Democratic-
Republican protests of their rival Federalists' Alien and Sedition Acts of
1798, on one hand, and Virginians' willingness to separate and restrict the

---

[3] Patrick Rael, *Eighty-Eight Years: The Long Death of Slavery in the United States,
1777–1865* (Athens, GA: University of Georgia Press, 2015), 152 (first quotation);
Patrick Henry, "Give Me Liberty or Give Me Death," March 23, 1775 (second quotation),
online: http://avalon.law.yale.edu/18th_century/patrick.asp, accessed: July 8, 2016.

same liberties when claimed by African Americans, on the other. Gabriel discussed the hypocrisy of such an outlook with Charles Quersey and Alexander Beddenhurst, French-born Revolutionary War veterans living in Virginia. Quersey and Beddenhurst were two white expatriates who helped convince Gabriel and his allies that sympathetic whites would join an insurgency led by African Americans, and that class and not race was the common denominator among those who would finish the work of the American Revolution.

While Gabriel cultivated allies in Richmond, Byrd recruited in Petersburg, twenty-five miles south of Richmond. Ben Woolfolk went north to Hanover and Caroline counties. Gabriel approached black workers in tobacco warehouses. He also attracted free African Americans and working-class whites to his cause. Solomon later testified, "[m]y brother Gabriel was the person who influenced me to join him and others in order that (as he said) we might conquer the white people and possess ourselves of their property."[4]

Rumors of an armed revolt spread. A witness in Richmond's jail wrote Thomas Jefferson that "[a] number of [s]words were made in a clumsy enough manner out of rough iron; others by breaking the blade of a [s] cythe in the middle, which thus made two [s]words of a most formidable kind. They were well fastened in proper handles, and would have cut off a man's limb at a single blow." As the insurgents made plowshares into swords, Gabriel's plan came into focus. "The first places Gabriel intended to attack in Richmond were, the Capitol, the Magazine, the Penitentiary, the Governor's house and his person." The plan was to take prisoner Virginia governor James Monroe. "The inhabitants were to be massacred, save those who begged for quarter and agreed to serve as soldiers with them."[5] Jack Bowler co-organized the uprising. Bowler was nearly six feet five inches tall and had long hair tied back behind his head. New recruits like King expressed enthusiasm, pledging, "I am ready to join them at any moment. I could slay the white people like sheep."[6]

[4] Solomon cited in *A Documentary History of North America*, ed. Willie Lee Rose (Athens, GA: University of Georgia Press, 1999), 112.

[5] James T. Callendar to Thomas Jefferson, September 1800, cited in Scot French, *The Rebellious Slave: Nat Turner in American Memory* (New York, NY: Houghton Mifflin, 2004), 15 (first quotation); Solomon cited in *A Documentary History of North America*, 113 (second and third quotations).

[6] King cited in Douglas R. Egerton, *Gabriel's Rebellion: The Virginia Slave Conspiracies of 1800 and 1802* (Chapel Hill, NC: University of North Carolina Press, 1993), 57.

The revolt was planned for Saturday, August 30, but on the appointed day, a violent storm broke, washing out bridges and roads, making it impossible for the armed insurgents to gather. Two members gave into fears and reported to owners, who passed word to authorities. Governor Monroe called up the militia to guard the Capitol. Alarmed citizens locked up some of the rebels, and Gabriel fled on a merchant ship down the James River. He was captured in Norfolk nearly a month later. "They could hardly have failed of success," a jailed witness wrote Jefferson, "for after all, we only could muster four or five hundred men, of whom not more than thirty had Muskets."[7]

White responses were swift and decisive. Virginia authorities arrested and jailed scores of African Americans, and in the aftermath, courts in four counties and Richmond City tried fifty-eight, convicting and hanging twenty-six. One of the condemned compared himself to the martyrs of the American Revolution, announcing to his captors, "I have nothing more to offer than what General Washington would have had to offer, had he been taken by the British and put to trial by them. I have adventured my life in endeavouring to obtain the liberty of my countrymen, and am a willing sacrifice in their cause: and I beg, as a favour, that I may be immediately led to execution. I know that you have pre-determined to shed my blood, why then all this mockery of a trial?"[8] Governor Monroe pardoned thirteen, and eight were transported out of state. Twenty-five more were acquitted. Gabriel was tried on October 6 and hanged four days later. Jack Bowler turned himself in on October 9 and was convicted three weeks later, sentenced to transportation out of state. Ben Woolfolk detailed the plans to authorities in exchange for a pardon, and the two recruits who betrayed the plan in August were also released and rewarded. Wealthy white Virginians breathed a collective sigh of relief as the rebels were hanged or exiled and the uprising unraveled.

But concerns over the black insurgency lingered. Governor Monroe asked the then Vice President Thomas Jefferson for advice on how many public executions Virginia should stage in order to deter other would-be rebels. Jefferson, then running for president, wrote from his Albemarle County home, "there is a strong sentiment that there has been hanging

---

[7] Callendar to Jefferson, September 1800, cited in French, *The Rebellious Slave*, 16.
[8] "A lawyer," cited in Robert Sutcliff, *Travels in Some Parts of North America* (York: C. Peacock, 1811), 50.

enough. [T]he other states & the world at large will for ever condemn us if we indulge a principle of revenge, or go one step beyond absolute necessity."[9] He did not want to provoke a further uprising of the kind roiling Haiti. Diffusing Virginia's slave population seemed more attractive.

An emerging slave market gave enslavers what they claimed was a safety valve. Jefferson argued that selling off bondspersons concentrated in high-density areas would reduce danger to whites. Rather than hanging Bowler and losing the work capability of his strong arms and his keen leadership skills, authorities cleared his sale to slave traders who took him to Spanish New Orleans. But diffusion was a shallow hypocrisy.[10] Other rebellions took shape as Gabriel's comrades were hanged or sold off. The Easter Plot of 1802 reflected the discontents of thousands of enslaved people. Even as its leader, Sancho, and members of his network were tried and executed, and as ripples of panic roiled whites along the Roanoke and James Rivers, North Carolina insurgents organized, word traveling the inland waterways of a time when the insurgency would erupt. White strategies to isolate and root out rebellion met black counterstrategies to recruit and mobilize bondspersons and free people of African descent who would carry on the work of rebellion.

Two years after Thomas Jefferson left the White House, the republic's largest armed domestic slave rebellion erupted in the heart of his Louisiana Purchase. The German Coast slave rebellion began in 1811 in southern Louisiana when some 500 African-descended rebels marched "On to New Orleans" with plans to kill white people and form a republic modeled on Haiti. (The German Coast on the Mississippi River was named for eighteenth-century Europeans who settled there.) In January, Charles Deslondes – a light-skinned Louisiana Creole – organized enslaved people on the sugar plantation of his owner after killing the son of his owner, Manual Andry. Deslondes had worked as a driver or an enslaved overseer, and after taking over the plantation, he recruited and enrolled other young men in an upstart militia in St. John the Baptist and St. Charles parishes. The men were multiethnic and multiracial. Some were born in Africa and others in America. Some spoke French; others spoke English, Akan, or Kikongo. Some were Christian, others Muslim. Charles, Harry Kenner,

---

[9] Thomas Jefferson to James Monroe, September 20, 1800, *Encyclopedia Virginia*, online: www.encyclopediavirginia.org/Letter_from_Thomas_Jefferson_to_James_Monroe_September_20_1800, accessed: April 10, 2017.

[10] Edward E. Baptist, *The Half Has Never Been Told: Slavery and the Making of American Capitalism* (New York, NY: Basic, 2014), chap. 1.

and Joseph joined Cupidon, Kooche or Kook, Quamana, Mingo, Diaca, Al-Hassan, and Omar, all united in determination to overthrow white rule.[11]

As in Gabriel's Virginia, the lower Mississippi River Valley was alive with unrest as slave labor camps were built to furnish their owners with cotton and sugar. But the German Coast uprising was inspired by the Haitian Revolution, which brought people together against a common adversary. Many of the enslavers were castoffs or legatees of the uprising in Haiti. Unable to win that struggle, they used the same strategy in Louisiana, forcing people of African descent to toil for their sake and, in an emergency, calling on another army to protect their interests.

Unlike Gabriel's insurgents, the German Coast rebels wore uniforms and faced both US soldiers and local militiamen in the canebrakes. Deslondes's recruits enrolled others, some runaways living along the Mississippi River and others enslaved on adjoining plantations. They raised flags and beat drums, marching down the River Road carrying long knives, axes, and sharp tools, attacking plantations, capturing provisions, and even conscripting some less-than-willing recruits, burning buildings in their wake and killing one enslaver who stood his ground. Deslondes's militia rested after closing half the distance between Andry's plantation and New Orleans, by which time terrified whites had alerted federal authorities in the city. Governor William C. C. Claiborne sent a company of light cavalry upriver to raise alarms, attract local militias, and face the rebel force.

The wounded planter Manual Andry had managed to raise an alarm on the opposite bank of the Mississippi River, and as Deslondes's force pivoted to avoid the US cavalry advancing on its position, it fell between two other white militia forces. About 200 members of Deslondes's army were caught in open sugar fields, the ratoon cane, and young plants offering no cover. The result was a bloodbath of insurgents falling before musket fire, the whites advancing and butchering the survivors, mutilating the corpses. Faced with the enemy on three sides, Deslondes's army fractured, many fleeing into a swamp. Deslondes himself fell on the battlefield, the advancing whites stepping in, cutting off his arms, breaking his thighs with the butts of muskets, and then burning him alive. The whites' fury burned bright.

---

[11] Albert Thrasher, *On to New Orleans! Louisiana's Heroic 1811 Slave Revolt* (New Orleans, LA: Cypress Press, 1995) (quotation); Walter Johnson, *River of Dark Dreams: Slavery and Empire in the Cotton Kingdom* (Cambridge, MA: Harvard University Press, 2013), chap. 1.

Reprisals were swift. Twenty-one captured soldiers were taken to a nearby plantation and tried by a kangaroo court of local planters. All received death sentences. After the executions, Louisiana enslavers cut off the heads of those condemned in the makeshift tribunal, spiked them on polls, and hung them up along the Mississippi River levee as ghastly "insignia of the regime" that condemned them. Twenty-nine more were tried in a New Orleans court where twenty-four were condemned to death, two to flogging and a return to forced labor, and two acquitted. Several of those condemned were executed by hanging on rude scaffolds, their corpses left in nooses to rot, unmistakable symbols that the Empire of Liberty envisioned by architects of the Louisiana Purchase was an empire of slavery as well.[12]

Unlike Jefferson and Monroe in Virginia, Louisiana's territorial governor, William C. Claiborne, gave no doubts that an overwhelming armed response to the German Coast uprising was the way to Americanize Louisiana and prevent future insurrections. He insisted that citizens must be "aware of the many casualties, internal and external to which the [t]erritory is exposed, and must be sensible of the importance of a well-regulated [m]ilitia." The language of the Second Amendment was applied to controlling the internal enemy that was also the labor backbone of the lower Mississippi River Valley.[13] In addition to armed surveillance, Americanization meant stripping rights like Spanish *coartación*, a legally binding covenant between an enslaver and bondsperson in which she paid for freedom in installments, along with the time to work for the wages to do so. It meant incorporating whites into the militias, drawing a color line ever more boldly, and closing other passageways to freedom among the enslaved. The German Coast rebellion was brutally put down and the plantation complex became a series of slave labor camps patrolled by armed guards. Yet uprisings did not end.

The Corotoman plantation in Lancaster County, Virginia, was an unlikely place for an insurgency. It was tucked away on the north shore of the Rappahannock River in Virginia's Northern Neck. It was an old plantation. In 1807, it came into the possession of Joseph C. Cabell, whose wife inherited half, and the new owner ran it like a business, pushing bondspersons to work harder or be sold off. Productivity soared. And Corotoman flourished as a plantation, yielding grain, meat, and other

---

[12] Johnson, *River of Dark Dreams*, 21 (quotation); 18–22.
[13] Daniel Rasmussen, *American Uprising: The Untold Story of America's Largest Slave Revolt* (New York, NY: Harper Perennial, 2011), 171.

produce in abundance from 1808 to 1812. Into that cauldron of conflict British warships entered the Chesapeake in February 1813, and enslaved people cautiously greeted the invaders as lifelines to freedom. Charles Ball was living along the Patuxent River in Maryland at the time, a refugee from slavery in South Carolina. He had his own reasons for serving his Patriot masters, but watched as "several thousand black people deserted from their masters and mistresses, and escaped to the British fleet. None of these people were ever regained by their owners," Ball reported, "as the British naval officers treated them as free people."[14]

The Chesapeake uprising during the War of 1812 revealed a great internal enemy. For the bondspersons enslaved there, the freedom struggle was not so much a second American Revolution as it was a shortcut out of grinding labor and the everyday violence to which they were subjected. Instead of reaching out to Revolutionary principals, black people made use of the British naval presence in 1813–14 to run away in groups. Some fled as families and parts of kinships. Others escaped plantation by plantation. History caught up with enslavers in the War of 1812 as estates that had been handed down whole under colonial laws were divided up among American inheritors. With estate divisions came family destruction at the hands of heirs who received parts of estates. Sons, brothers, and sons-in-law divided up enslaved people, splintering neighborhoods and kinships, rifling families for moveable human property. The Corotoman plantation in Lancaster County was one such place that became a microcosm of the liberating potential of a foreign force.

Enslaved people were cautious at first as American owners warned that the British would simply re-enslave them in the Caribbean should they flee. Instead, British vice admiral Sir Alexander Cochrane welcomed them onto his ships. The official British position was that enslaved Americans were not to be taken as slaves but as defectors eligible to serve in "the Black Corps." Cochrane's appeals convinced many to try their luck with the enemy. After British warships anchored in Lynnhaven Bay near Norfolk, Virginia, African-descended people fled in throngs. A British officer reported in 1813, "[t]he [s]laves continue to come off by every opportunity and I have now upwards of 120 men, women and children on board." He reported plans to send them to Bermuda. "Amongst the Slaves

[14] Charles Ball, *Slavery in the United States: A Narrative of the Life and Adventures of Charles Ball, a Black Man, Who Lived Forty Years in Maryland, South Carolina and Georgia, as a Slave under Various Masters, and Was One Year in the Navy with Commodore Barney, during the Late War* (New York, NY: John S. Taylor, 1837), 469.

are several very intelligent fellows who are willing to act as local guides . . . and if their assertions be true, there is no doubt but the [b]lacks of Virginia and Maryland would cheerfully take up [a]rms and join us against the Americans."[15]

When four British barges paddled up Carter's Creek off the Rappahannock, chasing American vessels, several young adults, including Canada Baton, Ezekiel Loney, and Tom Saunders, fled their owner and joined the British. Around midnight three days later, they returned, guiding British raiders to Cabell's property, going ashore and rousing family members, friends, and others. Sixty-nine bondspersons fled under cover of darkness, nearly half of Corotoman's bondspersons. One young woman was in labor, reaching the British brigantine HMS *Jasseur* just in time to give birth aboard the small warship.[16]

But not all fled from Corotoman. Some were confused, and armed white responders prevented others from escaping. Young adults, especially parents in their twenties and thirties, led the exodus, and families generally fled together. Tom Saunders persuaded his extended family to flee, taking children and young cousins. Twelve of twenty-four adults fleeing Corotoman were a Saunders or a spouse of one. Twenty-one of forty-five children had a Saunders parent. But it was not just male relatives who led the uprising.

Men may have contacted the British, but women took charge of the escape. Sukey Saunders Carter pulled her husband, Dick Carter, out of slavery by insisting that he join her and their four children, along with her brother. Dick Carter told the furious overseer he was leaving at his wife's behest. "Sisters apparently led the decision to go," argues a historian of the uprising, "for nine of the fourteen departing siblings were women, and they were the oldest in five of the seven lines." Some elderly men stayed put, likely because of weary legs and light work. Ezekiel Loney's older sister Fanny Loney helped persuade several of his nieces to leave parents behind and flee, and the kin of Ezekiel and Tom Saunders who fled were related to other enslaved women, who also escaped.[17] But some families were parted by the flight itself and the confusion of a midnight exodus.

The same month as Saunders and the others fled Corotoman, Admiral Cochrane went a step farther, proclaiming all slaves who presented themselves on British vessels could serve with them or be resettled in Canada or

---

[15] Jeremy Black, *The War of 1812 in the Age of Napoleon* (Norman, OK: University of Oklahoma Press, 2009), 220.

[16] Taylor, *The Internal Enemy*, 235.   [17] Taylor, *The Internal Enemy*, 238.

the West Indies. Cochrane began incorporating willing ex-slaves into the Colonial Marines based on the southern tip of Tangier Island in the lower Chesapeake Bay. About 200 African-descended men mustered into the Corps of Colonial Marines, trading their rags for red uniforms. And many others served as scouts, spies, cooks, cleaners, or laborers on fortifications. Thirty black Colonial Marines helped 130 British troops capture an American battery at Pungoteague Creek near Tangier Island, and they supported the British in the Battle of Bladensburg and the burning of Washington, DC, in August 1814. Some African-descended marines rose to become corporals and sergeants, and when African-descended soldiers marched into the national capital to burn it, locals were horrified that they were the advance guard of an insurrection force, memories of Gabriel haunting the British advance and sack of Washington. Three weeks after Bladensburg, the Colonial Marines supported British forces that had been turned back from the invasion of Baltimore.

Uprisings shook but did not shatter slavery in the Chesapeake. The flight of some 6,000 enslaved people jarred enslavers, but did not cause a significant rethinking of slavery. Six thousand was about 1 percent of Maryland and Virginia's slave population counted in 1810, or about equal to twice the number of enslaved people in Lancaster County, Virginia. Instead the defections hastened a process the legislature set in motion in 1806 when liberal manumission laws of the 1780s were repealed and replaced by a statute forbidding any freed black person to remain in Virginia a year after slavery – or face re-enslavement. Enslavers opted for greater security. And south of the Chesapeake African-descended refugees from slavery sought advantages across borders.

While Chesapeake enslavers heightened security, black freedom fighters established a stronghold in Spanish Florida. In 1814, enslaved people fled from American owners south from Georgia and east from Pensacola. British marines officers directed recruitment efforts, beckoning Red Sticks, Seminoles, and African Americans to join them. The strategy was to divert American attention away from British forces and toward maroon and Indian allies south of the border. British recruiters sent volunteers to a fort under construction fifteen miles up the Apalachicola River in Spanish Florida. The fort at Prospect Bluff, called the British Post, was sixty miles south of US territory, and escaped bondspersons joined British-allied Indians there. As elsewhere, British officers offered uniforms and arms, enrolling male recruits into three companies of Colonial Marines. Jackson's forces moved on Pensacola in November 1814, driving out

British and Spanish forces. Beleaguered British forces handed the British Post over to African-descended Colonial Marines and their Indian allies.

As the British abandoned the War of 1812, African-descended refugees were increasingly responsible for their own security. American victories drove the British from the region following the Battle of New Orleans and the Treaty of Ghent, which ended the war. One British force sailed to the Georgia–Florida border, appealing to fugitives from slavery to join the evacuating forces and gain freedom. Some made it aboard British ships bound for Bermuda. Hundreds more former slaves gathered on Dauphin Island in Mobile Bay. And despite the treaty requirement obliging British forces to return American bondspersons, officers left it to Americans and Spaniards to retake their human property, carrying off those African-descended allies who stuck with them.

The departure of British forces exposed black refugees to violent reprisals, but the British Post – soon renamed Negro Fort – was a rebel stronghold. By the summer of 1815, the British Post was chiefly occupied by African-descended defenders and Seminole allies. One Creek visitor reported that there were "no British troops there at present now but negroes." He explained that "[t]hey [k]eep [s]entry & the [n]egroes are [s]aucy & insolent, and say they are all [f]ree." Besides "a vast deal of ammunition," the fort's defenders had five cannon and ample stores of corn and rice, and nearby were pastures and plots suitable for growing corn and vegetables.[18]

Negro Fort was a beacon to refugees from slavery and Indians determined to resist American incursions. It was the last stand of the insurgency that broke out during the war. In command of about 300 African-descended men, women, and children were three captains, veterans of the Colonial Marines. One was known as Garçon or Garson, a refugee from the Haitian Revolution who had fought with the British. Thirty-year-old Garson had risen to the rank of sergeant major under British command. The two other captains were Prince and Cyrus, each about twenty-six and also veterans of the Colonial Marines. Despite being abandoned by the British, their position seemed secure in 1815.

---

[18] Matthew J. Clavin, *Aiming for Pensacola: Fugitive Slaves on the Atlantic and Southern Frontiers* (Cambridge, MA: Harvard University Press, 2015), 52–53 (quotations); Adam Rothman, *Slave Country: American Expansion and the Origins of the Deep South* (Cambridge, MA: Harvard University Press, 2005), chap. 4; Jane Landers, *Black Society in Spanish Florida* (Urbana, IL: University of Illinois Press, 1999).

They were in Spanish territory, beyond American law and General Andrew Jackson's reach. Besides generous provisions and arrivals of insurgent African Americans, the fort itself had earthen walls fifteen feet tall, eighteen feet thick, and surrounded by a fourteen-foot-wide moat four feet deep at a strategic defensive point on the river. By the summer of 1815, Negro Fort was home to about 1,100 soldiers guarding the sprawling encampments of black and Indian refugees whose settlements were fanning out up and down the river.[19]

But the fort was soon destroyed in an American counterinsurgency campaign. By the spring of 1816, Jackson's forces were chasing enemies he reckoned were still in league with the British or the Red Stick Creeks he had defeated at the Battle of Horseshoe Bend. As cotton rose in importance following the war, so did the imperative of controlling bound laborers. Americans treated a fort controlled by former bondspersons in Spanish Florida as a security risk, and Jackson demanded the Spanish governor destroy the fort. Without orders from Spain, the governor sent a military detachment to scout the fort and return any bondspersons belonging to Spanish owners.

The Americans were not satisfied. Jackson wrote General Edmund P. Gaines that the fort "ought to be destroyed."[20] Gaines ordered US Lieutenant Colonel Duncan L. Clinch to attack the fort. American-allied Coweta Creeks assisted. Besides continuing intra-Creek hostilities, these soldiers were promised a fifty-dollar bounty for capturing ex-slaves. Two US Navy gunboats were sent up the Apalachicola River. The fort's defenders attacked the boats on July 17, killing a handful of American sailors. Garson warned he would sink any vessel attacking the fort, but the Americans now had provocation to attack a fort on foreign soil. They moved in and surrounded the fort. On July 27, 1816, Negro Fort's defenders raised their red flag under the British Union Jack and fired on encroaching forces.

The next day a heated American artillery projectile – a hot shot – landed in Negro Fort's powder magazine. It exploded. "In an instant," a US soldier wrote, "hundreds of lifeless bodies were stretched upon the plain, buried in sand and rubbish, or suspended from the tops of the

---

[19] Kerry Walters, *American Slave Revolts and Conspiracies: A Reference Guide* (Santa Barbara, CA: ABC-CLIO, 2015), 87–94.

[20] Andrew Jackson cited in Clavin, *Aiming for Pensacola*, 56 (quotation); Ada Ferrer, *Freedom's Mirror: Cuba and Haiti in the Age of Revolution* (New York, NY: Cambridge University Press, 2014).

surrounding pines. Here lay an innocent babe, there a helpless mother; on the one side a sturdy warrior, on the other a bleeding squaw. Piles of bodies, large heaps of sand, broken guns, accoutrements, etc. covered the site of the fort."[21] About fifty more survivors died of their wounds soon afterward, and the Coweta–American forces gathered up 250 dead bodies, burning them on a massive pyre. Several survivors surrendered and were either returned to owners or sold back into slavery. Garson survived but was shot soon afterward, along with one of his Indian lieutenants, who was scalped. And at a blow, the largest maroon fort in American history was destroyed.[22]

Destruction of Negro Fort seriously weakened but did not end the black insurgency in the Florida borderlands. Formerly enslaved African Americans allied with Seminoles. Seminoles relied on their military prowess, language skills, and knowledge of American politics and geography. Freed people relied on Seminole patronage, paying tributes in some cases to live in Seminole areas in towns in which they governed themselves. Several such enclaves were sites of Seminole–black cooperation and mutual defense from American forces. Spanish authorities relied on such coalitions to strengthen their position against American belligerents. The results of that trilateral cooperation included settlements clustered along the Suwanee River in central Florida such as Bowlegs Town, which collected refugees from the destroyed Negro Fort. Other defensive outposts were Powell's Town on the Withlacoochee River and the free black enclave known as Mulatto Girl's Town south of Alachua, which flourished from 1818 to about 1823.[23]

To American citizens, such maroon communities were insurgent outposts. And like Negro Fort, they beckoned runways from cotton country. Still leading volunteers in 1817, Andrew Jackson provoked a crisis with Spain while starting a war against Seminoles in the name of eliminating the internal enemy from the southeast mainland of North America. In doing so, he accentuated an emerging racial justification for making war on Native Americans, now allied with African Americans. Indians and maroons were subject to ethnic cleansing, anticipating Jackson's Indian removal policies as president.[24] In November, General Gaines

[21] Quoted in Walters, *American Slave Revolts and Conspiracies*, 92.
[22] Jane G. Landers, *Atlantic Creoles in the Age of Revolutions* (Cambridge, MA: Harvard University Press, 2010), chap. 3.
[23] Landers, *Atlantic Creoles in the Age of Revolutions*, chaps. 3–5.
[24] Deborah A. Rosen, *Border Law: The First Seminole War and American Nationhood* (Cambridge, MA: Harvard University Press, 2015).

attacked and burned the Mikasuki–Seminole village of Fowl Town, which provoked Seminole retaliations. Secretary of War John C. Calhoun appointed Jackson commander of American forces in the area. And Jackson escalated the conflict, starting the First Seminole War and instigating a fight with Spain in the southeastern borderlands. Spain ceded Florida to the United States under the terms of the Adams–Onís Treaty of 1819, extending slavery and invigorating the cotton economy. The Seminole Wars became America's longest-running and most expensive military commitment until the Civil War and a preview of a Manifest Destiny argument for the expansion of a continental empire. And it was relentless. The Third Seminole War did not end until 1858, more than forty years after the destruction of Negro Fort.

As American soldiers pursued rebels in Florida, Denmark Vesey used his church network in Charleston, South Carolina, as a hub of the black insurgency, organizing one of the largest uprisings in American history in 1822. Vesey was born on St. Thomas, then a Danish possession, in 1767, and spent his boyhood on St. Thomas in a polyglot Creole community. At age fourteen he was sold to slave traders sailing to St. Domingue, the hellish French sugar island that became Haiti. On board a merchant ship, he attracted sailors' attention. Called Telemaque, Vesey was described as physically striking, and the ship's master, Joseph Vesey, bought him and resold him to a sugar planter, who sent him back for a refund. Captain Vesey took him back in 1781 and employed him aboard his slave ship for another two years before settling him in Charleston, South Carolina.[25]

Religious networks and evangelical fervor explain how Vesey's planned uprising and the black insurgency of which it was a part changed in the generation after Gabriel's Rebellion. Evangelical Christianity washed over the landscape. In backwoods revivals and in urban meeting houses, the new evangelicals became fishers of converts. When African-descended Americans heard the Word and read Scripture, they took unintended lessons: that all people were spiritual equals in the sight of God, that all were equally loved by Jesus Christ, and that the Holy Spirit was working for all. Christianity leveled republican hierarchies and elided democratic divisions.[26] Denmark Vesey was among a cadre of evangelical

---

[25] Douglas R. Egerton, *He Shall Go Out Free: The Lives of Denmark Vesey*, rev. edn. (Lanham, MD: Rowman and Littlefield, 2004).

[26] James Cone, *Black Theology and Black Power* (New York, NY: Harper & Row, 1969); Sylvia Frey and Betty Wood, *Come Shouting to Zion: African American Protestantism in the American South and British Caribbean to 1830* (Chapel Hill, NC: University of North

African Americans who preached a theology of liberation that became a strategy of emancipation.

That liberation network formed with black congregations. In Charleston, Vesey acted as his owner's agent and servant, forming a wide network of associations in the bustling city. There he married an enslaved woman named Beck, learned trades and literacy, and met numerous potential recruits. In 1799, the thirty-three year-old Vesey's fortunes turned when he bought a winning lottery ticket. With $1,500, he bought his freedom from Joseph Vesey, now a plantation owner. Denmark Vesey worked as a carpenter, but rather than distancing himself from his enslaved friends and acquaintances, as many free African-descended Charlestonians did, he remained close, answering a vocation. He became a minister, preaching equality among men and rebelliousness to whites who refused to acknowledge Christian equality. It was a time when evangelicals were planting churches and broadening their work.

Vesey became a class leader in the Methodist Church, cultivating a black following at a time when evangelicals were dividing along racial lines. The African Methodist Episcopal (AME) church was the first independent black Protestant denomination in America, and in 1818, under the leadership of Morris Brown, Charleston's AME church seceded from the white Methodists. African-descended people were like the children of Israel, Vesey argued. And the New Testament liberation theology of the biblical Apostle Paul of Tarsus was also operating in the potent evangelical upwelling in Vesey's Charleston. One witness said "he would speak of the creation of the world in which he would say all men had equal rights, black as well as whites, &c. all his religious remarks were mingled with [s]lavery."[27]

And as Paul defied Roman authority, African-descended Christians defied whites' authority. In retaliation for exercising religious autonomy, authorities arrested 140 AME church members in June 1818, and several black ministers were given the choice of fines or jail time or leaving the state. Morris remained, serving a month in jail. And as the conflict deepened, Vesey formed ties with enslaved men such as Rolla Bennett, Monday Gell, and Peter Poyas, their conversations turning on the injustices swirling around them.

Carolina Press, 1998); Eddie Glaude, *Exodus! Religion, Race, and Nation in Early Nineteenth-Century Black America* (Chicago, IL: University of Chicago Press, 2000).

[27] Ex-slave, quoted in Lawrence W. Levine, *Black Culture and Black Consciousness: Afro-American Folk Thought from Slavery to Freedom* (New York, NY: Oxford University Press, 1977), 76.

A plot formed to throw off slavery's chains. As AME leaders were perse-cuted and driven underground, they linked Christian liberation theology with historical processes like the Haitian Revolution and some traditional African practices. At some point before the summer of 1822, Vesey's ministry turned from Christian salvation to earthly revolution. The 1820 Missouri Crisis convinced him that the tide was turning against slavery in the United States. He and Monday Gell looked to Haiti as an ally. They authored a letter to Jean-Pierre Boyer, who had become Haiti's president in 1818 and was working to unify the country. A black sailor promised to deliver it. Angola native Gullah Jack allied with Vesey's insurgents, which helped broaden the revolution's appeal to Africans shipped to Charleston as slaves before the 1808 ban. Jack organized an Angolan band of insurgents. Monday Gell organized fellow Igbos from West Africa into a regiment. Mingo Harth was another West African who organized Mandinka recruits. Some of these ethnic companies maintained cultural discipline: dissenters or those who refused to join the planned rebellion would suffer the scorn of fellow Africans from the old country. This pan-African coalition joined a wider vision Vesey offered, "that if we did not put our hand to the work, & deliver ourselves, we would never come out of [s]lavery." And with a growing insurgent network reaching into the church, out to various ethnic groups, and beyond Charleston to Haiti, Vesey's planned revolution quickly took shape in 1822.[28]

Vesey's would-be revolution had the potential to succeed, even more than Gabriel's 1800 uprising. Lowcountry South Carolina was majority black and majority enslaved, unlike Richmond and Henrico County, Virginia. Vesey's insurgent network was broad, and perhaps 9,000 enslaved people knew some part of the uprising planned for July 14, 1822, Bastille Day, commemorating the start of the French Revolution in 1789. But such a wide-ranging conspiracy was also a weakness. A bondsman named Peter betrayed the plot in May. Governor Thomas Bennett was disinclined to believe that his bondsman Rolla was involved in any planned uprising so sweeping and ambitious, even after Rolla – Vesey's friend – was implicated. But evidence coming from informants – including two enslaved men who traded betrayal for freedom – blew up the plan.

South Carolina and Charleston authorities began rounding up accused conspirators and torturing confessions out of them. Vesey fled but was caught, along with 130 other African-descended people. Panic spread

---

[28] Bernard E. Powers, *Black Charlestonians: A Social History, 1822–1885* (Fayetteville, AR: University of Arkansas Press, 1994), 32 (quotation); Egerton, *He Shall Go Out Free*, chap. 6.

among whites as the magnitude of the planned rebellion came to light. Two courts were convened in Charleston, and as a result of the proceedings, thirty were released, thirty-seven were exiled from the state, and twenty-three were acquitted. Two died in custody, and courts convicted and sentenced thirty-five to death by hanging. Vesey, Rolla Bennett, Peter Poyas, and several others were hanged on July 2 outside the city limits, their bodies taken by surgeons. Even in death black bodies had "ghost values" or a postmortem slave commodity price.[29]

The decision to hang Vesey and some of his coleaders in an out-of-the way place was meant to deprive them of martyrdom. Yet South Carolina officials created a ghastly spectacle of executing others. On July 12, two more insurgents were hanged at a portion of Charleston called the Lines, a stone wall at the city's northern limits. Twenty-two were led to the Lines on July 26, where a group of benches was set up and nooses thrown over the walls in a gallows spectacle staged as a theatrical display of vengeance. But authorities botched the executions, miscalculating the drop. And instead of seeing the necks of the condemned breaking, the large crowd – including children – watched as twenty-two men were slowly strangling. The captain of the city guard then opted to shoot each one by one. When five more conspirators were hanged at the Lines in late July and August, the nooses were dangled from a deadly height.[30]

In the aftermath of the abortive Vesey rebellion, South Carolina imposed harsh new security measures meant to control the contagion of liberty among would-be black insurgents. Black preachers were banned, the AME church was destroyed, and independent congregations were disbanded. The state passed new black codes in December, including the mandatory arrest of any black mariner who arrived in port (though he could be released to leave). South Carolina's Negro Seaman's Act of 1823 enacted harsh penalties for violators. Charleston beefed up its police force, built a new arsenal, and created a surveillance association to watch and control black people. City bondspersons had long worn badges, and that regime was more strictly enforced along with slave patrols and increased penalties for bondspersons hiring their own time.

Eight years after Vesey's execution, a fresh wave of religious antislavery activism stoked enslavers' fears. North Carolina native David Walker

---

[29] Daina Ramey Berry, *The Price for Their Pound of Flesh: Black Bodies for Sale in the Building of America* (Boston, MA: Beacon Press, 2017), chap. 6.

[30] Jack Shuler, *The Thirteenth Turn: A History of the Noose* (New York, NY: PublicAffairs, 2014), 102–05.

extended Vesey's liberation theology into a call for massive uprisings in his 1829 *Appeal, in Four Articles; Together with a Preamble, to the Coloured Citizens of the World, but in Particular, and Very Expressly, to Those of the United States of America.* Born free in North Carolina in 1785, Walker became an antislavery lecturer, traveling widely before settling in the 1820s in Boston, where he ran a used clothing business. He rejected the gradualism of the American Colonization Society, which sponsored schemes to manumit American bondspersons and exile them to Liberia. Instead he urged an immediate uprising.

Walker's *Appeal* was in important ways an expression of a rising tide of democracy and evangelical religion. Words and political speech were becoming powerful democratic forces as more people could read and buy copies of newspapers, books, tracts, pamphlets, and magazines. Democratic appeals were beginning to infuse politics as they had religious debates. And seizing that democratic entitlement, Walker picked up a pen mightier than many swords. It provoked an antidemocratic response.

When copies of the *Appeal* were found circulating among African Americans in Wilmington, North Carolina, in 1830, whites' frenzied response sent a murderous wave across the eastern part of the state. Governor John Owen led a frantic effort to suppress the *Appeal*, sending notices to thirty-two state senators and urging law enforcement to be on high alert. Suspicion soon centered on the large free African American networks in Pasquotank and Craven Counties. New Bern was thought to be at the center of an insurrection planned for Christmas Day, 1830, and enslavers arrested and detained hundreds of African-descended people suspected of conspiring against them. In Chowan County, a mob destroyed a black church, rifled the dwellings of Edenton residents, and forbade gatherings. No conspiracy was uncovered, but fears simmered as the state legislature passed a raft of repressive legislation.

North Carolina tightened security, forbidding bondspersons' gaming and whites' gaming with them. Sheriffs were empowered to sell fugitives caught as runaways and to prevent free blacks from selling wares outside the county in which they resided. It forbade "the circulation of seditious publications" or those advocating rebellion, established new county slave patrols, punished harboring runaways, and threw up barriers to black people entering the state and to manumitted bondspersons remaining. Once freed or manumitted, black North Carolinians had ninety days to leave the state for good. It forbade intermarriage among blacks and whites and, perhaps most ominously, the legislature passed a law "to Prevent All Persons from Teaching Slaves to Read or Write, the Use of Figures

Excepted." Numeracy could serve enslavers' ends, but literacy was dangerous. State-enforced ignorance was the price North Carolina was willing to pay to prevent an organized black insurgency.[31] Across the South, enslavers undercut public education in a furious attempt to foreclose the possibility that black protests could find their way into print and through it the circulation of ideas. And then enslavers' worst fears came to pass.

On the moonlit early morning of August 22, 1831, Nat Turner climbed up a ladder into his owner Joseph Travis's house in Southampton County, Virginia, slipped in through an attic window, crept downstairs, and unbolted the door, letting in two fellow insurgents, Will Francis and Hark Travis, also called Hark Moore. "I entered my master's chamber, it being dark," Turner testified. He raised a hatchet with deadly intent, then faltered. "I could not give a death blow, the hatchet glanced from his head, he sprang from the bed and called his wife, it was his last word, Will laid him dead, with a blow of his axe, and Mrs. Travis shared the same fate, as she lay in bed." Downstairs two white boys, Putnam Moore and Joel Westbrook, were also sliced to death with axes. The most deadly slave uprising in American history had begun.[32]

The Nat Turner Rebellion brought home the ever-present possibility that enslaved people would rise up and murder their owners in bed. And the Turner rebels did not spare non-enslavers. Every white person in their path was targeted for being connected to an enslaver in some way. The uprising was calculated to spread terror. It was planned, not spontaneous. And it came from within the black neighborhood local whites claimed to have mastered. The terror of that August rocked the state and nation and rattled the foundations of slavery in Virginia.

Nat Turner was about thirty, born the year Gabriel was executed in Virginia and Denmark Vesey bought his freedom in South Carolina. He was recognized as particularly intelligent and gifted. "I was intended for some great purpose," he testified. He professed Christianity, and as Turner grew, he began a ministry to fellow bondspersons. Unlike Vesey, he did not become part of an institutional church. Rather, he claimed that the Holy Spirit spoke to him as a prophet. Turner witnessed several prophesies such as when he "discovered drops of blood on the corn as

---

[31] Jean Fagan Yellin, *Harriet Jacobs: A Life* (New York, NY: Basic Books, 2005), 35 (quotations); Claude A. Clegg III, *The Price of Liberty: African Americans and the Making of Liberia* (Chapel Hill, NC: University of North Carolina Press, 2004), chap. 3.

[32] Nat Turner, *The Confessions of Nat Turner, the Leader of the Late Insurrection in Southampton, Va.* (Baltimore, MD: T. R. Gray, 1831), 12.

though it were dew from heaven," and also found "on the leaves in the woods hieroglyphic characters, and numbers, with the forms of men in different attitudes, portrayed in blood." This was evidence of a divine commission of which he was the fulfillment: "I should arise and prepare myself and slay my enemies with their own weapons."

After the murders of Mr. and Mrs. Travis, one of the rebels returned to the Travis house to kill an infant left behind, beheading it and throwing the body in a fireplace. The band then moved south a quarter mile to the cabin of Salathiel Francis, killing him, taking his guns and horses, and moving in the early morning darkness southward to the Reese farm, killing Piety Reese and her eighteen-year-old son, William. Both the Francis and Reese properties were home to free and enslaved African Americans, and the Turner rebels spared their lives while recruiting others.[33]

As dawn approached, Turner's men then headed for the Elizabeth Turner plantation, where Nat Turner had once abided. There an insurgent shot and killed a white overseer, but "as we approached, the family discovered us, and shut the door," Turner recalled. "Will, with one stroke of his axe, opened it, and we entered and found Mrs. Turner and Mrs. Newsome in the middle of a room, almost frightened to death." Will Francis killed Elizabeth Turner, and Nat Turner killed Sarah Newsom. The rebels ransacked the estate and recruited insurgents from the slave dwellings. Having killed nearly eleven whites connected to Turner's rebels by legal ownership, the group split up.[34]

Turner directed a detachment to attack neighboring estates while he led men south. Hark Moore and Jack Reese killed four non-slave owners, including an infant. Alarmed whites in the neighborhood had begun fleeing the insurgents. Turner led nine more rebels who mounted horses and rode to the Whitehead cotton plantation, killing seven, including a two-year-old toddler. A terrified Harriet Whitehead hid in a bedroom and was left alive. Enslaved people belonging to the Whiteheads fled, but on leaving the plantation Turner's men recruited two enslaved men returning from an early morning hunt. Now numbering seventeen, the band split again, fanning out into the county.

As the sun rose higher on that summer morning, Turner's rebels raced against warnings sent out by whites in the neighborhood about the

---

[33] David F. Allmendinger Jr. *Nat Turner and the Rising in Southampton County* (Baltimore, MD: Johns Hopkins University Press, 2014), chaps. 5–6.

[34] Turner, *The Confessions of Nat Turner*, 13.

uprising, splitting up. As the killings continued, Turner recruited more rebels. Some joined willingly while others were coerced. By then whites were counterattacking. Tom Barrow had received word the rebels were heading to his farm and loaded two guns, lying in wait for the insurgents led by Nat Turner II (another Nat Turner involved in the raid). While his sister-in-law Mary T. Vaughn escaped through a garden, aided by an enslaved woman, Barrow fired at the rebels but was overrun and killed along with his brother-in-law George Vaughn.[35]

At ten in the morning, white volunteers chased about Southampton County on the bloody trail of the insurgents. Evading them, Nat Turner and the two other rebel detachments regrouped at the Newt Harris farm, then attacked the Levi Waller farm, killing ten, including six children, before advancing on the farms of William and Jacob Williams, killing a dozen more whites. A little after noon, the insurgents shot three more at the Rebecca Vaughn farm. To avoid the betrayals that undermined Gabriel and Denmark Vesey's uprisings, Turner had kept his plans to himself, acting as a military commander. He even took the name "General Jackson" (Andrew Jackson was president at the time) or "General Cargill" while his captains also referred to themselves as generals.[36]

The moonlight raid had become a daylight skirmish. About thirty of Turner's insurgents encountered an eighteen-member white posse at Parker's Field, about three miles from the town of Jerusalem (today Courtland). Whites formed as if to fight. Turner's men advanced after he ordered them "to fire and rush on them." And the militiamen fled, Turner's insurgents pursuing until they met another posse of white volunteers reinforcing the first, counterattacking and pushing back Turner's men. "The insurgents," Captain William C. Parker contended, "after receiving a few raggling fires, retreated."[37] Turner recalled that "several of my bravest men being wounded, the others became panick [sic] struck and squandered over the field; the white men pursued and fired on us several times."[38]

White militiamen fell back while the insurgents tried an alternate route to Jerusalem, halted by whites guarding a bridge. By nightfall, about

[35] Allmendinger, *Nat Turner and the Rising in Southampton County*, 181–82.
[36] Thomas C. Parramore, "Covenant in Jerusalem," in *Nat Turner: A Slave Rebellion in History and Memory*, ed. Kenneth S. Greenberg (New York, NY: Oxford University Press, 2003), 58 (quotation); Allmendinger, *Nat Turner and the Rising in Southampton County*, 184–90.
[37] Parker, quoted in Allmendinger, *Nat Turner and the Rising in Southampton County*, 193.
[38] Turner, *The Confessions of Nat Turner*, 16.

twenty surviving members of Turner's force gathered at Buckhorn Quarter four miles west of Jerusalem, including both Nat Turners, Hark Moore, and Sam Francis. They spent the night there, moving at about five in the morning to the house of Dr. Samuel Blunt. There Blunt and some neighbors fired on the rebels. As the Turner rebels moved to the Newt Harris farm again to regroup, they encountered mounted militiamen from nearby Greensville County. Most of the insurgents disbanded. Turner went into hiding near Cabin Pond. The Turner Rebellion had ended.

But whites in Virginia and North Carolina panicked, it not being clear whether Turner's insurgency was isolated or one part of a vast and coordinated uprising. Locals in Southampton County and its vicinity summarily executed African-descended people with near impunity, perhaps twenty-five to forty in the days after the uprising. Alfred, owned by Levi Waller, was captured by Southampton volunteers shortly before the skirmish at Parker's Field. To restrain him, they cut his Achilles tendons. When the Greensville militia came upon Alfred, they shot him dead, cut off his head, and placed it on a post by the roadside. And Jordan, a black man who had joined Dr. Blunt in shooting at insurgents on August 23, was killed anyway. One black man was shot dead by a jittery militia company just for being in Southampton County. Militiamen from Norfolk took home the severed heads of several enslaved people, placing them atop poles to warn any would-be insurrectionaries.

Misinformation led to hysteria. Reports indicated that the Southampton insurgent leaders had fled to the Great Dismal Swamp straddling the Virginia–North Carolina border. "Excessive agitation prevailed in [Wilmington, North Carolina]," a Maryland newspaper reported, "the men were under arms, and the women and children half-distracted by their fears; and thus it was in several parts of North Carolina, and the people hastily prepared themselves to encounter reported armies of slaves!" About 1,000 militia and federal troops responded, rounding up suspects and hunting for conspirators. And by September, perhaps 100 African-descended people in southern Virginia and northern North Carolina had been killed by militia and other white mobs.[39]

---

[39] *Baltimore Gazette and Daily Advertiser*, August 25, 1831, 2; *Niles' Weekly Register* [Baltimore] September 24, 1831, 67 (quotation); Lacy K. Ford, *Deliver Us from Evil: The Slavery Question in the Old South* (New York, NY: Oxford University Press, 2009), 338–53; Alfred L. Brophy, "The Nat Turner Trials," *North Carolina Law Review* 91 (May 2013): 1817–80.

The meanings of the uprising and the identity of Nat Turner remain controversial matters. To some, he was a holy warrior. To others, he was a thief and a murderer. To yet others, he was a general. But unlike Gabriel, Turner's insurgency targeted whites regardless of class or whether they were enslavers. Even babies were not spared, a tactic suggesting vengeance for so many black infants and children snatched away. And unlike Vesey's uprising centered on a church, the 1831 rebellion in Southampton focused on a determined leader, one whose ministry attracted some followers and repelled others.[40] Turner hid for nine weeks in Southampton County before being captured, and legend spread of "Captain Nat Turner" and "Gen. Nat Turner." He was compared to Gabriel in the press.[41] In jail pending trial, he gave an interview to a local lawyer, Thomas Ruffin Gray, detailing the uprising and his putative motives. Gray published it as *The Confessions of Nat Turner*. Authorities treated it as an admission of guilt.

It was a shrewd one indeed. Turner drew all the responsibility for the rebellion to himself while announcing its overarching theme, "it 'twas my object to carry terror and devastation wherever we went." The "terror" was deliberate. Turner gave no indication that he had been persuaded by abolitionist appeals or that he was head of an expansive revolutionary movement. Rather, his uprising was a response to a divine call. "The Spirit instantly appeared to me and said the Serpent was loosened," Turner argued, "and Christ had laid down the yoke he had borne for the sins of men, and that I should take it on and fight against the Serpent, for the time was fast approaching when the first should be last and the last should be first."[42]

Virginia declared war on that kind of terror. Authorities tried suspected insurgents, executing fifty-five, equal to the number of whites killed. Some suspects were acquitted while others were sentenced to transportation out of state. After Turner's execution, spectators dismembered his body. Some took souvenirs. His head probably made it to Wooster, Ohio, though the corpses of many of those hanged were taken off to the medical school at the University of Virginia, where cadavers were in short supply. In North

[40] James Sidbury, "Reading, Revelation, and Rebellion: The Textual Communities of Gabriel, Denmark Vesey, and Nat Turner," and Douglas R. Egerton, "Nat Turner in a Hemispheric Context," in *Nat Turner*, 119–47.

[41] *Baltimore Gazette and Daily Advertiser*, August 29, 1831, 2 (first quotation); *Vermont Republican*, September 10, 1831, 3 (second quotation); *Salem* [Mass.] *Gazette*, September 9, 1831, 2.

[42] Turner, *The Confessions of Nat Turner*, 14 (first quotation); 11 (second quotation).

Carolina, by year's end, fifteen African Americans were lynched and another fourteen convicted of insurrection. Twelve of them were hanged.[43]

Although Nat Turner insisted his rebellion was divinely ordained, it came amid a chain of uprisings that were part of a wider revolutionary movement sweeping Europe and the Americas in the early 1830s. In Europe came the July 1830 Revolution in France and uprisings in Poland, Italy, and the German states. Belgium split from the Netherlands in 1831, and Greece won its independence from the Ottoman Empire in 1832. West Indian bondspersons were mobilizing too. In February 1831, a slave rebellion in Martinique involved some 300 bondspersons and a pair of white revolutionaries. In the aftermath, twenty-two African-descended people were executed in Saint-Pierre, and French authorities imposed a strict color line. In 1831, enslaved insurgents on British Tortola planned to kill all the white males on that sugar island and seek refuge in Haiti. In December 1831, Samuel Sharpe led nearly 20,000 African-descended people in the Christmas Rebellion in Jamaica, burning sugar plantations, stores, and sugar houses, and taking large swaths of the island under rebel control. British forces put it down early in 1832, executing 138, including Sharpe, and maiming many more.

But British legislators were forced to confront the issue of why so many were following insurgent leaders like Sharpe. Abolitionist and Member of Parliament Thomas Fowell Buxton warned the House of Commons that "if the question respecting the West Indies were not speedily settled, it would settle itself in an alarming way." Buxton and his abolitionist colleagues were able to persuade Parliament to pass a gradual abolition scheme that would rid Britain of West Indies slavery starting in 1834 while compensating owners financially.[44] It was the last nail in the coffin of the old West Indies sugar lobby, and Parliament calculated it was far better for Americans to pay the security costs of enslaved people to produce cotton bound for England than for Britain to risk uprisings for diminishing returns in sugar. Virginia too debated whether African American slavery was worth the costs the Turner Rebellion tallied.

After Turner was executed, the Virginia General Assembly weighed the expenses of a slave security state against the financial interests of

[43] David Grimsted, *American Mobbing, 1828–1861: Toward Civil War* (New York, NY: Oxford University Press, 1998), chap. 5.

[44] Buxton quoted in Gelien Matthews, *Caribbean Slave Revolts and the British Abolitionist Movement* (Baton Rouge, LA: Louisiana State University Press, 2006), 168.

enslavers. Some antislavery delegates recommended colonization – sending manumitted bondspersons out of the country – and thereby ending slavery gradually. Colonization was the persistent outcome of racial thinking that stumbled on the logic of inclusive societies.[45] But the Assembly sided with enslavers, narrowly defeating a gradual abolition petition early in 1832. That was no accident.

Slavery promised greater returns than in the 1820s. In 1830, slave prices in the United States had begun their steepest ascent in fifteen years. Cotton prices were leading the rise. British demand for American slave-grown cotton rippled back to Virginia, the state with the largest enslaved population. With each slave sale, Virginia enslavers collected some of the wealth flowing into the state from lower south sugar and cotton planters demanding more workers. Would-be revolutionaries could be sold off with greater ease and efficiency as bondspersons became liquid assets.[46] The slave market therefore seemed to diffuse the dangers of future uprisings. But states did not let the market alone solve their security problems.

In the wake of the Nat Turner Rebellion, Virginia and bordering states passed sweeping new restrictions on people of African descent. Since religion and abolitionist agitation seemed to be at the root of the rebellion, Virginia took steps to limit black preaching and everything associated with it. The legislature outlawed teaching people of African descent, free or enslaved, to read or write. Many teachers disobeyed the law and instructed black students anyway. The legislature forbade religious worship without a licensed white minister. Some African American congregations went underground, meeting in secret. Other black Christians joined white worshippers, under their surveillance, rather than go unchurched. Virginia's measures were part of a wave of restrictive legislation enforcing a color line in worship, mobility, and education, which also enlisted whites of all social classes as monitors of African-descended people.[47]

Deep South states countered Virginia's efforts to dispose of rebels in the interstate slave trade. A month after Turner was executed in Virginia, Louisiana forbade entry of enslaved people brought to the state for sale based on rumors that traders bought up other Southampton rebels for

---

[45] Nicholas Guyatt, *Bind Us Apart: How Enlightened Americans Invented Racial Segregation* (New York, NY: Basic Books, 2016).

[46] Baptist, *The Half Has Never Been Told*, chap. 7.

[47] Rebecca Hartkopf Schloss, "The February 1831 Slave Uprising in Martinique and the Policing of White Identity," *French Historical Studies* 30.2 (Spring 2007): 203–36.

export. To prevent the volatile conditions leading to the German Coast uprising twenty years earlier, Louisiana already required certificates of good character for any bondsperson arriving in the state for sale. Alabama also passed emergency legislation that was a mix of Virginia restrictions on literacy and Louisiana restrictions on bondspersons entering the state. The Alabama legislature refused to allow enslaved people entering with any but a resident owner or migrant owner and outlawed teaching African Americans to read or write and gathering in groups of five or more, and forbade anyone addressing groups of black people – a prohibition on public worship. Mississippi wrote a slave-trading ban into its 1832 constitution. Yet some enslavers scoffed at such restrictions. "London and Paris have much more to dread from their rabble than Louisiana will ever have from her blacks," banker Edmond Jean Forstall wrote a New York correspondent in 1832. Demographics favored white surveillance and control over black workers, he argued, since Louisiana's population was roughly equal free and enslaved.[48] Forstall's explanation is the kernel of why there were not more Nat Turner-like uprisings.

But in preventing another rebellion, Virginia and other states permitting slavery doubled down on war capitalism while foreclosing what would later be called Schumpeterian capitalism, which was capitalism characterized by an intellectual class of creative entrepreneurs. Theorized by economist Joseph Schumpeter, entrepreneurial, change-oriented capitalism flourished in places with schools, free exchanges of ideas, and encouragement of innovation. It led to experimentation and invention rather than merely growth. Instead, Virginia and other states that remained committed to slavery knocked down opportunities for education and with it the creativity that led to economic diversity in states and regions in which slavery was outlawed.[49]

The process had been unfolding for decades, but the draconian restrictions on literacy and dissemination of literature put in place after 1831 meant that creativity foundered on the overriding imperatives of the slave security state. In restricting schooling and literacy to enslaved people, it denigrated the same for poor whites. In enlisting whites to police

---

[48] Robert H. Gudmestad, *A Troublesome Commerce: The Transformation of the Interstate Slave Trade* (Baton Rouge, LA: Louisiana State University Press, 2003), chap. 4; Edmond Forstall to Thomas Wren Ward, November 19, 1832, Baring Papers, Ottawa, Canada, quoted in Reginald C. McGrane, *Foreign Bondholders and American State Debts* (New York, NY: Macmillan, 1935), 171 (quotation).

[49] John Majewski, "Slavery and Schumpeterian Capitalism," paper presented at the Business History Conference, April 1, 2016, Portland, Oregon.

nonwhites, the state became consumed with suspicion and security, focusing on terror rather than on hope. Free speech sank in importance, so great was the fear that another *Appeal* would circulate. In choosing the interests of enslavers Virginia chose the expansion of commodity capitalism over economic diversification and a more creative and dynamic variety of capitalism. And so the 1830s became a great fulcrum of American history, thanks in no small measure to the Turner Rebellion erupting in the context of a growing financial interest in chattel slavery.

Enslaved rebels brought home to enslavers the towering social costs of slavery, and by the 1830s, the slave security state developed in reaction to the black insurgency. Southern whites traded liberty for security, forbidding educational opportunities for African-descended residents, closing churches, curtailing meetings, and restricting unsupervised movement. In the process they sacrificed economic diversity and democracy to the imperatives of slave labor production. Rebels were captured, tortured, sold off, or executed. Their tactical objectives failed. Gabriel, Sancho, Deslondes, Vesey, and Turner met gruesome fates, and they did not spark a Haitian revolution in the United States. But collectively they forced enslavers to choose a repressive regime that squashed economic vibrancy in the service of war capitalism. It was that move to a society of suspicion and the overriding imperative of protecting enslaved property that divided the Slave South from states in which slavery was prohibited. And slave security set the groundwork for the meteoric expansion of slavery in the 1830s.

5

Financial Chains

Money made enslavers' world go around, and the ordeals of three young African-descended Americans in the slave market in 1835 reveal both the human costs and financial connections that made the slavery business. That summer, Norfolk slave trader Bernard Raux and his partners bought a shipload of captives in Virginia and North Carolina to sell in New Orleans, where prices were much higher. One was Virginia native Venus Giles. She was sixteen years old and stood five feet three inches tall. In late June, Raux bought her, handing her Norfolk owner $550, probably in banknotes from the Bank of the United States.[1] The kind of money he used was important. Banknotes were not the familiar greenbacks of today featuring Andrew Jackson or Alexander Hamilton. The Federal Reserve notes of a later era were issued by government authority and backed by confidence in the nation's solvency. Instead, banknotes in the 1830s were expressions of trust in particular financial institutions. In 1835, the Bank of the United States was a quasi-public bank issuing its own notes alongside some 700 state-chartered banks throughout the country. Notes embodied confidence in the promises made to redeem them. Banknotes also point to a towering irony of the slave trade: its violence and destruction was built on confidence and trust.

Confidence tied the promise of future repayment to the imagination of entrepreneurs, even slavery's entrepreneurs. And that relationship of trust was at the heart of capitalism. Yet money was not all equal, and slave

---

[1] Bill of sale from [?] Cox (Venus), June 29, 1835, folder 35, Bernard Raux Slave Trade Papers, 1828–36 (MS Am 790), Houghton Library, Harvard University (Raux Papers, HU).

traders were as concerned about particularities of money and finance as they were about risks and captives' security. Their business took place over a vast geography. Norfolk and New Orleans were separated by several states and thousands of miles of ocean. Within that space, most money was local. Americans – if they had money – spent a hodgepodge of promissory notes, state banknotes, foreign coins, and a few federal ones. Most did business on local credit. And much of what changed hands when something was bought or sold was not widely spendable. A typical state banknote was worth less the farther it traveled from the bank that issued it. Silver and gold were scarce, cumbersome, and expensive to use. After all, coins were bulky and could be stolen easily. But paper money held certain advantages, especially notes from a strong state bank (a privately held bank chartered by a state) or the Bank of the United States. Notes from the Bank of the United States were typically the best suited for spending across state lines. And all banknotes were negotiable instruments, meaning that in theory they could be redeemed in silver or gold and so embodied trust in future repayment. That is why owners were willing to part with such valuable human properties in exchange for pieces of paper.

To buy Giles and the others, Raux wrote a $11,469 draft on his account at the Bank of the United States branch in Norfolk ($322,000 in 2017 real price equivalent), cashed by his partner Paul Pascal, and with the money in hand, he scouted for young enslaved people.[2] And those notes were part of what held the economy together. The Bank of the United States exercised a central banking function that organized a national economy. Its policies also stabilized and promoted the interstate slave trade, if unintentionally. In the previous decade, the Bank had become an engine of slavery's growth by regulating the domestic or national exchange of money (mostly bills of exchange, another type of negotiable instrument) to ensure steady growth in the North Atlantic cotton economy. After assuming the presidency in 1823, Bank president Nicholas Biddle instituted monetary policies that integrated sections of the country. By buying and selling bills – called exchange – the Bank smoothed out seasonal variations in the national money supply, promoting foreign trade and national growth.[3] And the confidence Biddle built

---

[2] Bernard Raux, check payable by the Second Bank of the United States, July 29, 1835, Series 3, Folder 15, Raux Papers, HU.

[3] Howard Bodenhorn, *A History of Banking in Antebellum America: Financial Markets and Economic Development in an Era of Nation-Building* (New York, NY: Cambridge University Press, 2000).

attracted foreign investment in both the Bank of the United States and the economy it shepherded. And to do that Biddle and the Bank relied on British backers.

London was the financial capital of the North Atlantic, and merchant bank Baring Brothers and Company of London extended Biddle and the Bank a revolving credit line to cover the Bank's exchange business. In addition to buying and selling domestic bills, the Bank's exchange business involved accepting foreign bills of exchange and turning them into dollars and, through merchants, putting those dollars into circulation or loaning them out. The British connection was important because most American cotton was sold in Britain, and many of the goods Americans imported came from there. Broadly speaking, Americans imported goods credit and exported raw materials, much of it the product of slave labor. The Bank's financial transactions generated profits, and Biddle wielded a great deal of economic power (which generated charges of favoritism and corruption).

But the important consideration for slave traders was the soundness of the paper money used to buy bondspersons. Barings' British pounds crossed the ocean to become dollars drawn by slave traders to pay for captives like Venus Giles. And with Biddle at the helm, the national economy sailed along. State banking and credit facilities grew steadily as growth accelerated under the Bank's stewardship. The Andrew Jackson administration defunded the Bank in 1834 in favor of smaller state banks run by Democratic supporters. But even by 1835, the Bank's notes were the best banknotes in the country since they could be redeemed in many places.[4] And enslaved people were part of a constellation of interests. In the eyes of slave traders, African-descended Americans were investment properties. To bankers, they were working capital. To enslavers, they were both laborers and "collateralized labor."[5] And the main strategy of slave traders was to align the enforced movement of enslaved people with the flow of money among centers of banking and the domestic slave trade that was part of a larger process of slavery's commodification.

Capitalism transformed American slavery by radically commercializing it. And finance was decisive in that transformation. Without banking

---

[4] Sharon Ann Murphy, *Other People's Money: How Banking Worked in the Early American Republic* (Baltimore, MD: Johns Hopkins University Press, 2017).

[5] Joseph C. Miller, *The Problem of Slavery as History: A Global Approach* (New Haven, CT: Yale University Press, 2012), 142 (quotation); Robert W. Fogel, *Without Consent or Contract: The Rise and Fall of American Slavery* (New York, NY: W. W. Norton, 1991), chap. 1.

and credit there would have been no war capitalism and no cotton empire. Credit availability was the main limiting factor to growth. But unlike the violence done to bodies of bondspersons, the actions and movements of credit were relationships that built confidence in financial transactions. Financing the bloody violence of the pushing system, the commercialization of slavery was a process of handshakes, confident words, and honorable signatures on lifeless paper that passed from hand to hand. That process was largely hidden from enslaved people themselves.

Whether Venus Giles saw the banknotes exchanged for her body, the transaction was terrifying. Her world shattered as she was led away from home and family. After a month locked in the Norfolk City Jail, she met another forlorn captive, Israel Dyson. He was twenty-three years old and from North Carolina. Dyson stood five feet five inches tall and had been exchanged for $900 in banknotes. Venus Giles had spent more than two months in a hot, humid, crowded jail when Lewis Hancock was tossed in among the captives that first Monday in September. Hancock was twenty-one and stood five feet eight inches tall. Lewis Hancock's world shattered when his legal owner handed him over to slave trader Paul Pascal for $900 in banknotes. Most understood that the journey to Louisiana was one of no return.[6] But those sales were part of a booming economy.

Financial expansion closely tracked slave market growth. The domestic slave trade rose 84 percent in the 1830s. Bank money per capita in Virginia rose 66 percent between 1830 and 1840. Upper South sellers insisted on cash, and slave traders made sure they got it. Meanwhile, the lower South and the lower Mississippi Valley in particular became the most monetized and credit-abundant parts of the country as buyers of lands and enslaved people accessed foreign and northern capital to grow at unheard of rates between 1828 and 1836. Bank money per capita in Louisiana rose 567 percent between 1830 and 1840, and eightfold in Mississippi.[7] All that money sped enslaved people to market.

Beginning in the 1820s, Bernard Raux and his Norfolk partner Nathaniel built a slave supply chain, and as money and credit expanded, so did their slaving business. They bought bondspersons in Norfolk and

---

[6] Bill of sale from Peter Hancock (Lewis), September 7, 1835, folder 32; bill of sale from Charles Hatcher (Israel), September 5, 1835, folder 29, Raux Papers, HU; Inward Slave Manifest, New Orleans, September 26, 1835 (*Ariel*), National Archives and Records Administration, Washington, DC. Microfilm M1895 (NARA M1895), Roll 7, images 879–82.

[7] Howard Bodenhorn, *State Banking in Early America: A New Economic History* (New York, NY: Oxford University Press, 2003), 252, 289.

incarcerated them in the city jail until a merchant ship loaded for Louisiana. And once the slaves were shipped to New Orleans, a partner met the ship, jailed the captives, and began selling. By the late 1820s, the interregional slave trade was flourishing, and Raux and Currier were poised to cash in. Agricultural prices were rising faster than real estate. Foreign investors were looking for Southern investment opportunities, and cotton exports were rising. As the 1808 US ban on imported bondspersons was enforced, Chesapeake ports like Norfolk, Virginia, became a strategic embarkation port on the domestic slave route. Raux's consignments were by and large individuals, mainly young people. By 1830, the average incarceration time was 117 days.

What they could see and hear in Norfolk, Virginia, in the summer of 1835 was Nathaniel Currier turning the iron locks on the jail doors one day in late September and calling the names of seventy captives he, Raux, and Pascal owned. Pascal led them down to the city dock, and each climbed aboard the two-mast sailing ship *Ariel*. Other slave traders put their coffles aboard. And by the time Pascal bid adieu to his partners and Captain Banks gave the order to push off, 192 African Americans were aboard – as cargo. In the depths of the ship, Giles, Dyson, and Hancock were cramped in a floating prison. Each had thirty-seven cubic feet of dedicated cargo space below decks, about the size of a kitchen cupboard – or a convenience store drink refrigerator today – and that does not count the cargo that was also consigned to the voyage.[8] Most had never been to sea, and the initial terror of movement through water, shouts and thuds of sailors on deck, and threats screamed through hatches down at captives packed like cordwood gave way to seasickness as scores of forced migrants' stomachs gave up their meager rations as their bodies were tossed about on the salty waves. That relentless motion did not stop for three weeks, until the *Ariel* sailed up the Mississippi River, docking at New Orleans in mid-November.

The timing of the shipment coincided with a financial as well as a climatic calendar. Summers were deadly in places like New Orleans and Natchez, with periodic outbreaks of yellow fever, cholera, and smallpox. Fall brought a break from some mosquito-borne diseases. But cotton planters hungry to expand or replace dead, injured, or sick workers were also flush with credit in the form of advances from factors or middlemen who consigned their cotton bales to ships sailing to New York and Liverpool.

---

[8] Inward Slave Manifest, New Orleans, September 26, 1835 (*Ariel*), NARA M1985, Roll 7, images 879–82.

In New Orleans, Pascal disembarked Giles, Dyson, and Hancock, along with the other Raux–Currier captives, who walked down the wooden plank into a city nearly five times the size of Norfolk and much louder, busier, and more cosmopolitan. And there Pascal jailed them. Offered for sale, they were picked over, prodded, groped, and appraised by strangers assessing how much cotton they might make, how well they might serve or scrub, or – like fashionable cars of a later age – how their young bodies and youthful vigor might boost the status and prestige of the owner.

Slave trader Paul Pascal waited for the right price rather than to make a quick sale. Venus Giles spent thirty days incarcerated in New Orleans before he sold her to a city resident at a 45 percent markup. The terms were "ready money" or banknotes. Pascal sold twenty-one-year-old Lewis Hancock to a Rapides Parish enslaver for what today would be $34,000 in real price equivalent, or a 36 percent markup. Hancock was taken aboard steamboats up the Mississippi and the Red Rivers and into a forest that was quickly becoming cotton country through unpaid labor. Arriving on that changing ground was jarring, and enslaved people often did not survive the transition to a new disease and work environment as they were forced to cut timber, grub stumps, drain malarial swamps, and lay up furrows on which to plant cotton. Any ties Hancock and Dyson had made disappeared as they were sold apart. Fifty-eight days after Israel Dyson arrived, Pascal sold him to a New Orleans physician for cash, a 22 percent markup.[9] And with the proceeds Pascal was able to extend financing to willing buyers without ready cash.

And like every aspiring trader, Bernard Raux needed to lay hands on the proceeds of sales in New Orleans in order to count banknotes into the hands of buyers in Norfolk. That is, he did not have enough capital to buy and ship slaves constantly during a sales season that could stretch over nine months, from September to May. Instead, the New Orleans sales agent had to send money back to Virginia. And since buyers tended not to pay in full at the time they bought a bondswoman in New Orleans, slave traders needed to access a credit chain to remit funds. To do so they tapped into an interregional financial network linking the lower South and the mid-Atlantic centers of finance on which they relied.

---

[9] Notary William Boswell, Vol. 37, Act 1236, December 15, 1835 (Giles), [quotation]; Notary William Boswell, Vol. 36, Act 1119, November 14, 1835 (Hancock); Notary William Boswell, Vol. 37, Act 1225, December 12, 1835 (Dyson), New Orleans Notarial Archive.

The main challenge Raux and Pascal faced was not so much delivering captives to New Orleans but remitting the proceeds of their sales. As they sailed to Louisiana, enslaved people generally appreciated in value. But money traveling back to Virginia generally depreciated. The exchange of state banknotes was like foreign exchange today. A Louisiana state banknote was worth less, sometimes substantially less, back in Virginia than it was in Louisiana, and banks were happy to see notes disappear in long-distance traders' wallets since the farther they traveled from the bank, the less likely they would be presented for redemption in gold or silver. So the cost and logistics of money were of highest importance to Raux and his partners.

There were several other considerations and expenses having to do with a long-distance trade in human captives. Incarceration was one. At twenty-five cents a day, jail fees ate up more capital, adding to the costs of captives. Venus Giles's eighty-nine-day term in the Norfolk jail accounted for about 4 percent of her purchase price. Counting her thirty-day incarceration in New Orleans, jailing Giles cost 5.4 percent of her purchase price, to say nothing of 119 days total spent in at least two jails and exposure to abuse and disease.[10]

And shippers wanted their cash up front. Robert H. Banks, master of the slave ship *Ariel*, charged about $18 per captive for sea passage from Norfolk to New Orleans. And on arrival, enslavers customarily paid the captain a gratuity for safe and prompt delivery. Clothing and medical care cost money. In addition, Raux and his partners had to pay postage, marketing, mortgage certificate fees, and financial fees such as the price of discounts on bills. All told, fees and expenses added about 10.5 percent to each captive's purchase price. And with stiff competition from rival slave-trading firms like Franklin & Armfield, every dollar saved contributed to a competitive advantage.[11]

To be competitive, Raux sent back funds in ways that lowered his firm's transaction costs. To do that, his New Orleans sales agent Paul Pascal bought financial instruments that could retain their value over long distances. Pascal remitted Raux the proceeds of sales in the form of checks payable at Northern banks. In June 1834, Raux entered a $1,000 cashier's check issued by the Union Bank of Louisiana payable at the Merchants'

---

[10] Notary William Boswell, Vol. 37, Act 1236, December 15, 1835, New Orleans Notarial Archive.

[11] Calvin Schermerhorn, "Slave Trading in a Republic of Credit: Financial Architecture of the US Slave Market, 1815–1840," *Slavery & Abolition* 36.4 (2015): 595–96.

Bank of New York. Such bank drafts were cheaper than sending cash across country. And safer. Stuffing Bank of the United States notes in an envelope in New Orleans and posting them to Norfolk risked theft. Checks were hard to steal. And when they arrived in the mail from Louisiana, Raux cashed the checks in Virginia for a small fee, and the Norfolk bank then sent the draft to be paid in full at the Merchants' Bank of New York or sold them to merchants with business in New York. And remitting monies payable at that New York state bank was no accident.

The same British bank that backed the Bank of the United States also invested in key state banks in states like Louisiana. Foreign banking firms pumping investment capital into the South created the financial network Raux used to cut costs. The Union Bank of Louisiana and the Merchants' Bank of New York had a correspondent tie, meaning that they shared information and accepted each other's checks at par or face value. Raux could cash such checks at a small discount (or percentage off the face value) in Norfolk, and reinvest in captives. That tie and the efficiencies it provided slave traders was a direct result of how London's Baring Brothers and Company capitalized the Union Bank of Louisiana. It did so by marketing Louisiana State bonds to its British and European customers and by using its New York merchant banking affiliate Prime Ward King and Company to sell Union Bank bonds to US customers. Prime Ward King and Company had ties to the Merchants' Bank of New York. So financing the Norfolk-to-New Orleans trade used preexisting ties between New York and New Orleans banks, which were clients of Baring Brothers of London. Slave trading fit neatly into that credit chain.

Slave traders also drew credit from the same network. Just as Baring Brothers lent the Bank of the United States a revolving credit line, it also lent the Union Bank of Louisiana a revolving credit line of £40,000 for its exchange business. Pascal had an account at the Union Bank in New Orleans, which permitted him to access that money to remit to Bernard Raux and Nathaniel Currier to turn into more captives. And so Baring Brothers, through its backing of a US central bank in the 1820s and through its support of Louisiana banking in the 1830s, increased liquidity in the US slave market, while it helped monetize the South and extend credit to enslavers. And that network was merely one efficiency slave traders seized.

Pascal was also using the architecture of the cotton export market to cut costs and remit revenues. To reinvest in captives, Pascal sent Raux a $2,000 check written by New Orleans cotton merchant Andrew Hodge, payable at the Commercial Bank of Pennsylvania. Raux cashed it in Norfolk for a small discount, preserving as much value of the captives sold in Louisiana as possible. Even though Hodge did business in New Orleans, he was a Pennsylvania native with ties to the Commercial Bank. Following the money again leads out of the South. Neither Hodge nor the Commercial Bank need know their cotton bills were used to buy slaves.[12] But the irony is that Pascal and Raux's use of their bill made it stronger by endorsing its value.

It was a time when private money was public currency. A well-regarded merchant's promise to pay at a future date could be written down and traded as if it were cash. It was another expression of trust. Bills of exchange were negotiable instruments. Confidence in the promise of payment was strengthened when that bill was sold or endorsed. And a bill that paid for cotton in New Orleans could pay for slaves in Norfolk on its way to being cashed to pay for imported merchandise in Philadelphia. Neither the drawer nor the payer need have known that their bill paid for slaves. But as a bill circulated through arteries of exchange, its value was endorsed multiple times. Those who accepted it for payment placed confidence in the promise written on its face. Whether or not cotton merchants or importers approved of the slave trade, their bills sped the movement of captives.

Cotton, captives, and those who bought and sold each were therefore connected through a network of financial confidence. The money that paid advances on cotton in New Orleans were bills of exchange, checks, or promissory notes drawn by private merchants like Hodge that obligated a third party to pay at a future date. And how much value such a private note had depended on the standing of the merchant or drawer within a financial network, which in turn relied on the broader North Atlantic cotton market.

Cotton bills, so called because they were derived from the value of cotton, stood at the center of the North Atlantic financial network of the 1830s. And Southern commission merchants relied on Northern credit and shipping facilities. Measured in dollars, the distance cotton traveled from New Orleans to Liverpool was shorter through New York or Philadelphia than directly because shipping and financial services firms were located there. So in the 1820s, a cotton triangle formed, linking Liverpool, New York, and Southern ports. And when slaves were bought

[12] Bernard Raux, Account of slaves bought and sold: MssS, 1832–34, Series 2, Folder 14, Raux Papers, HU.

and sold, the financial transactions that caused such bereavement in black families were also expressions of confidence in an international credit chain.

In other words, when Giles, Dyson, and Hancock were bought with paper money withdrawn from the Bank of the United States in Norfolk using bills of exchange linking New Orleans to Philadelphia and New York City, they were bought with trust in the commercial relationships binding cotton sellers in Louisiana to merchant bankers in Pennsylvania and New York. More broadly they were bought on the confidence in London bankers' bills of exchange, the Liverpool cotton market, and the fruits of Manchester, England, factories producing cotton goods shipped to New York, all working in concert. And a slaving triangle fit neatly into that larger cotton triangle since enslavers used the same credit chain. Virginians reaped the returns on a massive transfer of wealth moving in countermotion to captives, and enslavers in the Deep South got the labor backbone of their cotton fields and sugar estates.

Banking technology was key to expanding slave-intensive production. By expanding the money supply, banks and other lenders promoted growth. Borrowers could buy more acreage and more bondspersons. To the ambitious enslaver, the main constraint on growth was his credit limit. But a new kind of lender – property banks – allowed enslavers to leverage their productive assets, including plantations and slaves. Invented by slave trader Jean Baptiste Moussier in the 1820s, Louisiana property banks permitted stockholders to mortgage lands and chattels – enslaved people – and borrow back a portion of the assessed value. At a time when most enslavers accessed credit based on the actual crops they made, this scheme allowed productive assets to work for them twice: once as producers of goods and again as working capital. Slaves became collateralized laborers, and banks bundled those assets. Anything with a cash flow can be securitized, and that is what bankers did, turning collateralized bondspersons into bonds, selling the financial expressions of workers like Venus Giles on world markets. Property banks gave enslavers new leverage when they mortgaged or hypothecated enslaved people.

Hypothecation was similar to its English cognate, a hypothetical. It was the act of mortgaging a property without actually surrendering title. In theory, stockholders could leverage their holdings with minimal risk since they were, as stockholders, borrowing from themselves. Mortgaging bondspersons as a practice had been around a long time, and the great boom in mortgaging slaves in the 1830s was a variation on an old theme.

Slave mortgaging had been the key to building the political economy of colonial America from the Chesapeake to the lower Mississippi Valley. Enslaved people became collateralized labor in plantation economies where they embodied enslavers' borrowing power and underwrote growth. In colonial-era Virginia and Louisiana, equity mortgages using slaves accounted for the majority of borrowing. Equity mortgages tend to be associated with homeowners' mortgaging property in order to fund improvements. In early America, the same principle applied. Borrowers put up lands and chattels to secure loans that permitted expanded production. In colonial Virginia, 43 percent of equity mortgages included slave property, and those mortgages raised 68 percent of money borrowed. In colonial Louisiana, 51 percent of equity mortgages included slave property, and those mortgages raised 67 percent of money borrowed.[13] Enslaved people were both capital investments and leveraged investment properties.

Mortgaging patterns diverged after the Revolution when Virginians liquidated slave property and Louisianans went deep in debt to buy more. In early national Virginia, 28 percent of equity mortgages included slave property, and those mortgages raised 33 percent of money borrowed. In Virginia, the proportional value of equity mortgages using slaves halved from colonial times. Much of that lending was local, but some privileged borrowers accessed credit from foreign financial houses. (To build Monticello, for instance, Thomas Jefferson mortgaged 150 slaves to a Dutch firm.) In early national Louisiana, by contrast, 47 percent of equity mortgages included slave property (down 4 percent from colonial times), but those mortgages raised 88 percent of money borrowed, up by 21 percent from colonial times.[14] The divergence is explained by the fact that Louisianans were taking on debt and increasingly mortgaging slaves to expand production of cotton and sugar. Prices diverged as a result. Just before the 1819 financial panic, a bondsman selling for $800 in Virginia sold for $1,100 in Louisiana.[15] The limit on growth in cotton or sugar was how much credit enslavers could access, and slave mortgaging was the key to much of that.

Collateralized slaves were securitized, meaning that their asset values were pooled and portions sold off as securities. The asset value of slave

[13] Bonnie M. Martin, "Slavery's Invisible Engine: Mortgaging Human Property," *Journal of Southern History* 76.4 (November 2010): 837.

[14] Martin, "Slavery's Invisible Engine"; Henry Wiencek, *Master of the Mountain: Thomas Jefferson and His Slaves* (New York, NY: Farrar, Straus and Giroux, 2012), 96–98.

[15] Ulrich B. Phillips, *Life and Labor in the Old South* (1929; repr. Columbia, SC: University of South Carolina Press, 2007), 177.

property was used as the basis of a credit expansion that boosted production. Finance capitalism liberated the value of enslaved property, permitting it to work for owners while the bodies of bondspersons toiled in the fields. Property banking institutionalized slave mortgaging in the 1830s as it securitized collateralized slave property in such a way as to transfer an interest in slaves to investors outside the South. While they labored in a canebrake or kitchen, bonds representing a slice of an asset pool comprising mortgaged enslaved workers were sold on an open market. Enslaved people could sicken, die, or disappear, but slave securities were undying promises that crossed borders and oceans. New Orleans merchants Hugues Lavergne and Edmond Jean Forstall developed Moussier's idea into Louisiana's first property banks, the Consolidated Association of the Planters of Louisiana (chartered in 1827) and the Union Bank of Louisiana (chartered in 1832).[16] Not all went smoothly.

Mortgaging human property involved a risk, not the least of which was whether a basic component of a collateralized asset – an enslaved person – might perish in a field, flee the state, or rise up in rebellion. And investors were wary of bank securities derived from collateralized slaves. Initially, the Consolidated Association could not find investors to buy its bonds. Thomas Baring, soon to be junior partner at Baring Brothers and Company, considered investing but refused unless the state guaranteed the bank's bonds. Despite an attractive 5 percent interest rate, he was wary of the risk of failure lest the state assume a contingent liability. Over ferocious objections to socializing that risk, Louisiana lent its faith and credit to the Consolidated Association in 1828 and issued $2.5 million in state bonds (it would issue $7 million in state-backed bonds by 1836). In the summer of 1828, Lavergne traveled to London to make the deal, and after Baring Brothers agreed to buy $1.67 million worth of Consolidated Association bonds (mostly to resell), the Consolidated Association opened its doors in 1829.[17]

Privileged borrowers like Lavergne took out loans with human collateral, turning lands and mortal property into immortal promises. For forty-six shares of Consolidated Association stock – a $23,000 loan – Hugues

[16] Irene D. Neu, "J. B. Moussier and the Property Banks of Louisiana," *Business History Review* 35.4 (Winter 1961): 550–57; Edward E. Baptist, *The Half Has Never Been Told: Slavery and the Making of American Capitalism* (New York, NY: Basic, 2014), chap. 7.

[17] George D. Green, *Finance and Economic Development in the Old South: Louisiana Banking, 1804–1861* (Stanford, CA: Stanford University Press, 1972), chap. 4; Calvin Schermerhorn, *The Business of Slavery and the Rise of American Capitalism, 1815–1860* (New Haven, CT: Yale University Press, 2015), chap. 4.

Lavergne and spouse Marie Adele Villeré put up half of their Plaquemines Parish sugar plantation and "the undivided half of sixty slaves" named in the mortgage, from sixty-three-year-old "Old Abraham" to mothers and their children like "Anna 28 and Melina 7 and Henry 5 years," who were promised to the bank, along with "the undivided half of all the unborn infants of the above named negresses," an endorsement of the enduring nature of the mortgage. Individual bondspersons such as Abraham might not outlive their mortgage, but the agreement bound the bondswomen's offspring to the bank. "Should the security furnished by this present act diminish," the mortgage stipulated, "whether by expropriation, or death of the slaves, or otherwise, the said Mr. and Mrs. Lavergne obligate individually and separately to give additional guarantees when the [Consolidated Association] Board so requires."[18] Perpetual slavery backed enduring promises of repayment, which could collateralize the babies not yet conceived when Lavergne and his wife took out the mortgage. And they stood at the head of a long line of eager borrowers.

The credit available from the Consolidated Association was soon used, and would-be stockholders demanded more opportunities to collateralize labor and leverage bondspersons' rapidly rising market value. And what became a familiar pattern emerged of investors looking to offload risk at the public's expense. After Louisiana approved the Union Bank in 1832, investors again demanded guarantees. And again, over furious objections to what seemed like state favoritism, Louisiana amended the bank's charter, making citizens responsible for Union Bank debts if it failed. Other lower South states followed suit. Arkansas, Mississippi, and the Florida Territory also chartered property banks.

Bank charters were public policy matters, and only unchartered banks were actually private. It was common before 1838 for states to impose charter restrictions on banks and in some cases force them to lend to certain enterprises, say, a railroad, canal, or gasworks. Before reforms of the late 1830s, banking was closely tied to political patronage. The Union Bank's charter obligation to lend to planter-stockholders was part of why legislators decided its success was a matter of public interest. What was good for planters was thought to be good for the state. So Louisiana issued bonds capitalizing the bank. And after the Union Bank offloaded its risk, Baring Brothers marketed Louisiana state bonds to British and European investors. The firm also marketed Louisiana's Union Bank bonds to

---

[18] Notary Amadée Ducatel, Vol. 22, Act 8, February 18, 1840, New Orleans Notarial Archive.

American investors through its New York affiliate Prime, Ward, King and Company. That firm's Merchants' Bank of New York was part of the credit chain Currier, Raux, and Pascal used to buy captives in Norfolk, and its Louisiana affiliate provided credit to buyers in New Orleans.

The Union Bank financed sugar plantations and slave sales, and demand for its money soon exceeded its capacity. And after killing the "monster" Bank of the United States, the Jackson administration had removed limitations on growth. By the time Louisiana chartered the Citizens' Bank – a third property bank – in 1834, the Bank of the United States was out of business as an orchestrator of national monetary policy. In its absence state banks proliferated, and the Jackson administration was by then paying its obligations out of Bank funds. It deposited revenues in client banks like the Union Bank, founded by Democratic allies like Forstall. That amplified the credit expansion already under way, giving states more reason to borrow and lend and no reason to restrain growth other than their own preservation. Forstall's Citizens' Bank was capitalized at $12 million in state bonds ($347 million in 2016 real price equivalent). And as before, Louisiana socialized its risk by issuing bonds capitalizing it.

By the time Giles, Dyson, and Hancock arrived in New Orleans, the Deep South was the most credit-rich and highly monetized part of the United States. Virginia jurist Joseph Glover Baldwin traveled the Deep South in 1835 and exaggerated only slightly that "[t]he State banks were issuing their bills by the sheet ... and no other showing was asked of the applicant for the loan than an authentication of his great distress for money." Between 1834 and 1836, the national money supply grew by 30 percent a year on average compared to 2.7 percent between 1831 and 1834. The domestic slave trade also peaked during those two years.[19]

Raux, Currier, and Pascal cashed in on the bonanza. In New Orleans, slave prices surged by 50 percent from 1830 to 1833 then another 50 percent between 1833 and 1836, more than doubling in six years. Slave traders struggled to keep up with demand. Cotton production more than doubled, and Louisiana sugar production more than tripled between 1827–28 and 1834–35. Nationally, prices of agricultural products like cotton rose almost 51 percent between 1829 and 1836, during which time overall prices increased 18 percent. The federal government sold

[19] James G. Baldwin, *The Flush Times of Alabama and Mississippi: A Series of Sketches* (New York, NY: D. Appleton, 1854), 83 (quote); Bodenhorn, *State Banking in Early America*, chap. 10.

1.2 million acres of land in 1829, 3.9 million acres in 1833, 4.7 million acres in 1834, and 20 million acres in 1836. Receipts for land sales in 1836 were five times what they had been five years earlier.[20] Eager investors saw no end to such abundant growth.

So in the flush times, even the bodies of bondspersons became leveraged investment properties. The value derived from backs, heads, and hands turned into more captives. Such schemes expanded the slave market by permitting property owners to leverage their lands and chattels in order to buy more. In 1836, sixty-year-old Bernard Marigny and his wife, Anna Mathilde Morales, mortgaged 139 bondspersons and considerable land-holdings, borrowing more than $253,000 ($156 million in 2017 income value).[21]

And with that money, enslavers like Marigny bought more real estate and enslaved people using credit furnished by banks financed by Northern, British, and European investors. As people like Lewis Hancock labored in the fields, their value also worked to the putative advantage of enslavers like the Marignys as leveraged investment proper-ties. Following the Marignys' money leads from Louisiana state banks to London's Baring Brothers, F. de Lizardi Co. of London, and Hope and Company of Amsterdam. All those investment banks plowed money into Louisiana lands and slaves.

Financial creativity and foreign confidence flooded the state with capi-tal. By 1837, Louisiana's sixteen banks had more than $39 million in paid-in capital, more than half of which was raised in England and Europe in the form of state-backed bonds. (That was $467 billion in terms of 2016 US GDP, about the value of the global illegal drugs trade or Belgium's 2016 GDP.) Boston, New York, and Philadelphia investors had purchased another $7 million in state-guaranteed bonds.[22] Yet confidence in ever-rising prices ran out late in 1836.

Early in 1837, financial panic spread to New York and New Orleans as investors reacted to Bank of England policies reflecting a loss of confi-dence in cotton bills of exchange. US banks raised the discount rate on notes, which constricted credit. And the price of cotton plummeted, falling 30 to 40 percent by year's end. Credit froze. Banks and merchants in the

---

[20] Schermerhorn, *Business of Slavery*, chap. 4.

[21] Notary Theodore Segers, Vol. 18, Act 57, May 2, 1836; Vol. 18, Act 93, June 9, 1836; Vol. 18, Act 118, June 22, 1836; Vol. 18, Act 119, June 23, 1836; Vol. 18, Act 120, June 23, 1836; Vol. 18, Act 131, July 5, 1836, New Orleans Notarial Archive.

[22] Green, *Finance and Economic Development in the Old South*, chap. 3.

cotton trade began to fail on both sides of the Atlantic. New York's involvement in financing cotton and slavery was laid bare when 250 merchant houses failed in April 1837. And as if to ratify the disaster, a Hessian fly outbreak from Pennsylvania to Georgia devastated the wheat harvest, hurting farmers and causing flour prices to rise.[23]

After financial confidence collapsed, enslavers decided that the way out of hard times was to force bondspersons like Lewis Hancock to produce more cotton. Cotton, it was thought, was the South's economic lifeline. Good cotton would extinguish bad debt. But after a brief recovery in 1838, cotton crashed in 1839, and many merchant bankers and bond investors came to the awful realization that much of the collateralized property backing their bonds was African-descended men, women, and children.

Enslaved people felt debt evasion in intensely personal ways. During the hard times, delinquent borrowers fleeing obligations hid human assets. In the wake of the panic, foreclosing on land was easier than foreclosing on slaves, although banks like the Union Bank of Louisiana fought tenaciously to recover mortgaged slave property stashed in dark places or spirited out of state. In the lower South, sheriffs and bank agents attempted to seize assets of deadbeat borrowers, who absconded with astonishing rapidity.

For enslaved people who had been turned into collateralized labor, that meant a new round of disruptions as they were forced to march away from plantations, fleeing their owners' debts. And even if held by a conscientious debtor, delinquencies resulted in the sale of assets. Sheriffs seized bondspersons and sold them for the benefit of creditors, which was the moral equivalent of the theft from loved ones that had begun the journey for many. Another irony of the post-panic social landscape is that hard times brought calmer seas to the slave market. The interstate slave trade of the 1840s declined by a third compared to the 1830s. But enslaved people who were leveraged tumbled through a landscape of bad debt.

Some fleeing debtors simply chalked "G.T.T." on their doors – *Gone to Texas*. After gaining independence from Mexico in 1836, Texas remained an independent republic until it joined the United States in 1845. Migrant

---

[23] Scott Reynolds Nelson, *A Nation of Deadbeats: An Uncommon History of America's Financial Disasters* (New York, NY: Knopf, 2012), chap. 6; Jessica M. Lepler, *The Many Panics of 1837: People, Politics, and the Creation of a Transatlantic Financial Crisis* (New York, NY: Cambridge University Press, 2013).

debtors, one Texas chronicler explained, sought "to rescue themselves and their families from utter ruin; so shouldering their rifles, and arming the more trustworthy of their negroes, they departed secretly for Texas" to start over planting cotton where no warrants would reach them.[24]

And enslaved people were reintegrated into the slavery business there. The anti-bank spirit followed migrants to Texas. After statehood in 1845, Texans refused to charter banks and were left having to use the more primitive means of finance. The bodies of enslaved people became circulating media in some cases, and earlier patterns of slave mortgaging became prime means of financing plantations and ranches. Factors took payment in slaves and disbursed others as profits.[25]

The slavery business reformed. After recovering in the 1840s, New York credit flowed south by southwest. New York City's fortunes rose on a tide of cotton in the 1850s, eclipsing Baltimore, Boston, and Philadelphia. Credit propelled specialization, and like Liverpool of a generation earlier, cotton merchants in New York controlled the shipping business as well as the financial services essential to the cotton trade of the South, along with the distribution networks of foreign manufactures Southerners consumed. They also financed and drew profits from the slave trade among the Southern states. The slave market rebounded with cotton in the late 1840s and boomed again in the 1850s, slave prices reaching their apex just before disunion in 1860–61. Northern financial interest in slavery was generally hidden since the violence abolitionists brought to national attention seemed to be localized in the South. But in 1858, when that state's abolitionist Republican senator William Seward proposed limiting the interstate slave trade, New York City merchants howled in opposition. "The root of the evil," Seward gasped in reaction, "is in the great commercial cities and I frankly admit, in the City of New York."[26]

---

[24] Philip Paxton [pseudonym for Samuel A. Hammett], *A Stray Yankee in Texas* (New York, NY: Redfield, 1853), ix–xii (quotations); Nelson, *A Nation of Deadbeats*, chap. 6; US Supreme Court, *Union Bank of Louisiana v. Stafford*, 53 U.S. 12 How. 327 (1851).

[25] Steven E. Woodworth, *Manifest Destinies: America's Westward Expansion and the Road to Civil War* (New York, NY: Alfred A. Knopf, 2011); Nicholas Onuf and Peter S. Onuf, *Nations, Markets, and War: Modern History and the American Civil War* (Charlottesville, VA: University of Virginia Press, 2006), chaps. 8–10.

[26] Sven Beckert, *The Monied Metropolis: New York City and the Consolidation of the American Bourgeoisie* (New York, NY: Oxford University Press, 2001), 22 (first two quotations); Eugene R. Dattel, *Cotton and Race in the Making of America: The Human Costs of Economic Power* (Chicago, IL: Ivan R. Dee, 2009), 91 (final quotation).

Capital crossed slavery's boundaries with ease. And following the money of the 1850s slavery business led from plantations to Southern ports to New York City and abroad. On the eve of disunion in 1860, British bankers held a considerable portion. Baring Brothers and Company's fortunes rose on American cotton shipments and financing slavery, although after 1848 they diversified, turning to California gold. Other merchant banks like the George Peabody Bank of London joined in and also funded railroad construction, which was fast becoming a vehicle of the slavery business in the South. N. M. Rothschild and Sons of London invested in Kentucky, Missouri, Tennessee, and Virginia railroad bonds in the 1850s, which helped "finance their slavery-built railroads," according to one historian.[27]

But when civil war came, British bankers like Baring Brothers and Company did not forget the lessons of the flush times of the 1830s and the quickly broken promises of states when it came to their bonds. When lower South states tried selling bonds to finance their war against the United States in 1861, British investors refused to buy in. The Confederacy secured a large loan from the private Paris bank of Erlanger and Company, but British financial houses followed the British government in waiting for Confederate independence before investing. And English textile manufacturers looked east instead of west for their cotton.

Israel Dyson survived all that, but just barely. In 1863, the former bondsman was fifty-five when he entered a St. Louis, Missouri, hospital with a skin infection. Dyson could recall the days twenty-eight years earlier when he was taken from his native North Carolina, sold in Norfolk, Virginia, jailed, and held captive aboard a merchant ship sailing to New Orleans. There Dyson was sold to a Louisiana physician for a $200 markup over his purchase price. And there he spent most of his life in slavery. But Dyson did not live long enough to return to Norfolk or his native North Carolina. He died of infection and was buried in a public cemetery.[28]

---

[27] William G. Thomas, *The Iron Way: Railroads, the Civil War, and the Making of Modern America* (New Haven, CT: Yale University Press, 2011), 138.

[28] *Missouri Death Records*, 1863, State Archives, 132, online: www.ancestry.com, accessed: October 19, 2015, 4.

6

Life in the Quotidian

Enslaved Americans were not merely American slaves. They were people. In everyday life, the enslaved were people with faith and friendships, loves and animosities, interests and fears, songs and sorrows. Concerns focused on the big picture issues of God, freedom, and evil in the world. But they also dwelled in the everyday. Most were gnawed by hunger, and many were chronically sick, their quotidian lives lurching from crisis to crisis as friends and loved ones got ill, were sold, suffered injury, or disappeared. Enslaved people were constrained by the interlocking strategies of enslavers to take without asking, hurt with impunity, and force labor without paying.

But slavery was a constellation of constraints rather than an identity or a totalizing experience. *Slave culture, slave religion*, and the *slave experience* refer to categories of analysis rather than walls of separation between the culture, religion, and experiences of enslaved and non-enslaved people. Each established human ties against a dehumanizing institution. Growing up enslaved in Maryland, a young Frederick Douglass met an older African American lay preacher, Charles Lawson. Douglass was just thirteen, living in Baltimore, and awakening to God. Lawson was a man of faith. "His life was a life of prayer," Douglass warmly recalled decades later, "and his words ... were about a better world." Lawson formed a bond with the youth from the Eastern Shore. Douglass remembered "becoming deeply attached to the old man, I went often with him to prayer-meeting, and spent much of my leisure time with him on Sunday." Lawson became a father figure to the fatherless Frederick. "The old man could read a little," Douglass smiled, recalling their Bible lessons, "and I was a great help to him, in making out the hard words, for

I was a better reader than he. I could teach him 'the letter,' but he could teach me 'the spirit,' and high, refreshing times we had together, in singing, praying and glorifying God." Their friendship deepened and "went on for a long time," and though he lost Lawson when he was sent back to the Eastern Shore after the death of an owner, their mutual affection and fellowship built Douglass's character and kindled in him an abiding Christian faith. Their friendship was forbidden by Douglass's Baltimore master. But Lawson's influence was beyond enslavers' control. And Douglass's faith grew into a calling when, soon after escaping from bondage in Maryland, he became a lay preacher in New Bedford, Massachusetts.[1]

Yet Douglass's friendship with Lawson illustrates the personal connections African American slavery interfered with. Contingency governed relationships because enslavers inserted obstacles that limited contact or disrupted a fellowship, family relationship, or friendship. Slavery dehumanized by tearing at the social fabric and violating the bodies of bondspersons. But enslaved people's humanity did not disappear or erode under the constraints even as enslavers set the rules. For instance, men assigned to a gang or work group tended to form friendships in those male spaces. When they evaded patrols or drank alcohol, gambled, or fought, in violation of enslaver strictures, they also tended to deepen interpersonal bonds.[2] And enslaved people dwelled with their own concerns as they made life choices.

Life began in adversity and, for many, squalor. When born, an enslaved baby entered a world of constraints. Owners allowed little prenatal care, and babies were born to mothers who were poorly nourished and sleep deprived, and who were often forced to work right up to birth and then rejoin the workforce immediately afterward. That partly accounts for 10–15 percent of births of stillborn babies. Most African American babies were born in the cabins their mothers shared with family and fellow bondspersons. Those dwellings were often drafty in winter, sweltering in summer, lacking plumbing and anything but rough furniture and cooking implements. Mothers lacked diapers except for what they could improvise, and the dwellings enslaved people inhabited were unavoidably filthy.

---

[1] Frederick Douglass, *My Bondage and My Freedom* (Auburn, NY: Miller, Orton, and Mulligan, 1855), 167.

[2] Sergio A. Lussana, *My Brother Slaves: Friendship, Masculinity, and Resistance in the Antebellum South* (Lexington, KY: University of Kentucky Press, 2016); Joshua D. Rothman, *Flush Times and Fever Dreams: A Story of the South and America in the Age of Jackson* (Athens, GA: University of Georgia Press, 2012).

Partly as a result, black infant mortality was 2.2 times higher than that of whites. Fifty-one percent of African American mortality was children younger than nine in 1850.[3]

High infant mortality and childhood death seemed to work against the value of property in people, but owners collectively implemented a grim calculus: it was less expensive to buy a bondsperson than to grow one. Careers of enslavers were generally shorter than the span of time it took to raise children to productive ages, and enslavers stinted young people of food, shelter, and necessaries of life. And most enslaved people were young. In 1820, more than 43 percent were under age fourteen; throughout the antebellum period, average life expectancy was just over thirty years. Because of lack of food and poor nutrition, enslaved people were shorter in stature than free Americans. If possible, enslavers sent toddlers and young children to elderly or otherwise disabled caregivers. Frederick Douglass was raised until the age of six by his maternal grandmother since his mother's owner decided she was needed in the fields. African Americans strove for a two-parent-headed family, but such aspirations were constantly undermined by enslaver strategies. "Slavery does away with fathers, as it does away with families," Douglass argued. "Slavery has no use for either fathers or families, and its laws do not recognize their existence in the social arrangements of the plantation."[4]

Instead of attending school or receiving lessons, children were introduced to work. Jacob D. Green was put to work doing light housework as a child. He was Douglass's near contemporary, enslaved on Maryland's Eastern Shore. North Carolina native Moses Grandy was put to work in the fields tending animals. He recalled being "compelled to go into the fields and woods to work, with my naked feet cracked and bleeding from extreme cold: to warm them, I used to rouse an ox or hog, and stand on the place where it had lain."[5] Enslaved girls and boys generally realized they were enslaved early in childhood, around six years old. In the nineteenth century, middle-class families designated childhood as an organic stage of development in which children were supposed to be kept from scenes of violence and nurtured. But enslaved children had no such childhood. It was a time filled with dread, Virginia native Madison Jefferson argued,

---

[3] Wilma A. Dunaway, *The African American Family in Slavery and Emancipation* (New York, NY: Cambridge University Press, 2003), 141–42.

[4] Douglass, *My Bondage and My Freedom*, 51.

[5] Moses Grandy, *Narrative of the Life of Moses Grandy, Late a Slave in the United States of America* (London: C. Gilpin, 1843), 11, online: http://docsouth.unc.edu/fpn/grandy/grandy.html, accessed: November 11, 2014.

"for we don't know how long master may keep us, nor into whose hands we may fall."[6]

In cabins and fields, children witnessed a full range of human ordeals. They saw parents and family members beaten and humiliated, and in domestic settings, they witnessed loved ones burning with fever, couples making love, and mothers in labor. If children were fortunate enough to be cared for by one or both parents, they also lived with others in dwellings centered on a hearth. Often they lived with extended family and others who were tossed in together under a roof. Not infrequently one parent lived across a property or county line, and children might spend most of their time with one and not the other except for Sundays and the customary break at Christmastime when bondspersons received some small respite from toils.

Most work was determined by the routine of the seasons. It varied by region, but in the cotton belt, winter was a time for clearing fields, fixing irrigation channels, mending fences, cutting wood, and tending winter vegetable and grain crops. In sugar regions, winter was the most arduous time of the year, when sugar cane was cut and crushed, and the mattresses (units of sugarcane production) seeded in preparation for the next growing season. In the Chesapeake, men might harvest oysters, and in cities and hiring-intensive areas, the first few weeks of the year were the time when yearly contracts turned over. Either the contract was renewed or the enslaved person was bound out to another employer. Winter was also part of the slave-selling season in Deep South markets like New Orleans and Natchez since it was both a low-disease time and also when planters took advances on cotton bales loaded onto ships and sent to market.

The coming of spring brought planting season for cotton, corn, and other crops. Fieldwork replaced ditching and repairing. Birthing animals needed tending, and in places with finicky crops like tobacco, the cycle of weeding and removing pests (before an era of chemical pesticides) required attention. On many agricultural sites of slave labor, the enslaved themselves oversaw and directed those activities, and enslavers relied on bondspersons' knowledge of crops, climate, soil, and other variables that ensured their bounty. By the same token, enslavers shifted much of the burden of care and maintenance onto workers themselves. They granted plots of land to raise vegetables and fowl like chickens and guinea hens.

---

[6] John W. Blassingame, ed., *Slave Testimony: Two Centuries of Letters, Speeches, Interviews, and Autobiographies* (Baton Rouge, LA: Louisiana State University Press, 1977), 218.

Men fished and hunted game, and as spring roads became passable, enslaved people visited and held clandestine parties called frolics.

Summer brought dangers from water- and mosquito-borne disease like cholera, dysentery, yellow fever, and malaria. Transmission was the result of unwashed hands or undercooked meat, which could spread pork tapeworm, causing cysticercosis. Diseases were picked up in the field and transmitted in cabins through fecal matter. Enslaved people associated hookworm with bad air. Infected workers grew anemic, lost weight, and succumbed to infections. The sufferers' symptoms began with a dermatitis, "ground itch" or "dew poison," which was the hookworm larvae penetrating the skin and entering the blood stream. Enslaved people used a wealth of medical knowledge, mostly folk and herbal remedies, but most nevertheless spent most of their lives ill.

The turn from summer to fall compounded the woes of workers since harvest time was when enslavers instituted the pushing system. Cotton was slow to ripen and needed to be picked two or three times from late summer to late fall. Enslaved wagoners or draymen took it to market. Tobacco needed special attention since it was a weed. It bolted or put forth flowering stalks that needed to be cut, and the leaves needed to be harvested at just the right moment, then cured for processing. Corn too needed to be picked, and often enslavers would organize corn-shucking gatherings. Some served whiskey and made it into a festivity or contest reaching late into the night. Hogs and other animals were slaughtered in the fall, and then came the tricky work of processing all the meat and byproducts, smoked into ham or otherwise preserved in an era before reliable refrigeration. Harvest time was just about the only time of the year enslaved people ate well or received a break from the monotonous diet of corn or rice porridge and stewed vegetables or tubers. And the two weeks off surrounding Christmas and the New Year were times when loved ones could visit or expect to see family members separated during the working year. Many enslaved people celebrated with games and parties, but some took the opportunity to care for household chores neglected during the harvest rush. And interspersed with the routines of the seasons were the interpersonal concerns enslaved people had as they went about in their world.

Enslaved people sought relationships that lasted, or at least had the potential to last. Jacob D. Green seemed at times like a love-sick teenager. Green's bid to court a sweetheart featured a range of interpersonal conflicts and overwhelming emotions that involved enslavers solely when they got out of hand. He fell in love with Mary, who was a few years older.

"One glance of her large dark eyes broke my heart in pieces," he sighed. "In spite of either [slave patrollers] or dogs, who stood in my way, every night nearly I was in Mary's company." By the cabin fire they talked of past and future. "I learned from her that she had already had a child to her master in Mobile," Green recalled. The jealous mistress had her sold to Maryland "for revenge" to hide the husband's infidelity; "her baby she said her mistress sold out of her arms, only eleven months old" to a Kentucky owner. Mary had faced hardships, but Green was smitten. "I could not sleep at night for thinking of this almost angel in human shape." Six weeks he courted her, and besides her history he learned – to his "annoyance" – that "Mary was adored by every negro in the neighbourhood, and this excited my jealousy and made me miserable." Green's biggest rival was Dan, "a sweet and easy talker," Green recalled, "and a good bone and banjo player." "One night I went over to see Mary, and in looking through the window, saw Mary – my sweet and beloved Mary – sitting upon Dan's knee." Dan too was risking punishment to court Mary. Jacob Green was thunderstruck. "My teeth clenched and bit my tongue – my head grew dizzy, and began to swim round and round," and he considered killing his rival but shook it off, settling on another tactic to make Mary choose him. Green called one afternoon at Mary's – she was the domestic servant of a local physician – and asked whom she would be, his or Dan's? "Dan's, she replied, with an important toss of her head, which went through my very soul, like the shock from a galvanic battery." Green then pulled a trick he'd soon regret. He threatened to hang himself if Mary didn't change her mind. "To this she replied, hang on if you are fool enough," whereupon Green pulled out a length of rope, secured it to a ceiling beam in the kitchen, tied a noose, slipped it over his head, climbed on a three-legged stool, and fastened the rope around his neck. Mary was unimpressed. "I stood upon the stool for some considerable time," Green confessed, "groaning and struggling, and making every kind of noise that might make her believe that I was choking or strangling; but still Mary sat deliberately smoking her pipe with the utmost coolness, and seemed to take no notice of me or what I was doing." "I stood like a fool," Green admitted, waiting for his would-be lover's intercession. Mary got tired of the act and departed. Then the owner's dog burst in, "racing after the cat, right across the kitchen floor, and the dog coming in contact with the stool, knocked it right away from under my feet, and brought my neck suddenly to the full length of the rope, which barely allowed my toes to touch the floor." The trick went bad as the noose closed around his neck, leaving him choking and shaking. "I roared out, Mary! for God's sake cut the rope! No, answered Mary, you went up there to hang yourself, so now hang on." Green pleaded, confessing that he didn't want to hang – just to get her to love him, not Dan. "I roared out like a jackass, and must too have fainted," Green recalled, and when he regained consciousness, he looked up at the doctor, along with his wife and Mary. They were resuscitating him. "Next day my neck was dreadfully swollen, and my throat was so sore that it was with difficulty that I could swallow meat for more than a week," Green sighed. His owner learned of the trick and punished him with "seventy-eight lashes, and this was the end of my crazy love and court-ship with Mary."[7]

Jacob Green's account of his failed courtship is all too human, and besides the romantic idea of love it incorporates, Green shows a full range of emotions from jealousy and anger to humiliation and hope. He valued honor and defended it, even in a place in which enslaved males were not supposed to possess it. And while Mary was enslaved and the subject of sexual abuse and the trauma of having her baby taken away and sold, she too appears as a woman of moral propriety deciding to whom she would commit in a monogamous courtship and, Green contends, marriage.

Yet Mary and Dan's courtship soon turned tragic. A little while after Green gave up pursuing her, the son of Mary's owner cornered her in a barn and forced himself on her. Green reported that "she strenuously refused" his sexual advances. The doctor's son did not take no for an answer, but when Dan discovered the man assaulting his beloved, he murdered the assailant with a pitchfork. Mary and Dan fled. That night, a local cart driver called at Mary's owner's house, claiming he had a female corpse. To identify it, Mary's owner summoned Green. "The [d]octor ordered me to mount the cart and look at the corpse; I did so, and looked full in that face by the light of the lantern, and saw and knew, notwithstanding the horrible change that had been effected by the work of death, upon those once beautiful features, it was Mary. Poor Mary, driven to distraction by what had happened, she had sought salvation in the depths of the Chesapeake Bay that night." Dan was caught two months later and, according to Green, burned alive for the murder, the bondspersons of the neighborhood forced to witness his immolation. And a few years later, Green was "married" to an enslaved woman named Jane, who was already pregnant with their owner's child, whom Green

---

[7] Jacob D. Green, *Narrative of the Life of J. D. Green, a Runaway Slave, from Kentucky, Containing an Account of His Three Escapes, in 1839, 1846, and 1848* (Huddersfield, [England]: Henry Fielding, 1864), 16–18.

described as having near-white skin and blue eyes, "yet notwithstanding this we lived happily together, and I felt happy and comfortable, and ... I should never have thought of running away if she had not been sold." But after the death of the owner's wife and his engagement to the sister of the man Dan killed in the barn, the fiancée "made a condition that all female slaves whom he had at any time been intimate with must be sold, and my wife being one was sold with the children as well as any other female slaves." Green returned from an errand to find his wife and children sold, never to return again.[8] He was devastated and soon fled bondage himself, beginning a decade-long ordeal of clawing his way out of the South and, eventually, the United States. And by the 1860s, Green was lecturing in England.

Green's story of his doomed romance and dissolved marriage shows the full range of human intentions and emotion, tragically undermined by the levers of power enslavers manipulated. Green did not behave slavishly but humanly, in his midnight gallantry in Mary's cabin and afternoon foolery in the kitchen. Mary and Dan became tragic lovers in a plot worthy of the shrewdest dramatic poet. Their responses to enslavers' assaults on affections and bodies reveal a determination to assert a humanity enslavers could not dominate or possess. Their identities and intentions were their own, and each paid for asserting their authenticity and being true to their hearts.

The conflicts over friendship and family Douglass and Green's ordeals suggest were part of a larger struggle over identity. Beyond matters of individual identity, gender featured a contest between enslaved people's investment in manhood or womanhood over against enslavers' blunting of gender identities as part of a means of social control. The result was a gender fluidity that existed in the spaces between enslaved people's intentions and enslavers' constraints.

Enslavers' violence and degradation worked against any enslaved person's efforts to be entirely cisgendered, in the modern sense of identifying as wholly male or female. In the early nineteenth century, masculinity in the American South was characterized by citizenship rights like court testimony, militia eligibility, property ownership, earned income, and public contracts. Men became breadwinners and voters. Despite the honor shown by Jacob Green and his rival Dan, enslaved males had no civil or political rights and next to no social prestige, which white Southern men called their honor and defended, often, with public violence.

[8] Green, *Narrative of the Life of J. D. Green*, 18–22.

By the same token, middling adult females inhabited social identities as ladies, mistresses of a domestic realm, and moral exemplars as well as moral overseers. They were restrained by their own moral probity and were enforcers of order. Mary strove for a version of that idealized womanhood, which masked the fact that many women did not relish the role of moral enforcer or model. The sexual and gender-contoured violence to which African-descended females were subject distanced them from such femininity, however idealized. Most Southern women, white and black, performed farm and domestic work, endured reproductive labors including childbirth, and exercised more symbolic than actual restraints on male behavior. Married women's legal and social identity was bound up with that of their husbands. A fiancée might insist on purging an enslaver's household of his extramarital sexual partners and unrecognized offspring. But she had little such authority after marriage. By the same token, enslavers and other whites refused to treat African-descended females as ladies, wives, or even as women. And whether male or female the hard edges of that gender-fluid socialization began very young.

Enslavers stamped gender ambiguity onto children. When a baby was born on a slave ship en route to New Orleans, officials termed it an "infant slave," refusing to identify a gender.[9] Enslavers enforced ambiguous gender identities on young people like Leonard Black. After the Maryland native's parents were sold to New Orleans, he and his four brothers were hired out to work. While the master flogged and branded him with hot iron, the mistress, he recalled, "had a son about ten years old; she used to make him beat me and spit in my face. Here I was, a poor slave boy, without father or mother to take my part."[10] The spitting was not just a mark of racial inferiority. The mistress was teaching her son gender difference as well. Not only was Black African-descended and unequal to whites, he was not on a trajectory to manhood, in contrast to the white boy. Enslavers referred to adult bondsmen as Boy, a term of emasculation as well as derision. Former bondsman William Craft explained that "every man slave is called boy till he is very old, then the more respectable

[9] Inward Slave Manifests, New Orleans, March 19–23, 1822 (*Lapwing*) National Archive and Records Administration (NARA), Microfilm M1895 Roll 2, images, 637–47; 645 (quotation).

[10] Leonard Black, *The Life and Sufferings of Leonard Black, a Fugitive from Slavery. Written by Himself* (New Bedford, MA: Benjamin Lindsey, 1847), 7, online: http://doc south.unc.edu/neh/black/black.html, accessed: August 23, 2016.

slaveholders call him uncle. The women are all girls till they are aged, then they are called aunts."[11]

Enslaved people made their own meanings of such customs, refusing to accept emasculating constructions. Frederick Douglass explained that on the Eastern Shore plantation of his youth, "'Uncle Tony' was the blacksmith; 'Uncle Harry' was the cartwright; 'Uncle Abel' was the shoemaker; and all these had hands to assist them in their several departments." The title was "a mark of respect, due from the younger to the older slaves," even as enslavers used the titles to demasculize senior African Americans.[12]

Slavery made gender while making race. And even in abolitionist circles, formerly enslaved males struggled to assert a robustly masculine identity. After Douglass escaped to Massachusetts and began speaking at abolitionist gatherings, he was confronted with the gendered assumptions of his audiences and even his sponsors, and not merely the racial ones. In a Boston speech in 1842, William Lloyd Garrison "announced him, in his peculiarly arousing manner, as 'a thing from the South!'" the *Liberator* reported. The neuter-gender pronoun was intentional, setting up a contrast between free manliness and enslaved demasculization. Douglass was uncomfortable with the characterization. "The idea seemed to fire the noble fugitive with the indignation of outraged nature," the report continued. "His eyes flashed as he spoke in tones of appalling earnestness and significancy [sic]."[13] In his 1855 autobiography, Douglass argued that the essence of enslavement was treating a bondsman "as a thing destitute of a moral or an intellectual nature," or, more succinctly, "[m]anhood lost in chattelhood."[14]

Douglass framed his freedom as an existential and a gendered struggle, the defining moment of which came not when he exited a train in a free state, but when he established his honor in a fight with Edward Covey, a marginal white farmer who rented the sixteen-year-old on Maryland's Eastern Shore. Douglass argued that "this battle with Mr. Covey ... was the turning point in my 'life as a slave.' It rekindled in my breast the smouldering embers of liberty ... and revived a sense of my own manhood. I was a changed being after that fight. I was nothing before; I WAS

---

[11] William Craft, *Running a Thousand Miles for Freedom; or, the Escape of William and Ellen Craft from Slavery* (London: William Tweedie, 1860), 77.

[12] Douglass, *My Bondage and My Freedom*, 69.

[13] *The [Boston] Liberator*, February 18, 1842.

[14] Douglass, *My Bondage and My Freedom*, 152 (first quotation), 175 (second quotation).

A MAN NOW. It recalled to life my crushed self-respect and my self-confidence, and inspired me with a renewed determination to be A FREEMAN." This self-conception was also a cultural nod to the cluster of attributes of nineteenth-century American masculinity. "A man, without force," Douglass argued, "is without the essential dignity of humanity. Human nature is so constituted, that it cannot honor a helpless man, although it can pity him; and even this it cannot do long, if the signs of power do not arise."[15] In a society in which honor, force, and masculinity were fused, Douglass argued that enslaved males were men struggling against their chains rather than piteous beggars for whites' intercession.

In between the lines of Douglass's and others' argument for the humanity and dignity of enslaved men was a recognition that some men were attracted to other men. In early nineteenth-century America, there was no category of someone being gay or lesbian, bisexual, or transgender. Sexuality was an act rather than an identity. Speaking of his "fellow-slaves," Douglass remembered that:

They were noble souls; they not only possessed loving hearts, but brave ones. We were linked and inter-linked with each other. I loved them with a love stronger than any thing I have experienced since. It is sometimes said that we slaves do not love and confide in each other. In answer to this assertion, I can say, I never loved any or confided in any people more than my fellow-slaves.[16]

Although that passage can be understood within a heteronormative frame of fraternal closeness, mutual support, and solidarity, it also points beyond that to the intimate same-sex bonds that existed on the landscape of the American South among women and men, which were little understood and often feared even as gay, lesbian, and transgender enslaved people cherished them.[17] And in making the argument for men's intimacies Douglass was also arguing that enslaved people were fully formed human beings.

He was not merely arguing for his own membership in a masculine gender identity but telling how slavery prohibited millions of males like him from participating in it. And that celebration of masculinity was also one female bondspersons used to argue for their own emancipation.

---

[15] Douglass, *My Bondage and My Freedom*, 246–47.

[16] Frederick Douglass, *Narrative of the Life of Frederick Douglass, an American Slave, Written by Himself* (Boston, MA: Anti-Slavery Office, 1845), 82–83.

[17] Jim Downs, "With Only a Trace: Same-Sex Sexual Desire and Violence on Slave Plantations, 1607–1865," in *Connexions: Histories of Race and Sex in North America*, ed. Jennifer Brier, Jim Downs, and Jennifer L. Morgan (Urbana and Chicago, IL: University of Illinois Press, 2016), 15–37.

Former bondswoman Sojourner Truth took a similar tack when arguing for women's rights. "I am a woman's rights," she argued to an Akron gathering in 1851. "I have as much muscle as any man, and can do as much work as any man. I have plowed and reaped and husked and chopped and mowed, and can any man do more than that? I have heard much about the sexes being equal; I can carry as much as any man, and can eat as much too, if I can get it. I am as strong as any man that is now." Linking masculinity to civil rights and then applying for recognition as the equal of a man, Truth blended rather than differentiated gender characteristics. She tempered that appeal by emphasizing female differences in capacity. "As for intellect," Truth argued, "all I can say is, if a woman have a pint and a man have a quart – why can't she have her little pint full?" The nature of those capacities was not different, she contended, just the volume.[18]

Gender ambiguity sometimes paved the path out of slavery. Ellen and William Craft escaped from bondage in Georgia in 1848 by assuming opposite gender guises. William Craft dressed as a female servant, his dark skin accentuating the role. Ellen Craft was light-skinned and dressed and acted as a frail white enslaver traveling with his valet or personal servant. "I cut off my wife's hair square at the back of the head," William recalled of the plan, "and got her to dress in the disguise and stand out on the floor. I found that she made a most respectable looking gentleman." But the Crafts apologized for the gender ambiguity this caused. "My wife had no ambition whatever to assume this disguise, and would not have done so had it been possible to have obtained our liberty by more simple means; but we knew it was not customary in the South for ladies to travel with male servants; and therefore, notwithstanding my wife's fair complexion, it would have been a very difficult task for her to have come off as a free white lady, with me as her slave; in fact, her not being able to write would have made this quite impossible."[19] The apology indicates a self-conscious attempt to disavow transgender leanings, even though Ellen Craft's success hinged on her inhabiting the role with such conviction that she dined with a ship captain and conversed with a slave trader, talking of "breaking" in bondspersons under one of the most notorious enslavers in South Carolina.[20] When telling their story, Ellen and William Craft used

---

[18] Nell Irvin Painter, "Representing Truth: Sojourner Truth's Knowing and Becoming Known," *The Journal of American History* 81.2 (September 1994): 489 (quotations).
[19] Craft, *Running a Thousand Miles for Freedom*, 35–36.
[20] Craft, *Running a Thousand Miles for Freedom*, 48.

he and *she* to refer to the genders they inhabited during the escape and without which the strategy would have collapsed.[21]

The Crafts' gender swapping was part of a series of shrewd tactics throwing off suspicion used among many enslaved people fleeing their chains. "Put your hands in your pockets, and walk ricketty, like de sailors," a sponsor advised Harriet Jacobs when she fled her enslaver's sexual abuse in Edenton, North Carolina. As she walked through the town, "I passed several people whom I knew," Jacobs recalled, "but they did not recognize me in my disguise."[22] Disguised as a male sailor, the mother of two boarded a boat and braved the aptly named Snaky Swamp.

Gender fluidity worked too to make Harriet Tubman a "Moses" and a "hero" to those who escaped under her guidance before the Civil War.[23] Unable to recognize the strengths and perseverance of African American women, admirers turned Tubman into an honorary man. Masculinized, "General Tubman" became known as a fearsome warrior against slavery. Her military service was exemplary, requiring extraordinary valor on the part of someone who came up in Maryland and had never been south of the Chesapeake by the time she served in South Carolina from 1862 to 1865. It was not that those qualities were essentially masculine but that they were recognized as masculine at the time. The army did not enroll self-identified females. Yet Tubman was among a small group of combat women serving as soldiers and spies, many posing as males and others, like Albert D. J. Cashier, who was white and who made a permanent transition from female to male.[24] And while Tubman identified as a woman, there were certainly African-descended transgender people for whom slavery's gender ambiguity was part of a process of inhabiting a transgender identity, before sexuality was recognized as an identity and not merely a complex of behaviors.[25] Cisgender norms were part of an edifice of white male control, always more celebrated and idealized

---

[21] Barbara McCaskill, *Love, Liberation, and Escaping Slavery: William and Ellen Craft in Cultural Memory* (Athens, GA: University of Georgia Press, 2015).

[22] Harriet Jacobs, *Incidents in the Life of a Slave Girl, Written by Herself*, ed. Lydia Maria Child (Boston, MA: the author, 1861), 170.

[23] William Wells Brown, *The Rising Son, Or, The Antecedents and Advancement of the Colored Race* (Boston, MA: A. G. Brown and Company, 1882), 538.

[24] Milton C. Sernett, *Harriet Tubman: Myth, Memory, and History* (Durham, NC: Duke University Press, 2007), 42, quotation; Richard H. Hall, *Women on the Civil War Battlefront* (Lawrence, KS: University of Kansas Press, 2006), chaps. 3, 10.

[25] Joanne J. Meyerowitz, *How Sex Changed: A History of Transsexuality* (Cambridge, MA: Harvard University Press, 2002).

than actually practiced. In the United States, enslaved people themselves lived in gender-fluid ways from a combination of violent cisgender norms enforced on them and based on the creativity born of those constraints.

In the enslavers' stronghold of gender and color lines, enslaved women were condemned three times over, as bondspersons, as females, and as African-descended people. Like enslaved males, they were subject to arbitrary force, unpaid labor, and legally sanctioned punishments. But they also faced gender-specific constraints and perils in a patriarchal society. Growing up, enslaved girls had to be wary of predators of all classes and colors. Wives had no legal rights to husbands' protections and no legal protections from male violence either, whether the aggressor was free or enslaved. It was no crime in Virginia, say, to rape or abuse a black female. In that environment, the line between girlhood and womanhood was hazy too.

Enslaved children had no childhood marked off as an organic phase of development. Parents often did not instruct enslaved children about sexuality and childbirth, and many enslaved girls found out in violent and degrading ways. To keep children from slavery's torments as long as possible, parents of enslaved children apparently did not instruct girls extensively in sexual matters, and young women experiencing menarche seem to have been told what it signaled only reluctantly. When children asked where babies came from, parents sent them looking in clover patches or hollow logs, or instructed them to await the arrival of the physician or midwife. A young woman like Jacobs had to grow up very quickly.[26]

Yet Harriet Jacobs's attachment to her two children, Louisa Matilda and Joseph, led her to an extraordinary strategy. When she escaped from her legal owner, she hid in her grandmother's attic, just blocks from where her children were living in slavery, watching them through a hole in the wall. Jacobs relied on a social network centered on her grandmother Molly Horniblow, a free African-descended woman and small business proprietor, who hid her from 1835 to 1842.[27] Only when the father and

---

[26] Anthony S. Parent Jr. and Susan Brown Wallace, "Childhood and Sexual Identity under Slavery," *Journal of the History of Sexuality* 3.3 (January 1993): 363–401; John Brown, *Slave Life in Georgia: A Narrative of the Life, Sufferings, and Escape of John Brown, a Fugitive Slave, Now in England* (London: [W. M. Watts], 1855), 2.

[27] Jean Fagan Yellin, *Harriet Jacobs: A Life* (New York, NY: Basic Civitas, 2005), chaps. 3–4; *Edinburgh Gazetteer, The Edinburgh Gazetteer, or Compendious Geographical Dictionary*, 2nd edn. (Edinburgh: Longmans, Rees, Orme, Brown & Green, 1829), 167.

owner of Louisa and Joseph moved them from Chowan County to New York State did Jacobs make good her escape and reunite with them.

Strategies to keep families together were constrained by the fact that enslaved females had more limited work tasks than their male counterparts. That meant fewer opportunities to network. Trades were male gendered. If they showed aptitude, males were often apprenticed to learn barrel making or carpentry, or how to operate a boat or wagon. Gabriel learned blacksmithing in 1790s Richmond. Frederick Douglass learned the lucrative trade of caulking ships' hulls in 1830s Baltimore. Some enslaved males went to sea. And as Gabriel and Douglass discovered, urban networks could provide informal schooling. That did not forestall female learning, but it did hide it. Douglass discovered after his mother's death that "she could read, and that she was the only one of all the slaves and colored people in Tuckahoe who enjoyed that advantage." (A white kinswoman of Douglass's mother's owner countered that "many" in fact possessed literacy: "They were proud of the fact that they could read the [B]ible.")[28] Yet there were advantages that bondswomen could seize.

In the culture of surveillance and suspicion that prevailed after the Nat Turner Rebellion, enslaved women were able to cultivate and pass along literacy as Sunday school teachers, missionaries, and church extension workers. Like white women, African American women tended to prize church membership more than men, even though they were forbidden from being ministers, preachers, exhorters, or class leaders. But while enslavers kept strict watch on male pastors and preachers, churchwomen were able to offer religious instruction and lead informal worship, especially to the young. Despite males' having greater access to literacy, enslaved females helped steal an education from owners who forbade it. In a society in which relatively few whites could read and write, however, enslaved literacy remained low, perhaps no more than 5 or 10 percent of the population. Formal literacy statistics may hide folk and biblical literacy that was more aural and theologically sophisticated than grounded in the words of scripture. Sojourner Truth's biographer argued that Truth often asked children to read her passages out of the Bible since they would do so without the adults' habit of lapsing into commentary. When she

---

[28] Douglass, *My Bondage and My Freedom*, 57–58 (first quotation); Harriet Anthony quoted in Calvin Schermerhorn, "Working through the Double-Bind: Frederick Douglass's Intellectual and Literary Legacy, 1841–1855," *U.S. Studies Online: The BAAS Postgraduate Journal* 13 (Autumn 2008): www.baas.ac.uk/issue-13 -autumn-2008-article-5/ accessed: July 14, 2016 (second quotation).

challenged Seventh Day Adventists on one occasion, she met scriptural reasoning with scriptural reasoning arguing, "I am going to stay here and stand the fire, like Shadrach, Meshach, and Abednego! And Jesus will walk with me through the fire, and keep me from harm." Her opponents, "[white] ministers[,] were taken quite aback at so unexpected an opposer," concluding that "she had learned much that man had never taught her."[29] Informed by the Word of God, Truth's theology and mission – inseparable from abolition – was guided by the Holy Spirit, indicating a much more complex and rich interplay of literacy, religious education, and social activism than is indicated by formal literacy statistics. But females' experience of slavery was rarely a contest of letters.

Most were forced into agricultural or fieldwork. Cotton required dexterity and endurance rather than strength, and unlike sugar masters who preferred males, cotton enslavers put females to work in fields as soon as they could follow directions. A close second was domestic labor. Enslaved women toiling in the households of owners or hired out to staff middle-class white households were exposed to violence and abuse that complemented the punishing pushing system in the fields. Household service was a gender-fluid set of occupations. Children and adult males were trained in domestic arts, including those whose appearance flattered enslavers' sense of their own mastery, whiteness, and prestige.[30] Jacob Green, for instance, kept house as a boy.

But most domestic bondspersons were female, and they typically served two households. After performing the domestic drudgery of scrubbing floors, emptying chamber pots, cleaning dishes, cooking over open fires, serving food, washing, mending, ironing, sweeping, dusting, dressing, nursing, and diapering white babies, most had to remove one apron and put on another to cook, clean, wash, and nurse their own families, repeating the same female-gendered tasks around the hearth of their own family's cabin or urban tenement apartment. And that was just the everyday drudgery of domestic work. For enslaved females, labor carried a variety of meanings and manifestations.

Labor in childbirth complemented field and domestic toil for most enslaved women. US slavery was distinctive in the Americas and the

---

[29] Sojourner Truth, *Narrative of Sojourner Truth, a Northern Slave, Emancipated from Bodily Servitude by the State of New York, in 1828*, ed. Olive Gilbert (Boston, MA: the author, 1850), 112, online: http://docsouth.unc.edu/neh/truth50/truth50.html, accessed: August 25, 2016.

[30] Walter Johnson, *Soul by Soul: Life inside the Antebellum Slave Market* (Cambridge, MA: Harvard University Press, 1999), chap. 5.

Atlantic world because the enslaved population was self-reproducing. A healthy enslaved female was pregnant or nursing from her late teens to her early forties and sometimes beyond. And slavery robbed children of childhood while enslavers robbed mothers of important parts of motherhood. Laws of slave states held that the children born of enslaved women were also enslaved. Babies of enslaved men and free women were free, but slavery followed the mother's legal condition. Motherhood, the sacred bond between parent and child, was cut through by an owner's property relationship. A mother's precious baby was also the legal property of the mother's owner.[31] As former bondswoman Fannie Berry put it many years later, "[u]s [c]olored women had to go through a plenty, I tell you."[32]

And so the chattel principle fell doubly hard on mothers when enslavers ripped beloved babies from their mothers' arms through work regimes in which the mother was hired out, or through other geographic separations. Enslavers often gave babies or children as gifts, sold young people to pay debts, or removed nursing infants in order to put new mothers back to work in fields, kitchens, and parlors. Such babies were typically cared for by older kinswomen or female bondspersons past prime working age. Mothers of enslaved children could expect an inevitable separation at the point of sale or estate division after an owner's death. Birth labor began a tragic progression of joy and love followed by violence and traumatic loss, heartache, and both support and witness to other mothers and women enduring similar toils and trials.[33] Yet not all was anguish and loss.

Enslaved women were social joiners, healers, worship leaders, and even matriarchs. The flip side of domestic work was that enslaved women typically traveled through neighborhoods in domestic circuits. Through their unseen labor, enslaved females knit together families, neighborhoods, churches, and even communities as they cared for children, the sick, elderly, and disabled and made the business of living their business, protecting the most vulnerable along the way. Some grew small businesses selling handicrafts, eggs, poultry, and vegetables. So-called root doctors and midwives traveled local circuits practicing arts of healing, forging

---

[31] Marie Jenkins Schwartz, *Birthing a Slave: Motherhood and Medicine in the Antebellum South* (Cambridge, MA: Harvard University Press, 2006); Jennifer L. Morgan, *Laboring Women: Reproduction and Gender in New World Slavery* (Philadelphia, PA: University of Pennsylvania Press, 2004).

[32] Interview of Mrs. Fannie Berry (1937), online: www.encyclopediavirginia.org/_Interview_of_Mrs_Fannie_Berry_1937, accessed: April 24, 2017.

[33] Emily West, *Enslaved Women in America: From Colonial Times to Emancipation* (Lanham, MD: Rowman and Littlefield, 2015).

therapeutic ties among people, giving perinatal care, and practicing social medicine. Slave quarters were the closest thing to community clinics for most of the enslaved population residing in what amounted to slave labor camps. Enslavers often called on male physicians to treat sick, injured, or pregnant African Americans, but racist medical science and physicians' limited (and often counterproductive) repertoire of therapies and procedures made midwives and folk healers preferable in many cases. Black female medical providers' operating principles tended to start with empathy and compassion as opposed to enslavers' callous suspicion, and that by itself influenced better outcomes than the professional physicians who roamed the early nineteenth-century South.[34]

Enslaved women's medical repertoires were sometimes generations deep. Neighborhoods often had a female healer who made rounds dispensing herbal remedies. And African American women shared herbal remedies with one another, from mother to daughter, transmitting a pharmacopeia of folk medicines, many of which had originated back across the Atlantic Ocean. The same is true with the recipes and the foodways that enriched slave cabins' hearths and were incorporated into Southern regional cuisines. Men may have held the secrets to tasty barbecue. But enslaved female cooks prepared nearly everything else, including dishes of fowl and vegetables, grains, dairy, eggs, and even desserts.[35] Since domestic labor was at its core female, enslaved women shaped much of the material culture outside the kitchen as well.

Enslaved women sewed dresses and other garments, did one another's hair, crafted ornamental jewelry, and transmitted knowledge of cosmetics and sewing to females in their network. Rather than imitating mistresses' styles, African American women made homemade relaxers to straighten hair while others braided cornrows, plaited, or opted for "tidy Afros," hiding styles under wraps during hours in kitchens and fields.[36] As they made clothes for one another, did one another's hair, and passed along medical knowledge, enslaved females formed networks sometimes powerful enough to upend the strategies of enslavers.

---

[34] Herbert C. Covey, *African American Slave Medicine: Herbal and Non-Herbal Treatments* (Lanham, MD: Rowman and Littlefield, 2007); Sharla M. Fett, *Working Cures: Healing, Health, and Power on Southern Slave Plantations* (Chapel Hill, NC: University of North Carolina Press, 2002).

[35] Michael W. Twitty, *The Cooking Gene: A Journey through African-American Culinary History in the Old South* (New York, NY: Amistad, 2016).

[36] Stephanie M. H. Camp, *Closer to Freedom: Enslaved Women and Everyday Resistance in the Plantation South* (Chapel Hill, NC: University of North Carolina Press, 2004).

In some contexts, enslaved women formed gossip networks in which anecdotes and stories, true or not, could end up in court testimony impeaching an enslaver, if repeated strategically enough in the neighborhood. The power of suggestion and rumor could and did influence local elites, making enslaved women a formidable moral authority even in places in which they lacked civil and political rights.[37] Such gossip networks dovetailed with escape networks, and the most famous conductor on the Underground Railroad, Harriet Tubman, was able to orchestrate an elaborate network of allies reaching down into her native Dorchester County, Maryland, up through Philadelphia and Auburn in upstate New York and eventually to Saint Catharine's, Canada. Harriet Jacobs, too, in her quest to keep close her children, Joseph and Louisa, was able to hide out in her grandmother's attic for the better part of seven years, all while sending letters to her owner in Edenton that were postmarked from New York, and watching her children as they grew up through a hole in the garret of her grandmother's house. Her grandmother Molly Horniblow, who was formerly enslaved, carried enough clout in the neighborhood to protect Jacobs and eventually head an escape network.[38]

And so while enslaved males had comparatively much greater mobility and varieties of work, and therefore the ability to run off, make good their escapes, and mobilize as part of the black insurgency, enslaved females used the putative disadvantages of their gender as tools to network to serve and minister to one another, to organize defenses, and to knit neighborhoods, families, and communities together. Enslaved people were never merely slaves, and a constellation of contingencies ensured that there were no uniform cultural or religious experiences uniting bondspersons. Proximity and working environments fostered friendships and gendered understandings of work, knowledge, and sociality influenced gender identities. But violence and social instability worked against permanence in those relationships that were at the core of enslaved people's being. Each was the sum of the roles she lived in the human dramas of the everyday.

---

[37] Laura F. Edwards, "Status without Rights: African Americans and the Tangled History of Law and Governance in the Nineteenth-Century U.S. South," *American Historical Review* 112 (April 2007): 365–93.

[38] Calvin Schermerhorn, *Money over Mastery, Family over Freedom: Slavery in the Antebellum Upper South* (Baltimore, MD: Johns Hopkins University Press, 2011), chap. 3.

7

Landscape of Sexual Violence

Slavery took place on a landscape of sexual violence. Enslavers' sexual abuse, assault, and rape of African-descended subjects was pervasive. And it was no accident. The ability of whites to rape nonwhite people without fear of consequence was a cornerstone of American slavery. Sexual assault established mastery. Abuse enforced the racial hierarchy. Rape was an act of domination, discipline, and punishment. In using sexual violence to construct race-based slavery, enslavers racialized sexuality, making it intrinsic to the daily lives of and interactions among people in areas slavery touched. It was a tragic dimension of American slavery: enslavers construed African-descended people as racially inferior and unfit for citizenship, education, and social equality. But at the same time, sexual predation affirmed the utter humanity of those subject to it.

And as sexual violence made slavery, it unmade the dignity and integrity of human relations. Enslavers stole loved ones through sale and distance, but they also raped away childhood and ties that whites considered sacrosanct. In the words of a historian, "sexual violence was depressingly common: an inescapable itch for whites who discussed slavery, an everyday wound inflicted on people bought and sold as commodities."[1] Sexual assault and abuse undermined the human ties of African-descended people, traumatizing individuals and devaluing families, rending the fabric of neighborhoods and kinships. Rape tore at bonds of trust and affection between spouses and the sacred duty of

---

[1] Edward E. Baptist, "'Cuffy,' 'Fancy Maids,' and 'One-Eyed Men': Rape, Commodification, and the Domestic Slave Trade in the United States," *American Historical Review* 106.5 (December 2001): 1643.

parents to protect and nurture a child. Babies born to sex abuse survivors were often the legal property of the attacker. And the violence was not limited to enslavers. The ability to rape without consequence was a marker of manhood. White males everywhere slavery existed, including neighbors, employers, workers, or sailors, were empowered to assault and rape African-descended people. Once children and women transported in the slave trade reached their new homes, they were frequently raped by the men there, both white and black. Even African American men could rape black women without legal consequence in states like Mississippi.[2]

Sexual abuses began in childhood. After being kidnapped in Washington, DC, and shipped to New Orleans, Solomon Northup recalled the ordeal of seven-year-old Emily, the daughter of another bondswoman who was held captive on his ship. The slave trader separated Emily from her mother saying, "[t]here were heaps and piles of money to be made of her when she was a few years older." A nine-year-old could be sold for sexual exploitation, Northup explained: "There were men enough in New-Orleans who would give five thousand dollars for such an extra, handsome, fancy piece as Emily would be, rather than not get her."[3] Lurid accounts of such transactions hint at the terror of subjection.

Harriet Jacobs, enslaved in Edenton, North Carolina, gave a probing account of sexual abuse. When she was fifteen, she recalled, "[m]y master began to whisper foul words in my ear." That was a euphemism for sexual advances. "I tried to treat them with indifference or contempt," Jacobs recalled, but the owner, James Norcom, bided his time and increased the pressure. "He peopled my young mind with unclean images, such as only a vile monster could think of," previewing his fantasies of domination. "I turned from him with disgust and hatred," Jacobs remembered. "But he was my master. I was compelled to live under the same roof with him – where I saw a man forty years my senior daily violating the most sacred commandments of nature." Jacobs had a free grandmother living in the same town of Edenton, but she could do little more than whisper scandalous stories about the abuse-saturated Norcom household. "No matter whether the slave girl be as black as ebony or as fair as her mistress,"

[2] Jeff Forret, *Slave against Slave: Plantation Violence in the Old South* (Baton Rouge, LA: Louisiana State University Press, 2015), chap. 8.

[3] Solomon Northup, *Twelve Years a Slave, a Citizen of New-York, Kidnapped in Washington City in 1841, and Rescued in 1853, from a Cotton Plantation near the Red River in Louisiana* (New York, NY: Miller, Orton, and Mulligan, 1854), 86–87 (quotations); Edward E. Baptist, *The Half Has Never Been Told: Slavery and the Making of American Capitalism* (New York, NY: Basic Books, 2014), 241.

Jacobs argued. "In either case, there is no shadow of law to protect her from insult, from violence, or even from death; all these are inflicted by fiends who bear the shape of men." Jacobs resisted Norcom's advances in part by forming an alliance with another white man, Samuel Treadwell Sawyer, who was wealthier and of a higher social standing than her owner. Modern conceptions of sexual consent turn on a person's capacity and legal ability to consent, which is freely given and not subject to coercion, fraud, or the threat or use of violence. By any such measure, however, Jacobs's relationship with Sawyer was laden with coercion. She formed an alliance with him in a calculation of least-bad options. She had two children by Sawyer while enslaved in Edenton. It was a desperate tactic. Norcom refused to rape a pregnant or nursing teen, and Sawyer arranged to buy the children at a time when Norcom – their legal owner – needed money.[4] Jacobs loved her children and endured seven years' hiding from Norcom in her grandmother's attic to be near them, escaping when Sawyer moved away. In that Jacobs's situation was unusual. The unwanted pregnancies of rape weighed heavily on enslaved women.

"I was regarded as fair-looking for one of my race, and for four years a white man – I spare the world his name – had base designs upon me," Elizabeth Keckley recalled of her time in Hillsboro, North Carolina, in the late 1830s and early 1840s. She was enslaved and in her late teens when assaulted. "I do not care to dwell upon this subject, for it is one that is fraught with pain," she told readers thirty years later. "Suffice it to say, that he persecuted me for four years, and I–I–became a mother." The sparseness of Keckley's details and hesitation on the page merely hint at the torment, humiliation, and anguish she felt at a struggle that spanned months, seasons, and years. She left out mention of the particulars of the abuse or how she felt about the prospect of motherhood. "The child of which he was the father was the only child that I ever brought into the world," she wrote. "If my poor boy ever suffered any humiliating pangs on account of birth, he could not blame his mother, for God knows that she did not wish to give him life; he must blame the edicts of that society which deemed it no crime to undermine the virtue of girls in my then position."[5] Keckley wrote as one who valued the virtues she was denied, to choose – or deny – a sexual partner and spouse, and to prevent

[4] Harriet Jacobs, *Incidents in the Life of a Slave Girl, Written by Herself*, ed. Lydia Maria Child (Boston, MA: the author, 1861), 44.
[5] Elizabeth Keckley, *Behind the Scenes* (New York, NY: G. W. Carleton, 1868), 38–39.

an unwanted pregnancy or insist that intimacy be framed by love and not force.[6]

Enslavers' sexual abuse gave rise to "shadow families" whose members were publicly unacknowledged yet mapped onto the social and genetic landscape of Southern spaces.[7] "There was a whisper," Frederick Douglass wrote, "that my master was my father; yet it was only a whisper, and I cannot say that I ever gave it credence." But whispers in the shadows contrasted with the fact that "by the laws of slavery, children, in all cases, are reduced to the condition of their mothers," Douglass explained. "This arrangement admits of the greatest license to brutal slaveholders, and their profligate sons, brothers, relations and friends, and gives to the pleasure of sin, the additional attraction of profit."[8] An unacknowledged child of a white father and an enslaved mother could be disposed of in the slave market. She or he was also disinherited: instead of handing down social and real capital to the offspring of enslaved women, the father-enslavers sold their bodies for money and cut their social ties.

Practices of selling offspring of enslaved women gave rise to slave breeding, usually understood as owners' deliberately manipulating reproduction for profit. Narrowly defining enslavers' selling off human property born to other human property within a calculus of loss and gain, however, strips away historical context. As a business matter, the cost of raising a human child who was enslaved was higher than buying an enslaved worker. There was no profit in raising a child for the market. Socially, to the extent to which enslavers manipulated enslaved people's reproduction, they tended to diminish it. Forcing pregnancies for the sake of more children sparked resistance in would-be mothers. Some reached for abortifacients. Others committed suicide rather than have babies conceived through coercion. Breeding then signifies the extent to which enslavers used sexual violence for their own ends and transcends a biological or economic characterization. "It refers to more than the reproduction of human beings; it is a malleable narrative shorthand in which social norms, cultural values, and historical consciousness can be

---

[6] Thelma Jennings, "'Us Colored Women Had to Go through a Plenty': Sexual Exploitation of African-American Slave Women," *Journal of Women's History* 1.3 (1990): 45–74.

[7] Catherine Clinton, "Breaking the Silence: Sexual Hypocrisies from Thomas Jefferson to Strom Thurmond," in *Beyond Slavery: Overcoming Its Religious and Sexual Legacies*, ed. Bernadette J. Brooten (New York, NY: Palgrave Macmillan, 2010), 220.

[8] Frederick Douglass, *My Bondage and My Freedom* (Auburn, NY: Miller, Orton, and Mulligan, 1855), 58.

'bred,' or learned over time," as the memory and legacy of sexual violence.[9] And when enslavers violated African-descended people, the social trauma was not limited to subjects of abuse and aggression and their families.

Enslavers' sexual abuse linked to a chain of violence and trauma that pervaded social relations under slavery. "Men do not love those who remind them of their sins," Douglass argued, "unless they have a mind to repent – and the mulatto child's face is a standing accusation against him who is master and father to the child. What is still worse, perhaps, such a child is a constant offense to the wife."[10] In Harriet Jacobs's Edenton, Maria Norcom displaced her anger on a teenaged Jacobs for the supposed offense of tempting her husband. "The mistress," Jacobs wrote, "who ought to protect the helpless victim, has no other feelings towards her but those of jealousy and rage."[11] Moses Roper was nearly killed as a baby for his father's transgressions. Roper was born in eastern North Carolina around the same time as Jacobs. His father was his owner, and his mother's pregnancy infuriated his father's wife. Immediately after his birth, Moses Roper wrote, "Mr. Roper's wife ... got a large club-stick and knife, and hastened to the place in which my mother was confined." Moses's mother was recovering from childbirth when the owner's wife "went into my mother's room with a full intention to murder me with her knife and club, but as she was going to stick the knife into me, my grandmother happening to come in, caught the knife and saved my life." The wife soon got her revenge. As soon as Moses's mother had healed from the delivery, "my father sold her and myself," and so began a tumultuous childhood tumbling from one owner to another.[12] Such acts of sale set up and even invited further sexual violence. A witness in 1855 testified that enslaved females were offered at auction, "entirely naked surrounded by a profane and vulgar crowd while she writhes under the lash, or is offered for the purposes of prostitution to the highest bidder."[13]

---

[9] Gregory D. Smithers, *Slave Breeding: Sex, Violence, and Memory in African American History* (Gainesville, FL: University Press of Florida, 2012), 2–3.

[10] Douglass, *My Bondage and My Freedom*, 59.

[11] Jacobs, *Incidents in the Life of a Slave Girl*, 44–45.

[12] Moses Roper, *Narrative of the Adventures and Escape of Moses Roper, from American Slavery* (Berwick-Upon-Tweed, England: the author, 1848), 7.

[13] C. G. Parsons, *Inside View of Slavery; Or, A Tour among the Planters* (Boston, MA: W. P. Jewett and Company, 1855), 297.

But instead of owning up to an enslaver-made culture of rape and sexual abuse, enslavers twisted black sexuality into supposed deviance and then predicated their own mastery on it.[14] With pretzel-like logic, enslavers claimed that young African-descended women were hypersexual, morally unrestrained temptresses. Called *jezebels*, these rhetorical black women were masculinized and animalized, which contrasted African-descended female sexuality with their supposedly restrained and morally immaculate white counterparts. Enslaved woman who aged out of the jezebel stereotype were just as mythically designated *mammys* or desexualized caregivers, who were suitable to serve respectable white households. Rhetorically at least, enslavers assaulted and raped jezebels to assert mastery, turning them into virtuous mammys, pillars of the community, who nursed and tended the children of legitimate unions.[15] The tortured logic of enslavers' sexual rhetoric was like so many justifications: "it threatened to collapse at any moment under the weight of its own absurdity," were it not for the naked exercise of power that underlay it.[16]

Justifications for rape went beyond such rhetorical constructions and victim blaming to a foundational reason why African-descended people were enslaved in the first place. Enslavers contorted and twisted sexuality and intimacy into an excuse for mastery, setting themselves up as moral arbiters and white women as exemplars despite being responsible for creating the landscape of sexual violence. "The reversibility of power and the play of the dominated discredit the force of violence through the assertion of reciprocal and intimate relations," argues one scholar. "In this regard, the recognition of the agency of the dominated and the power of the weak secures the fetters of subjection, while proclaiming the power and influence of those shackled and tethered."[17] Enslavers flipped the narrative, justifying their own deviance while subjecting the vulnerable to their arbitrary power. Nowhere was that more clear than in the slave market.

---

[14] Aliyyah I. Abdur-Rahman, "'The Strangest Freaks of Despotism': Queer Sexuality in Antebellum African American Slave Narratives," *African American Review* 40.2 (2006): 223–37.

[15] Deborah Gray White, *Ar'n't I a Woman?: Female Slaves in the Plantation South*, rev. edn. (New York, NY: W. W. Norton, 1999), chap. 1.

[16] Walter Johnson, *Soul by Soul: Life inside the Antebellum Slave Market* (Cambridge, MA: Harvard University Press, 1999), 109.

[17] Saidiya V. Hartman, *Scenes of Subjection: Terror, Slavery, and Self-Making in Nineteenth-Century America* (New York, NY: Oxford University Press, 1997), 89.

Martha Sweart was bought and transported thousands of miles between her native Virginia and the lower Mississippi Valley as a sex slave. Sweart was from Albemarle County in central Virginia. In the winter of 1832, she was about sixteen years old, had light skin, and stood five feet two inches tall. Purchased for $350 by an itinerant trader working on commission, she was taken seventy miles east to Richmond and delivered to slave trader Rice C. Ballard.[18] He sized Sweart up as a sex slave.

Sweart underwent another sudden removal in late winter 1832, followed by a sea passage to New Orleans in tight conditions. Saltwater transport enforced a radical separation and the consequent utter reliance on captors. On a Sunday in mid-March – about a month after arrival – Sweart joined thirty-four other captives, mostly in their teens and twenties, processing through muddy streets to the Richmond city dock and a steamboat that took them down the James River. In Norfolk, Ballard embarked his consignment of captives on a company ship, the *Tribune*. The merchant vessel was already filled to capacity, and by the time it was cleared to sail out of Hampton Roads it had 222 involuntary passengers, about three and a half dozen more than it was built to confine.[19]

Sweart joined scores of captives who had also suffered sudden, jarring removals from the neighborhoods where they were born and families who loved them. The seasoned skipper sailed the *Tribune* to New Orleans in a speedy two weeks. But the passage was miserable. Measles broke out among the captives, who were each allotted twenty-nine cubic feet below decks, a cramped space roughly equivalent to a casket. As in company jails, captives were segregated by gender aboard company ships.[20]

Segregated shipboard compartments substituted white male subjection for what few vestiges of black male authority remained after sale. Although subject to enforced removal themselves, adult male captives retained social roles as protectors of females and children. White sexual predations (or their likelihood) sparked the uprising on the slave ship *Creole*, which sailed from Richmond in 1841. Leaders Ben Blacksmith

---

[18] Vol. 38, Ledger, Ballard and Co., 1831–34, subseries 5, folder 463, Rice C. Ballard Papers, Southern Historical Collection, University of North Carolina, Chapel Hill (UNC), quotation; Inward Slave Manifest, New Orleans, March 19, 1832 (*Tribune*), National Archive and Records Administration (NARA) M1895, roll 7, image 77.

[19] Inward Slave Manifest, New Orleans, March 19, 1832 (*Tribune*), NARA M1895, roll 7, images 77, 78, 81–84, 87.

[20] Calvin Schermerhorn, *The Business of Slavery and the Rise of American Capitalism, 1815–1860* (New Haven, CT: Yale University Press, 2015), 140.

and Madison Washington were punished for breaking rules against black men entering the part of the ship in which children and women were confined. Blacksmith and Washington uncovered sexual assaults on female captives.[21] Instead of taking their punishment, however, Blacksmith and Washington turned the tables on their captors and took command of the ship. They killed one slave trader and sailed to Nassau, Bahamas, where they sought British protection. All but three of the *Creole* captives were freed. But Rice Ballard's firm took steps to limit the possibility of such uprisings.

After the ship landed in New Orleans, Ballard's partner Isaac Franklin disembarked Sweart and the other captives, transferring them to holding cells and, shortly thereafter, the deck of a Mississippi River steamer bound for Natchez. At Forks of the Road, the firm's sales compound east of Natchez, sales agents including Isaac's nephew James Franklin completed the work of making Martha Sweart into a "fancy maid," advertising her for sale as a sex slave and enforcing that script.[22]

Isaac Franklin and his partners in the firm of Franklin & Armfield held a sexualized view of their trade, an attitude that infused the firm's culture. In 1834, Isaac suggested to Ballard that two female captives "could soon pay for themselves by keeping a whore house" in Alexandria, Baltimore, or Richmond, "for the exclusive comfort of the concern & those agents" in their employ.[23] Brothels were indeed kept by enslaved women who acted as madams for their owners. Some sex customers were enslaved. So were prostitutes. Implicit in Franklin's proposal, however, was the captives' indebtedness to the firm for their purchase price and maintenance, to be paid for by forced sex work.[24]

But after being offered for sexual exploitation, Sweart remained unsold that spring of 1832. James Franklin did not attract a buyer. About a month after she arrived, he wrote Ballard: "The fair maid Martha is still on hand. I think the chance to sell her ... as well and our white

---

[21] Walter Johnson, "White Lies: Human Property and Domestic Slavery aboard the Slave Ship Creole," *Atlantic Studies* 5.2 (August 2008): 237–63.

[22] Isaac Franklin, New Orleans, to RCB Esq., January 11, 1834, Series 1, Folder 13, Ballard Papers, UNC (quotation).

[23] Isaac Franklin to Rice C. Ballard, January 11, 1834, Series 1, Folder 13, Ballard Papers, UNC.

[24] Judith Kelleher Schafer, *Brothels, Depravity, and Abandoned Women: Illegal Sex in Antebellum New Orleans* (Baton Rouge, LA: Louisiana State University Press, 2009), 40–44.

Caroline is very bad."[25] One of Sweart's fellow captives was Caroline Brown, who was also offered for sale as a sex slave.

Brown sailed from Virginia three months before Martha Sweart. Brown stood just five feet one and three-quarters of an inch tall and was labeled "nearly white" on the slave ship *Tribune*'s slave manifest.[26] In the absence of a buyer, James Franklin raped her himself. "I have seen a handsome girl since I left Va that would climb higher hills & go further to accomplish her designs than any girl to the north & she is not to[o] apt to leave or loose her gold," he chuckled, hinting that Brown resisted him, "& the reason is because she carries her funds in her lovers purse or in Bank & to my certain knowledge she has been used & that smartly by a one eyed man about my size and age, excuse my foolishness. In short I shall do the best with & for the fancy white maid & excellent cook that I can."[27] His aggressive sexual banter was part brag and part business. Franklin equated Brown's genitals with the source of her worth, and in raping her he was symbolically robbing her "lover's purse" through sexual penetration, coyly equating it with market exploitation. Rape was discipline, enforcing the role of sex slave on an unwilling subject.

After failing to sell Martha Sweart, James and Isaac Franklin returned her to Ballard in Virginia. Ballard held on to her. After turning her into a sex slave, he showed no signs of reversing the process. In November 1833, some twenty months after Sweart's initial delivery to Richmond, Isaac Franklin wrote Ballard from Natchez, "I was disappointed in not finding your Charlottesvill[e] maid that you promised me." Apparently, Ballard and Franklin had discussed returning Sweart to Forks of the Road. In the same letter, Franklin reported "great demand for fancy maid[s]," and demanded Ballard "ship all the first rate house servants by the first shipment after you receive this."[28]

Ballard put Sweart back on a ship and sent her to his partner in New Orleans. It had been nearly two years since Ballard first laid eyes on her. Sweart had survived at least two sea passages between the Chesapeake and lower Mississippi Valley and was now returning at managing director

[25] James Franklin to Rice C. Ballard, May 13, 1832, Series 1, Folder 6, Ballard Papers, "UNC"; Kathleen Barry, *The Prostitution of Sexuality* (New York, NY: New York University Press, 1995), chap. 6.

[26] Inward Slave Manifest, New Orleans, November 17, 1831 (*Tribune*), NARA M1895, roll 6, image: 1213; James Franklin to Rice C. Ballard, March 27, 1832, UNC.

[27] James Franklin to Rice C. Ballard, March 27, 1832, UNC.

[28] Isaac Franklin, Natchez, to Ballard, November 1, 1833, Series 1, Folder 12, Ballard Papers, UNC.

Isaac Franklin's request. While waiting for Sweart to arrive in January 1834, forty-four-year-old Franklin boasted of his sexual exploits from New Orleans: "the way your old one eyed friend looked the pirate was a sin to Crocket but he is brought up all standing." The one eye was a reference to his penis. Unable to sell many slaves, Franklin demanded his partner send from Richmond "the Fancy Girl from Charlotte[s]ville." Franklin asked Ballard, "will you send her out or shall I charge you $1100 for her[?] say quick[!]" Franklin had either forgotten or refused to use Sweart's name. "I wanted to see her," he insisted. While bragging about erect penises, Franklin and Ballard reinforced a connection between sexual violence and slavery.[29]

Sweart soon arrived in New Orleans. She was about eighteen years old when Isaac Franklin took her into his private chambers. For nearly two months, she was subject to his sexual predations. Perhaps for his nephew's twenty-sixth birthday, Franklin embarked Sweart on a steamboat to Natchez and the Forks of the Road compound over which James Franklin presided.

Sweart moved from a New Orleans apartment to a Natchez rape room. "The old man sent me your [m]aid Martha[;] she is inclined to be compliant," the younger Franklin bragged to Ballard early in March.[30] About five weeks later, James Franklin wrote his partner again, boasting, "I have your Charlotte[s]ville [m]aid Martha on hand[;] she answers by the name of Big Cuff." The racist epithet hinted too that Sweart was pregnant. Whether that was the case or not, James removed her from Forks of the Road and took her across the Mississippi River. From White Hall, Louisiana, he joked to Ballard, "I am happy to say to you I have changed very much since I saw you," chuckling that, "[I] have become very virtuous." As he bragged of sexual overexertion, James hinted at Martha's strategy to leave the vicinity of Natchez. "I am nearly ruined," he wrote. "Martha sends her best respects & says she wants to see you very much."[31]

In the shadows of James Franklin's sexualized swagger is the glimmer of Martha Sweart's strategy to mitigate her abuse. She may have formed a traumatic bond with Rice Ballard, her legal owner, likely undergoing outcomes of traumatic stress. Perhaps expressing affection for or loyalty to

[29] Isaac Franklin, New Orleans, to RCB Esq., January 11, 1834, Series 1, Folder 13, Ballard Papers, UNC.

[30] James Franklin, Natchez, to Ballard, March 7, 1834, Series 1, Folder 13, Ballard Papers, UNC.

[31] James Franklin, White Hall, near Natchez, April 16, 1834, to Ballard Esq., Series 1, Folder 14, Ballard Papers, UNC.

Ballard was part of a desperate effort to return to Virginia. From Richmond she could hope to return to Charlottesville and reenter her old network of family and kin. But after two years of captivity, she may have lost such hope.

Sweart's response was one shrewd if anxious, evolving answer to the series of shocks Ballard and agents of his firm administered. Traumatic bonding may have played into the conceits of enslavers like Franklin and Ballard, who proved adept at disposing of captives pregnant with the children of white men.[32] In 1853, Ballard shipped another bondswoman, Virginia Boyd, off to Texas, where she gave birth to a partner's son, only to die soon after in the cotton fields.[33] While Ballard was shipping Sweart back and forth to Louisiana, he was also sexually involved with other captives, including Avenia White. Ballard's relationship with White led to the birth of a son, Preston, and her move to Cincinnati, Ohio. He wanted her and the baby out of the way. That was on the cusp of Ballard's marriage to a white woman of high status, Louise Cabois Berthe, in 1840.[34] What became of Sweart is unclear, but her near-invisibility in historical records is part of the landscape of sexual violence.

Some subjects of sexual abuse fought back, often with tragic consequences. An enslaved woman, Peggy, entered the house of her owner, John Francis, at midnight on August 22, 1830, and with an accomplice named Patrick attacked Francis with a stick and an ax. Francis begged for mercy, but none was given. And the farmhouse soon burned down around the body of the slain enslaver. At the trial in New Kent County, Virginia, a witness testified that "it was currently reported in the neighborhood that the deceased was the father of Peggy and that he wished to have illicit intercourse with her, to which she objected and that was the cause of their disagreement." The court found Peggy, Patrick, and another accomplice guilty and sentenced them to hang, but there was such an outpouring of sympathy from officials and other citizens that the Commonwealth of Virginia commuted the sentence to transport out of state.[35] Others were less fortunate. Male rapists had the law on their side.

---

[32] Baptist, *The Half Has Never Been Told*, 357–63; Steven Deyle, *Carry Me Back: The Domestic Slave Trade in American Life* (New York, NY: Oxford University Press, 2005), 262–64.

[33] Baptist, *The Half Has Never Been Told*, 363.

[34] Sharony Green, "'Mr. Ballard, I am compelled to write again.': Beyond Bedrooms and Brothels, a Fancy Girl Speaks," *Black Women, Gender + Families* 5.1 (Spring 2011): 17–40.

[35] Joshua D. Rothman, *Notorious in the Neighborhood: Sex and Families across the Color Line in Virginia, 1787–1861* (Chapel Hill, NC: University of North Carolina Press, 2003), 149–63; quote, 152.

John Newsom of Callaway County, Missouri, bought fourteen-year-old Celia in 1850, and he raped her on his return from buying her. That started several years of abuse. Newsom was a wealthy widower who housed Celia in a cabin on his property and continued to assault and rape her. She gave birth to two babies and was pregnant with a third by the spring of 1855. But she was in love with George, an enslaved man, who said if the owner's abuse did not stop, he could not continue courting her. So Celia tried – as she had so many times – blocking Newsom's advances and asking his adult daughters to keep their father from raping her again. But to no avail. And when Newsom entered her cabin on the night of June 23, she took a stick and clubbed him in the head, beating him to death, and burned his body in her fireplace. When the crime was discovered, Celia was arrested, jailed, and charged with murder. But her court-appointed attorneys argued that her actions were in self-defense under an 1845 Missouri law making it a crime "to take any woman unlawfully against her will and by force, menace or duress, compel her to be defiled."[36] The judge did not think the law applied to an enslaved person. The prosecutor sought the death penalty, and a jury of twelve white men who either owned slaves or who were sympathetic to slave owners found Celia guilty. She was allowed to give birth, but the baby was stillborn. And the state executed nineteen-year-old Celia that December.

Within that structure of oppression, some enslaved women made the choiceless choice of allying with their enslavers. Cooperation could mitigate the abuse, if not lead to an escape route. Corinna Hinton discovered that in Richmond, Virginia. In a sea of awful alternatives, occupational mobility was a raft. Intimate connections to enslavers helped them move out of being enslaved, if only by elevating them to the domestic partners of slave traders. Some exploited their exploiters. Hinton was about twenty years old when she was offered for sale in the Richmond slave market of the 1840s. She was enslaved but had light skin. Appraising her was Silas Omohundro, twenty years her senior, recently widowed, and an established slave trader who had come up under Ballard as a purchasing agent for Franklin & Armfield.[37]

Perhaps Hinton first looked at him with fear and loathing. But as words passed between them and he laid hands on her, she spied a strategy. In Hinton, Omohundro saw a striking woman, and his appraisal of her resale value shifted into his appraisal of her as a lover, a wife, and a mother.

---

[36] Melton A. McLaurin, *Celia, a Slave* (Athens, GA: University of Georgia Press, 1991), 107.

[37] Accounts of Silas and R. H. Omohundro's slave trade, 1857–64, mss. 4122, Small Library Special Collections, University of Virginia; Phillip D. Troutman, "Slave Trade and Sentiment" (PhD diss., University of Virginia, 2000).

In Omohundro, Hinton saw a way out of no-way. He was a mid-level trader cashing in on demand for bondspersons in the lower South, and his business caught the prevailing commercial winds. Out-of-state buyers lodged at his Richmond boardinghouse while shopping for human wares. The boardinghouse was part of a compound that included a private jail off 15th Street and a nearby dwelling place. Hinton pivoted quickly to enslaver, settling in as his domestic partner and helping to run the business. That relationship was one they both recognized as a marriage. Such arrangements existed on a knife-edge.

Those who moved from bondsperson to domestic partner could quickly move back, as was the case with Cynthia, whom William Wells Brown described as having light skin and a sterling reputation, and as "one of the most beautiful women I ever saw," from Saint Louis, bought by slave trader William Walker "for the New Orleans market." Walker cajoled and threatened Cynthia into taking up a domestic arrangement with him on a farm near where she was from. During Brown's time in Missouri, Cynthia had two children with Walker. But after two more babies, Walker decided he preferred marriage to a white woman and "sold poor Cynthia and her four children . . . into hopeless bondage," Brown reported.[38] The stakes were also high on Corinna Hinton's continuing arrangement with Silas Omohundro.

Rather than halt his business, Omohundro continued buying and selling females whom Hinton was tasked with costuming for sale. She publicly acted as Omohundro's agent doing business with local merchants. In 1855, for instance, Omohundro wrote in his accounts: "Bill of Negro Clothing to Corinner [*sic*] for this year," in the amount of "$587.25."[39] The same market and account book lists thousands of dollars in cash Corinna received, along with dresses, kid gloves, and jewelry, including a $200 diamond ring (the real price equivalent was $5,730 in 2016).[40] But there was an irony laced with tragedy. Her new role reinforced her vulnerability since Omohundro kept her enslaved, and she witnessed in a personal way the susceptibility to precisely the practices she honed as manager of her husband's enterprise.[41]

Hinton's social and geographic mobility combined with a new domestic role as mother of Silas's children. Hinton gave birth to six babies who

---

[38] William Wells Brown, *Narrative of William W. Brown, an American Slave, Written by Himself* (London: Charles Gilpin, 1849), 45–46.

[39] "Market and Account Book" (1855–64), Omohundro: Business & Estate Records, Library of Virginia (LVA).

[40] Omohundro Market and Account Book, LVA.

[41] Alexandra Finley, "'Cash to Corinna': Domestic Labor and Sexual Economy in the 'Fancy Trade,'" *Journal of American History* 104.2 (September 2017): 410–30.

survived infancy, all legally enslaved: Silas Jr., Alice, Colon, Riley, William, and George. Silas Omohundro apparently doted on his children, even as he deprived so many other young captives of their parents and siblings. He invested resources in them, lavished gifts on them, and sent them to school. But the sources of family wealth likely wore on Corinna. By the late 1850s, she and the children had departed Richmond. They stayed in Philadelphia for months at a time, and she was apparently planning another move, to Ohio. Omohundro bought a house in Philadelphia's 20th Ward. There Silas Jr. went to boarding school. There the Omohundros passed as white. There they also passed as free. A slave in law, Corinna Hinton-Omohundro was anything but an enslaved woman according to her local status.

During the Civil War, Omohundro continued to buy and sell captives. The business was too lucrative to leave. But he did not live to see Richmond burn and the end of legal slavery. Omohundro died in June 1864. In his will he ordered, "I do absolutely emancipate and forever set free, from all manner of servitude my woman Corinna Omohundro, and her five children ... who are also my children." (Silas Jr. had already passed away, at age thirteen, in December 1861.) Omohundro also gave her his compound in Richmond and if she chose not to live there a choice of his properties in Philadelphia. Hinton had honed her public persona as an honorable married white woman.

Her legal transformation was invisible as the burden of slavery lifted. Besides freedom, Omohundro willed most of his property to her. The month after his death, Hinton took possession of four enslaved people she claimed as part of her inheritance from one of her husband's business partners. That was not easy. The Civil War was raging across Virginia that summer, as it had for three years. Petersburg was under siege, Richmond was garrisoned, and two vast armies were colliding in places like Cold Harbor. But Hinton made her way to a war zone to claim her property, perhaps meeting a blue-eyed soldier from New Hampshire along the way. Mrs. Omohundro could play a Southern belle and a widow adrift in war. And that audacity enraged her ex-husband's other family. Littleton Omohundro, perhaps Silas's nephew or his son by a previous marriage, contended that Silas "had been building a house in Ohio for his wife (or reputed wife) and children, who resided there and where he was in the habit of visiting them till the rebellion broke out."[42]

---

[42] *Cooper, Executor* v. *Omohundro*, 86 U.S. 65, 22 L. Ed. 47, 19 Wall. 65 (1873), Lexis-Nexis Academic, accessed June 5, 2010.

But Hinton's transformation had many tangles. When she sued to collect her inheritance, which included property in Philadelphia and Lancaster County, Pennsylvania, she found out that her marriage was not legally recognized. Silas Omohundro chose to relinquish control over Hinton solely at his death. A Pennsylvania court decided that Omohundro had not freed her before marrying her, and consequently the marriage had no legal standing, even after 1865. The laws that gave Omohundro license to traffic in humans also threatened to wreck his legacy.[43] Having held the traffickers' reins over others, Hinton was fogged by them when denied what Omohundro claimed for her as a wife and mother to his children. She was unable to collect her inheritance in real estate.

Hinton was one of several female participants in the slave trade who allied with an owner and participated in the sexual economy of the slave market in an attempt to seize control over a seemingly uncontrollable momentum of events. Money, sexuality, and slave trading were linked in the cooperative endeavors of male traders and their female domestic partners who ran significant parts of the business.[44]

Human sexual contact in a loving adult relationship can embody the tenderest closeness and joy, the gift of love begetting the miracle of life. But similar physical acts can also express the most degrading and destructive violence, and their ritualization as the daily injuries and constant aggressions of slavery exemplifies the moral evil inherent in such human subjection. Enslavers' requiring the enslaved to perform sexual labor and, more generally, enslavers' control over the intimate lives of enslaved people was a central feature of American slavery. That sexual violence linked the individual experiences of solitary subjects to the sexual economy of the domestic slave trade. The constant threat and fear of rape served many disciplinary ends, but it was a power beyond the control of those who wielded it. "The whole commerce between master and slave is a perpetual exercise of the most boisterous passions," Thomas Jefferson wrote, "the most unremitting despotism on the one part, and degrading submissions on the other."[45] He knew that firsthand. When he wrote those lines in the 1780s, the future president of the United States was in a sexual relationship with his bondswoman Sally Hemings, which began

---

[43] Will book 2, Richmond City Circuit Court, 228, LVA.

[44] Alexandra Finley, *Household Accounts: An Intimate History of the Business of Slavery* (Chapel Hill, NC: University of North Carolina Press, 2020).

[45] Thomas Jefferson, *Notes on the State of Virginia* (1785), Query 18, online: http://xroads .virginia.edu/~hyper/jefferson/ch18.html, accessed: November 22, 2017.

when she was fourteen and he was forty-four. She would have six children with him in a relationship that some have romanticized and others have denied, and that historians have more recently concluded was a decades-long relationship in which the power differential between them prevented her from ever giving full consent.[46] Her and her children's value in the slave market was always part of his calculations, and his ability to dispose of her and her family members was undoubtedly part of hers.

[46] Annette Gordon-Reed, *The Hemingses of Monticello: An American Family* (New York, NY: Norton, 2008), 312–16.

8

Industrial Discipline

Enslaved people toiled in cities as well as on farms and in fields. The American South was overwhelmingly rural with most of the produce, including cotton and sugar or molasses, leaving the region for manufacturing and final processing. But in some regions, notably the Chesapeake and Virginia piedmont, the produce of the countryside was processed in Southern cities. There enslaved people added value to agricultural commodities. They flavored and pressed tobacco leaves, milled wheat into flour, and some even made iron. Mining and heavy transportation projects also used slave labor.

When railroads came south, owners staffed construction crews and section gangs with bound laborers. The burden of redeveloping Virginia in particular fell hard on African-descended people. Factory work was grueling and monotonous. Railroad work was demanding and dangerous. And employers wanted individual workers, not families. Each step in the region's redevelopment strained or splintered African American families as owners hired or sold individual workers to factory owners or railroad contractors. To meet complex labor demands, brokers matched employers and enslavers, selling slave labor on contract.

Mastery, once divided, was delegated, and brokers joined enslaved workers to supply chains reaching thousands of miles. Brokers were in the information business, negotiating on behalf of slave owners who had spotty knowledge of the actual labor market yet sought rents on slaves. Bondspersons inserted their demands and expectations. And over time, the enslaved themselves gained proficiency in an economy of knowledge, giving owners incentives to self-hiring arrangements.

The slave factory system had local consequences and far-reaching effects. Any consumer in New York, England, or Australia who bought a lump, cake, or twist of chewing tobacco was buying a slave-produced product and supporting the slave factory system. And long supply chain corridors reached deep into places where slavery had been abolished. Virginia bondspersons processed licorice shipped from southern Europe or laid down iron rails imported from northern England. And like the interstate slave trade, black families paid the social costs.

Henry Brown had a view from the inside. As a child on his mother's knee observing the autumn colors, he listened as she explained to him, "my son, as yonder leaves are stripped from off the trees of the forest, so are the children of the slaves swept away from them by the hands of cruel tyrants."[1] Her prophecy soon came to pass. At fifteen, Brown's owner died and his family was separated according to the owner's will, divided among his sons. Brown's mother kissed her son goodbye after he fell to William Barret, who staked his fortune in the city of Richmond, forty-five miles from Brown's Louisa County home. Barret bought a tobacco factory and put fifteen-year-old Brown to work in it. Many others did the same.

Tobacconists were the largest industrial employers of bound workers in Richmond. In 1840, tobacco manufacturers in Richmond employed 981 workers (about 73 percent of whom were enslaved). In 1850, the number more than doubled to 2,062 and then leaped to 3,254 in 1860 (about 8.5 percent of Richmond's total population), and between 1850 and 1860, a higher proportion of those workers was enslaved than before.[2]

Barret took Brown away from his parents and set him to work making chewing tobacco. The young man was resilient, resourceful, and strong. Brown grew to five feet eight inches tall and weighed some 200 pounds. He worked up the factory ladder to pressman, operating a screw press that shaped tobacco into a supple form customers craved. He became a Christian and joined a Baptist church, where he met Nancy. The two married in 1836, although the marriage had no legal standing. Nancy soon became pregnant with the first of their four children.[3] But Brown received no sympathy from his enslaver.

[1] Henry Brown, *Narrative of Henry Box Brown, Written by Himself* (Manchester, UK: Lee and Glynn, 1851), 2 (online: http://docsouth.unc.edu/neh/brownbox/brownbox.html, accessed: March 29, 2016).

[2] Midori Takagi, *"Rearing Wolves to Our Own Destruction": Slavery in Richmond, Virginia, 1782–1865* (Charlottesville, VA: University of Virginia Press, 1999), 18, 73.

[3] Jeffrey Ruggles, *The Unboxing of Henry Brown* (Richmond, VA: Library of Virginia, 2003), chap. 1.

Barret's tobacco factory was another slave labor camp with a system of small rewards and severe punishments. Owners and managers instituted a pushing system tasking individual tobacco workers with a daily quota. Brown recalled that a manager named William Bennett punished a worker named Pinckney, "and made him take off his shirt; he then tied his hands and gave him one hundred lashes on his bare back; and all this, because he lacked three pounds of his task, which was valued at six cents." It was a stern warning to the others. Bennett would creep up behind workers, but his attempt at eavesdropping was foiled by a wooden leg that inevitably struck something, giving him away.

Managerial style varied across the industry. In Barret's factory, Bennett's successor, Henry Bedman, tried cajoling work out of bondspersons. "He neither used the whip nor cheated the hands of what little they had to receive," Brown recalled, wringing more work with small incentives than with violence. Workers recalled Bedman as "a very good man" who encouraged workers to sing hymns to speed up work.

After Bedman died, Barret hired John F. Allen to oversee workers, and he had a flair for cruelty. He flogged a worker who failed to show up for work. The man was sick, but not sick enough to satisfy the manager. Brown reported that "Allen told him that his singing consumed too much time" and hurt his productivity. "This poor man was sick for four weeks afterwards, during which time the weekly allowance, of seventy cents, for the hands to board themselves with, was withheld, and the poor man's wife had to support him in the best way she could." Workers were afraid to go over Allen's head to the owner, but Barret was often absent anyway, taking his wife on long European vacations and managing his overseas distribution network. Leaving Allen in charge, Brown contended, Barret's "motto was, Mr. Allen is always right, and so, right or wrong, whatever he did was law, and from his will there was no appeal."[4] While managers used sticks, owners held out carrots.

Owners implemented an overwork system to boost production. With no wages on offer, they paid small cash incentives to exceed the daily quota. Brown used that system as a source of steady income, regarding himself as a top producer in Barret's factory. With those small payments, he arranged to rent wife Nancy for $50 a year and agreed to house and feed her and their children (the children legally belonging to the wife's owner, Samuel Cottrell).

---

[4] Brown, *Narrative of Henry Box Brown*, 20–21, 24–26 (quotations); Ruggles, *The Unboxing of Henry Brown*, chap. 1.

Overwork was a cornerstone of industrial slave labor discipline. New England reformer Elihu Burritt visited a Richmond tobacco factory in 1854, where he found all workers sweating in "the temperature of a bakery in July, and all engaged in skillful and rapid manipulations of the raw and unsavory material." Even so he found that workers responded to overwork incentives. "We are told that, almost without exception, every negro, young or old, was quickened to increased activity by this new impulse," some earning two or five dollars a week, and during short winter workdays striving for overwork "as long as the manager would consent to keep on the gas" in the lamps.

But factory owners designed the incentive system to produce tobacco and not workers' benefits. They understood what would be formalized in the twentieth century as scientific management. Central Virginia factories combined the worst of industrial Manchester, England, with the worst of plantation Mississippi. Like English factory workers, Brown and his colleagues had little control over the conditions under which they worked. They toiled relentlessly at repetitive tasks under strict control. And like the slave labor camps of the cotton South, managers stood ready with whips and other instruments of personal violence to coerce labor. And on such shop floors, owners applied principles of industrial management that drove workers apart by giving individual workers small but measurable incentives to exceed the daily quota.

That was good for production but tended to undercut worker solidarity. If owners had given workers collective goals, they would have incentivized cooperation. But individual quotas and overwork payments shifted the focus to individual productivity. Scottish journalist Alexander Mackay interviewed "a tall, athletic man at work" at a Richmond tobacco press in 1846. "He was married," he said, "had already purchased his wife's freedom, and was then labouring for the means of acquiring his own." "His expertness and activity were extraordinary," Mackay marveled, "sometimes earning for him, by extra work, no less than ten dollars a week." The equivalent income value of $10 in 1846 was $5,670 in 2016, and given prevailing Virginia slave prices, the tobacco worker could earn in sixty weeks of overtime enough to purchase his freedom if he saved it all. Historians have termed these kinds of arrangements "quasi-freedom," placing Brown and others on a continuum with forced labor and wage slavery.[5]

---

[5] Alexander Mackay, *The Western World; or, Travels in the United States in 1846–47: Exhibiting Them in Their Latest Development, Social, Political and Industrial; Including a Chapter on California*, Vol. 1 (Philadelphia, PA: Lea & Blanchard, 1849), 285 (first

But cooperation in the overwork system was for most a least-bad option. The Browns were no exception. As slave prices rose, Nancy's owner, Samuel Cottrell, added surcharges to the annual fee Henry Brown paid to live with his wife and their children. Owners Cottrell and Barret had good reasons to permit the Browns' domestic arrangement, beyond using Henry like a cash cow. Henry and Nancy were less likely to run off under the arrangement. For their part, the Browns' earning power also allowed them to buy consumer goods, easing a life of unrelenting toil.

Bound workers often chose to spend rather than invest their earnings. Mackay witnessed bondsmen dressed in finery on Sundays, sporting "gloved hands, flaunting frills ... spotless linen ..., with a dress of superlative fine broad cloth, evidently of the latest cut. ... This passion for dress exhibits itself, if possible, with tenfold intensity among the females."[6] Another visitor, English journalist James Silk Buckingham, witnessed similar displays. "On Sundays, when the slaves and servants are all at liberty after dinner," he reported, "they move about in every public thoroughfare, and are generally more gaily dressed than the whites." Enslaved people's clothing displays fascinated him. "The females wear muslin and light silk gowns, with caps, bonnets, ribbons, and feathers; some carry reticules on the arm, and many are seen with parasols, while nearly all of them carry a white pocket-handkerchief before them in the most fashionable style."[7]

Visitors seeing solely crimes of fashion missed the significance of enslaved people using clothing to critique slavery and escape it, if only culturally. "The young men, among the slaves," recalled Buckingham, "wear white trousers, black stocks, broad-brimmed hats, and carry walking-sticks; and from the bowing, curtesying, and greetings, in the highway, one might almost imagine one's self to be at Hayti, and think that the coloured people had got possession of the town, and held sway, while the whites were living among them by sufferance." The Haitian metaphor was as subversive as it was hidden to the general run of Richmonders. Bondspersons could act and dress as free citizens on the Sabbath. But the rebellious dress had limits. "On working days, however, the case is

quotation); Loren Schweninger, "The Underside of Slavery: The Internal Economy, Self-Hire, and Quasi-Freedom in Virginia, 1780–1865," *Slavery and Abolition* 12.2 (September 1991): 1–22 (second quotation).

[6] Mackay, *The Western World*, 285–86.

[7] James Silk Buckingham, *The Slave States of America, Volume Two* (Bedford, MA: Applewood Books, [1842] 2008), 427.

altered," Buckingham sighed, "for then they return back to their labour and dirty clothes again."[8]

Besides managers' whips and owners' relentless pressure to produce, occupational health and safety hazards abounded. When Swedish reformer Fredrika Bremer toured a Richmond tobacco factory, she pronounced it "no life of Canaan." Some tasks required little effort, but pressing tobacco into lumps or cakes required strength and endurance. Dust was not ventilated, and pressing "is so laborious that it not unfrequently produces diseases of the lungs, and costs the laborer his health and life," Bremer contended, such was the "smell and the dirt which always prevails in a tobacco manufactory, and which to me seems murderous, as they are employed in it from their very childhood."[9] The factory owner showed no shame as he handed her a tobacco cake as a gift. Little paternalism was displayed after hours either. When factory lamps were extinguished and the doors shut and locked, it was up to workers to find their own food and lodgings.

At the end of fourteen or sixteen hours in the factory, enslaved workers ceased to be supervised by factory employees. Rather than provide lodgings, tobacconists like Barret disbursed money for workers to buy their own food and shelter at the rate of seventy cents a week or about $35 - per year (not counting the two-week break at Christmas). In 2016 dollars, that amounts to an income value of $19,800. In today's terms, Brown's family of five would live at 70 percent of the 2016 U.S. federal poverty guidelines on the living-out stipend, excluding Brown's overwork and assuming Nancy earned no income. By the same measure, a single enslaved adult worker could live at the equivalent of 67 percent above the 2016 federal poverty level.[10] Outside the factory as well as inside it, that was no easy life.

Where factory owners' supervision ended, state supervision began. Black workers who ventured out of their neighborhoods or who attempted to visit friends or relatives in surrounding counties could be taken up and jailed on suspicion of running away. Authorities found the living-out system troubling since enslaved people had so much unsupervised time. Yet factory owners tended to be citizens of property and

---

[8] Buckingham, *The Slave States of America*, 427 (quotations); Monica L. Miller, *Slaves to Fashion: Black Dandyism and the Styling of Black Diasporic Identity* (Durham, NC: Duke University Press, 2009), chap. 2.

[9] Fredrika Bremer, *The Homes of the New World*, vol. 3, Mary Howitt, trans. (London: Arthur Hall, Virtue, 1853), 315.

[10] Brown, *Narrative of Henry Box Brown*, 25.

standing who were politically influential and economically savvy. Workers' free time was time they did not have to employ overseers, and so tobacconists effectively socialized the costs of security on civil authorities during the hours their factories were closed.

Police surveillance and poverty stipends tended to limit where factory bondspersons lived. Richmond's enslaved tobacco workers tended to reside in the poorest section of the city, clustered along Shockoe Creek. It was damp and dreary terrain. Some economized by living in alleys or piling in with other workers at rundown boardinghouses housing African-descended workers. They dined in kitchen shops catering to factory workers, and as proprietors, free people of African descent captured some of the monies owners paid to bound workers. As factories added thousands of bound workers in the 1850s, the arrangement became highly unpopular with white city residents. Richmond's Common Council banned enslaved people living out in 1858. But by then the practice was so engrained that enforcing the ban was impossible.

While authorities worried over enslaved factory workers' mobility, political economists extolled the business advantages of the slave factory system. Speaking of enslaved factory workers, Thomas P. Jones argued in 1827 that "experience has proved that they are more docile, more constant, and cheaper than freemen, who are often refractory and dissipated, who waste much time by visiting public places, attending musters, elections &c. which the operative slave is not permitted to frequent." In his view, production demands conflicted with democratic entitlements. Male wage workers expected to go to the polls on election days, attend militia musters, consume alcohol on the job, and agitate for higher wages and better working conditions. And that hurt productivity.[11] For similar reasons, factory owners in New England and old England preferred low-cost female and child workers. Southerners too saw advantages in workers with no rights.

Proponents of the slave factory system saw it as a model rather than as an aberration. Jones advocated expanding slave labor to spinning and weaving, contending that "slaves are competent [and] are capable of exercising many trades where much more intellect is required." At the time, New England's textile mills (and New York's tobacco factories) were staffed mainly by women and children who worked for below a family wage. But slave labor offered additional advantages, Jones

[11] Thomas P. Jones, "Domestic Manufactures," Natchez *Ariel*, October 5, 1827, 6 (quotations).

contended. "It surely requires little talent to draw out a thread with a mule, to join it to a spindle, or to apply the cotton to a carding apparatus," and slave factories would rival free ones for their efficiency. "New England now seems to imagine that the cotton growing states, with a million or two of the best operatives in the world, will continue incapable of using those simple machines which the very children of the white slaves of Europe can learn to manage in a month."[12] There was plenty of precedent outside factories and fields for slave labor's advantages. Most Southern railroads used enslaved labor. "That negro labor is perfectly adapted to the construction of works of internal improvement," the chief engineer of the Central Railroad and Banking Company of Georgia contended in 1839, "is now a well established fact."[13] But the competition for slave labor from cotton planters was overwhelming, and successful employers of slave labor in factories made products requiring specific knowledge.

Henry Brown's owner built a brand based on a secret recipe for his chewing tobacco and then marketed it as widely as possible. In Barret's case, the supply chain corridor was as long as the apparel industry's is today. Tobacco leaf came to Richmond from the western hinterlands, freighted on canal boats, wagons, or railroad cars. Other ingredients were sourced from thousands of miles away. Licorice auctioned in Richmond came from Calabria in southern Italy. Sugar arrived from the Caribbean and the lower Mississippi Valley. Barret's factory made a product that could not be imitated. After manufacture, the twists packed in boxes in Barret's Virginia factory sailed tens of thousands of miles around the tip of South America and across the Pacific Ocean to the merchants of Sydney.[14]

Anticipating the racial accents of brands like Uncle Ben (rice) and Aunt Jemima (pancake mix), tobacco chewers were invited to participate in consumerist bigotry by connecting the pungent, rich, and dark plug they popped in their mouths to idealized blackness. "NEGROHEAD" chewing tobacco was popular in Australia, and there were several popular brands. Barret's Virginia factory turned out tobacco flavored with licorice, a type known as Cavendish. A Sydney, Australia, newspaper in 1851 featured

[12] Thomas P. Jones, "Domestic Manufactures," Natchez *Ariel*, October 5, 1827, 6 (quotations).

[13] L. O. Reynolds, "Third Semi-Annual Report of the Central Railroad and Banking Company of Georgia, to the President, Directors, and Stockholders," *American Railroad Journal and Merchants Magazine* 9 (August 1839): 83 (quotation).

[14] Richmond *Enquirer*, October 8, 1845, 1; Sydney, Australia, *Freeman's Journal*, March 24, 1855, 1.

ads for "BARRETT'S TWIST" identified as "ANCHOR BRAND." Anchor was to Cavendish as Adidas is to athletic shoes. Barret's tobacco commanded premium prices, selling for about 30 percent more than molasses-flavored Honeydew, according to a London market report in 1854.[15]

Virginia's flour mills also produced a specialized product, known for its combination of high quality and long shelf life. It could be shipped to Brazil or the West Coast of North America and arrive unspoiled. As in tobacco, long supply chains hid slave labor in Richmond flour mills from distant customers. "It is from Richmond," Mackay claimed, "that the South American market is chiefly supplied with this necessary of life; the wheat of Virginia, when ground, being better adapted for tropical voyages than the produce of any other part of the country." Flour milled in Virginia was in great demand in Brazil and, by the late 1840s, California. Mackay argued that "the largest flour-mills in the United States [are] found here, one of which, when in full play, can turn out from 750 to 1,000 barrels of flour per day." Rio de Janeiro and San Francisco markets complemented capital and other connections with New York: Richmond millers used Northern capital to refine flour sold thousands of miles to the south and west.[16]

As a result, Richmond grew in tandem with the wealth of its hinterland and through the capitalist development that brought the market to the countryside and the produce of that countryside to the market. Between 1840 and 1860, the number of mills declined sharply in rural Virginia as wheat flour milling became centralized in Richmond and sold elsewhere. Eighty-seven percent of Richmond's flour exports went to South America. The mirror image of that process was happening in Brazil, which shipped slave-produced coffee to Virginia.[17] Rio de Janeiro flour merchants traded Richmond flour brands.

Niche products and slave labor did not scare away creditors, and the slave factory system attracted enough Northern investment to make Richmond an economic suburb of New York City. New York mercantile agency R. G. Dun and Company began collecting credit reports in

<hr>

[15] Sydney, Australia, *Empire*, January 24, 1851, 1 (quotations); Richmond *Enquirer*, October 8, 1845, 1; London *Daily News*, September 19, 1854, 2; Ruggles, *The Unboxing of Henry Brown*, chap. 1.

[16] Mackay, *The Western World*, 253 (quotation); *The [London] Morning Post*, April 10, 1854, 6; Takagi, *"Rearing Wolves to Our Own Destruction,"* chap. 2.

[17] Daniel Rood, "Bogs of Death: Slavery, the Brazilian Flour Trade, and the Mystery of the Vanishing Millpond in Antebellum Virginia," *Journal of American History* 101.1 (June, 2014): 19–43.

Richmond in the 1840s so that Empire City bankers and merchants could process applications for short-term mercantile credit. Such financial networks "helped to create a unified, national market in short-term credit during the antebellum era," argues a historian.[18] Haxall Mill owner William Henry Haxall's credit report listed him as the city's leading "capitalist" by the mid-1850s, doing "a heavy South American trade & some in Califa." Haxall and his brother Bolling Walker Haxall were "[m] en of high char[acter] & cr[edit] beyond a question. tip. top."[19] Slave hiring had long lent flexibility to flour mill owners, who employed thirty-five enslaved workers in 1840. The Gallego and Haxall mills together worked seventy-eight African-descended workers in 1850 and 136 in 1860. *DeBow's Review* of New Orleans applauded Haxall's firm in 1858, commending its "steadily increasing capacity and capital," along with an enslaved workforce of twenty turning out 1,000 barrels a day. Bound workers "have made large fortunes for their owners."[20]

William Barret's margins fattened on the theft of wages from enslaved workers. Henry Brown contended that "the greater portion of my earnings were stolen from me by the unscrupulous hand of my master." Agents of credit reporting agency R. G. Dun and Company reported that Barret "[s]tands high," in September 1848, while Brown was working in his factory. The New York mercantile agency got word in 1853 that Barret was doing a "heavy trade with the European [m]arket." By 1858, he had expanded his factory to two city blocks, and credit agents estimated him to be worth between $600,000 and $700,000 and "good as old cheese." The income value of that "cheese" was $296 million in 2016. Barret weathered the panic of 1857, which stunned the Richmond tobacco sector. Seven of eight Richmond manufacturers had to suspend operations when New York City creditors suddenly failed. By 1860, a Dun agent gushed that Barret was "A No 1 every way."[21]

And Barret had plenty of competition. Robert A. Mayo ran a slave labor tobacco factory in the same neighborhood. A Dun agent reported in

[18] Howard Bodenhorn, "Capital Mobility and Financial Integration in Antebellum America," *The Journal of Economic History* 52.3 (September 1992): 600 (quotation).

[19] Richmond, Vol. 43, pp. 259, 261, R. G. Dun & Co. Credit Report Volumes, Baker Library Historical Collections, Harvard Business School.

[20] *DeBow's Review*, 25 (1858), 582 (quotation).

[21] Brown, *Narrative of Henry Box Brown*, 39 (first quotation); Richmond, Vol. 43, pp. 279, 288, R. G. Dun & Co. Credit Report Volumes, Baker Library Historical Collections, Harvard Business School (subsequent quotations); Robert K. Heimann, *Tobacco and Americans* (New York, NY: McGraw-Hill, 1960), 154.

1855 that he owned good real estate "& is reputedly well off," with an annual income of $3,000, the income value of which was $1.21 million in 2016 dollars.[22] Another tobacco factory owner, Poitiaux Robinson, reportedly earned $25,000 in 1850 "[s]peculating on [t]obacco," an income value of $13 million in 2016. Robinson supplied plug tobacco to the US Navy and was said "to be the largest [t]obacco manuf[acturer] in the U.S." By 1852, the year he died, he was "work[ing] over 200 hands." Tobacco, according to the agent, "is a mo[n]ey mak[in]g bus[iness] just now & he is picking up the [output] v[er]y steadily. No 1 any day."[23]

And to meet growing demand, tobacco processors tended to hire rather than own bound workers, tapping a ready supply from old plantations in urban hinterlands. Brokers brought workers to the factory and took owners' demands to the countryside. Tobacconists preferred male workers, even paying a substantial premium for work that females could perform, preferring not to hire workers who might become pregnant. Factory owners did not grant maternity leave, but canceling a contract – firing the new mother – when the baby arrived disrupted production.

Philip M. Tabb's business illustrates the constellations of arrangements involved in such a slave labor market. In 1846, Tabb hired out fifty-five bondspeople belonging to Warner T. Taliaferro of Gloucester County. Most of the adult males went into tobacco factories, including eleven to Robert A. Mayo, whose factory was at the corner of Canal and Tenth Streets, three blocks downhill from the Capitol.

Robert was among the enslaved hirelings. In 1845, he'd worked in Poitiaux Robinson's factory, earning Taliaferro $50. But Tabb spied a more lucrative position and hired Robert to Mayo for $60 for the year beginning in January 1846.[24] While his owner made 20 percent more on his bondsman's hire than in the previous year (minus Tabb's commission), Robert eked out a few small benefits too. He had a shorter commute to Mayo's factory than to Robinson's. In 1846, Robert and a brother, Anthony, worked within a fifteen-minute walk to the residence of their mother and three siblings. Perhaps they ate and slept there. Tabb hired out

[22] R. G. Dun & Co., Virginia, Vol. 43, p. 24 (quotation), Baker Business Library, Harvard University; H. K. Ellyson, *Richmond Directory and Business Advertiser for 1856* (Richmond, VA: Ellyson, 1856), 175.

[23] R. G. Dun & Co., Virginia, Vol. 43, p. 101, Baker Business Library, Harvard University [quotations]; *Richmond Whig*, June 30, 1843, 2; August 11, 1848, 1; *Alexandria [Va.] Gazette*, November 21, 1850, 1.

[24] H. K. Ellyson, *Ellyson's Richmond Directory* (Richmond, VA: Ellyson, 1845), 73; *Montague's Richmond Directory and Business Advertiser, for 1850–1851*, 98.

Anthony too and paid his medical bills (deducted from his hiring fee). Tabb also hired out Robert and Anthony's mother Becky, along with three younger siblings, to a city bookkeeper.[25] Tabb knew much more than the owner about the working lives of Taliaferro's enslaved workers in Richmond.

And factory owners relied on brokers to fill their ranks on the factory floor, which permitted tobacconists to focus on production rather than recruiting a bound labor force. Slave labor brokers forced up rents on slaves based on their detailed knowledge of the labor market. A seasoned male worker like Brown could rent for $150; children were leased for less than a third of that price. And brokers acted analogously to the process of urbanization, bringing enslaved laborers to factory doors and taking employment opportunities to the hinterland while cultivating a network of slave owners.

As railroads and factories grew in scale, employers wanted regimented workforces hired under uniform contracts, railroads leading the way. Railroads such as the Richmond, Fredericksburg, and Potomac Railroad (RFPRR) used enslaved laborers extensively for construction, depot laborers, and even locomotive workers. The RFPRR standardized the language on its employment bonds, which enabled railroads to assemble mobile bound workforces the nuclei of which could be deployed hundreds of miles from the sites of their assembly. In 1856, a director of the Richmond and Danville Railroad wrote to the chief engineer of the Covington and Ohio (C&O) Railroad proposing that an assemblage of enslaved railroad workers then at Hanover Junction (now Doswell) build substantial parts of the new C&O Railroad. He offered to "push a negro force upon it which has been in our employment during the last five or six years and all now well used to the business." That would require moving the slave labor force some 200 miles west of Hanover Junction to a section between Covington and the bridge over the Greenbrier River, along the route that joined the Virginia Central to the C&O.[26] Such slave labor mobility was not unheard of. One South Carolina railroad company, facing owners who broke contracts and seized workers during the cotton harvest, solved the problem by hiring enslaved workers from Virginia and North Carolina owners hundreds of miles away. To help renew contracts,

[25] *Montague's Richmond Directory and Business Advertiser, for 1850–1851*, 82.

[26] James Hunter to Charles B. Fisk, April 25, 1856 [quotation]; Mss. BR 194, Orange and Alexandria Railroad, 1851–72, Virginia Railroads Collection, 1828–94, Robert Alonzo Rock Collection, Huntington Library.

the Charleston and Savannah Railroad sent bound workers back to Virginia each Christmas by steamship.[27]

Risk management became an issue for all involved. Owners required employers to post bonds as insurance against the bondsperson's being injured or killed. Life insurance companies took surcharges for covering enslaved people who worked in mines, factories, and railroads, but such policies were relatively uncommon. Some companies decreased risk through strict terms. The language of one policy on an enslaved person by the American Life Insurance and Trust Company of Philadelphia is typical. The agency refused to pay if the bondsperson covered was transported out of the South, used for military service, became addicted to alcohol that "induce[d] delirium tremens," committed suicide, worked in a mine or on a vessel, "or [was] employed as an [e]ngineer or [f]ireman in running a [l]ocomotive or [s]team [e]ngine, or as an [o]fficer or [b]rakeman upon a [r]ail [r]oad." Such occupations were dangerous in an age before mechanical brakes, couplers, or safety regulations. When brokers Branch and Company of Petersburg hired Michael to the Petersburg Railroad Company for 1848, it took out bond giving Michael's owner, a Mrs. MacFarland, insurance for her enslaved property.[28]

The contract MacFarland made for Michael's hire illustrates how female enslavers could avoid the impediments of negotiating contracts directly with employers. Beyond spanning a gender divide, brokers like Lewis Hill acted in the interests of enslavers whose direct negotiation with employers was complicated because they did not know the market adequately. Caroline County enslaver Sarah Brockenbrough directed Hill in April 1842 to collect late advances on two hired bondspersons. "I am not willing to loose [*sic*] any part of [the contracted fee]," she insisted. Besides finding employments, Hill hired lawyers to defend bondspersons accused of larceny and other crimes. He also sold bondspersons on commission and was a client of Rice C. Ballard, one of the largest slave traders

[27] Robert Starobin, "Disciplining Industrial Slaves in the Old South," *The Journal of Negro History* 53.2 (April 1968): 116.

[28] "Private Hiring for Year 1848," Branch & Company, Auction Sales, Mss3 B7327 a FA1, Virginia Historical Society, p. 41; American Life Insurance and Trust Company, policy #5152, March 16, 1860, Mss2 M9922 a 1, Virginia Historical Society; Jonathan Levy, *Freaks of Fortune: The Emerging World of Capitalism and Risk in America* (Cambridge, MA: Harvard University Press, 2012), chap. 2; Sharon Ann Murphy, *Investing in Life: Insurance in Antebellum America* (Baltimore, MD: Johns Hopkins University Press, 2010), 185–88.

in the 1830s.[29] If an enslaved laborer did not work out or stepped out of line too often, she could be sold to the cotton South.

But hired slave labor thrived in the South's industrial start-up phase. As the region's redevelopment progressed, industries and not just members of a particular sector competed with one another, which broadened the opportunities for enslavers looking to hire their bondspersons. Sixty-four female slaves were employed in Richmond's James River Manufacturing Company in 1840, the city's sole cotton mill. Mines were another slave-labor-reliant sector, and what locals called the coal pits west of Richmond produced bituminous coal in abundance. An 1850 London newspaper report contended that the port of Richmond "has been called into existence, within the last 15 years, by the unexampled development of the coal trade."[30] But American mining practices were dangerous. After an 1839 methane gas explosion at the Blackheath mines outside Richmond that killed scores of African-descended workers, the company president hired an expert English coal mining engineer who implemented a new safety regime. He appealed to slave owners: "There is no place in this country where slave labor commands as much, where the general health is better, and where the treatment and contentment of slaves are surpassed." Rather than inviting enslavers to show up to the mines, he directed interested parties to the offices of Robert Hill and Philip M. Tabb in Richmond, and D. H. Branch in Petersburg. They were the largest slave brokerage firms in the area and acted like recruiters. They served a variety of needs. Brokers could draw up contracts, collect bonds and fees, ensure that bondspersons showed up at the job site, and deal with matters should a hired bondsman run away, a bondswoman fall ill, or an enslaved worker become injured or killed.

When bondspeople disappeared, brokers turned into bounty hunters. John ran away from his employer in 1853, and the owner wrote Lewis Hill with instructions "to take immediate steps for his arrest, and after you have caught, sell him without delay, to the highest bidder." In June 1845, a resort manager wrote Hill in Richmond from Hot Springs, Virginia, some 160 miles to the west, asking for information on what became of eight hired bondspersons (belonging to at least three owners) who were

---

[29] Sarah Brockenbrough to Lewis Hill, April 26, 1842 [quotations]; Austin Brockenbrough to Lewis Hill, April 21, 1842, Lewis Hill Papers; Volume 38: Ledger: Ballard and Co., 1831–34, Subseries 5, Folder 463, Rice C. Ballard Papers, Southern Historical Collection, Wilson Library, University of North Carolina, Chapel Hill.

[30] London, *Daily News*, April 12, 1850, 4.

supposed to have arrived for service. Hill had not hired them, but the correspondent charged him with following up on another broker who had. He endorsed Hill's ability to find out what had become of them even though the broker was not party to the contracts.[31]

As the slave factory system developed, enslaved workers developed a knowledge of the labor market savvy enough for enslavers to delegate hiring to bondspersons themselves. Visitors were shocked to see throngs of enslaved people around New Year's congregating in what amounted to a hiring fair. By the late 1850s, enslaved people too were striking bargains that satisfied owners' interests in their wages while also seizing back some of the power over their employment taken away in the hiring process. A foreign visitor to Richmond in the late 1850s found Richmond "literally swarming with negroes, who were standing in crowds at the corners of the streets in different parts of the town." The visitor witnessed an enslaved woman making arrangements with a prospective employer, a market gardener. "The price that her owner had put on her services was not objected to by him," the visitor reported, but the woman refused to do gardening in addition to housework. After taking an "hour's walk in another part of the town," he returned and "met the two at the old bargain." On inquiring what the difficulty was, he "learned that she was pleading for other privileges – her friends and favourites must also be allowed to visit her."[32] No closer to freedom, she was attempting to soften the hard edges of the system.

There were limits on slave labor in Southern industries, and they had to do with the allure of cotton and the speculative nature of the slave market. When cotton prices rose, boosting slave prices, owners in Virginia demanded higher rents regardless of the local hiring market. Tobacconists, railroads, and mine companies had to compete with bidders in a slave market. And in the 1850s, slave prices in the Deep South became unmoored from cotton prices, indicating that enslaved people were being purchased not so much for the value of their labor products as for how much they could bring at auction in six months or a year. Rents or hiring fees on slaves rose too, but not in accordance with the value of chewing tobacco or railroad transportation. The largest iron manufacturer in the South illustrates the slave factory system's limits.

---

[31] Robert Ould to Lewis Hill, December 15, 1853 [quotation]; Thomas Goode to Lewis Hill, June 27, 1845, Lewis Hill Papers.

[32] Robert Russell, *North America: Its Agriculture and Climate, Containing Observations on the Agriculture and Climate of Canada, the United States, and the Island of Cuba* (Edinburgh: Adam and Charles Black, 1857), 151.

Richmond's Tredegar Iron Works was an industrial experiment in slave labor that stood out for its paternalism and reliance on skilled bound workers. Since the American Revolution, Richmond's ironworks had produced ammunition and construction materials. By the 1840s, enslaved ironworkers did much of the heavy labor, but white wage workers still performed skilled work as heaters, rollers, and puddlers. The Tredegar Iron Works' rolling mills turned out components of iron bridges and railroad parts such as axels. In 1842, director Joseph Reid Anderson hired skilled white workers to train an African-descended workforce as a way to save labor costs. In 1847, Anderson promoted skilled members of his enslaved workforce who had undergone apprenticeships under the tutelage of skilled wage workers. That led to a strike and the firing of a cadre of white workers. Richmond newspapers applauded Anderson's manhandling his wage workers and breaking the strike with slaves, hiring some and buying others. And after buying the company in 1848, Anderson became Richmond's chief industrial paternalist, housing bound workers in a man camp on company property, feeding them from company kitchens, and treating them at the company's hospital. They lacked the mobility of tobacco workers, but Anderson adopted tobacconists' practice of paying bound workers for overwork, giving them a source of income and an incentive to strive.[33]

The strategy bore fruit early in the 1850s, and Anderson's iron business diversified as a result. After partnering with machinists and other collateral industries in the late 1840s and early 1850s, the ironworks turned out locomotives as well as iron nails, castings, and farming implements. Despite holding some skilled jobs, African-descended workers were barred from the machine shop and locomotive works. Anderson's credit report endorsed his commercial probity. "He is A no. 1," an agent reported in the mid-1850s. Thought to be worth between $150,000 and $200,000 (an income value between $60.3 million and $80.3 million in 2016), "[h]e is of high char. & stand[in]g ... & is undoubted for any contract he will make." Anderson's experiment in industrial slavery also won large government contracts. His strategy of using bound laborers

---

[33] Sarah Bumgardner and Scott Reynolds Nelson, "Tredegar Iron Works: A Synecdoche for Industrialized Antebellum Richmond," online: http://srnels.people.wm.edu/antrichf95/bumgard.html, accessed: November 20, 2012 (quotation); Charles B. Dew, *Ironmaker to the Confederacy: Joseph R. Anderson and the Tredegar Iron Works* (New Haven, CT: Yale University Press, 1966).

helped make his enterprise one of the most distinctive industrial businesses.[34]

But as prices for slaves rose in the 1850s, free laborers became more cost-effective. Market pressures forced Anderson to hire back wage workers. Virginia iron lost some of its market advantages when Pennsylvania and English bar iron became cheaper. Nevertheless, Anderson's enterprise found a niche by accepting payment in financial paper from lower South customers. For a time, Richmond-built locomotives competed with those imported from England and with Northern-built engines on Virginia railroads.[35] The slave market frustrated Anderson's strategy, but the slave factory system did not come apart during the slave market boom of the 1850s. Tobacconists retained advantages foundries lost in the developing economy of the late 1840s and early 1850s as their profits remained steady even as the slave labor on which they relied soared in price.

On the individual level, the slave factory system devoured workers' best-laid plans. As Henry Brown toiled in the summer of 1848, events at home spun out of control. The fragile arrangement that held the Brown family together broke that August day when Nancy's owner Samuel Cottrell decided to sell her. As Henry prepared for work one morning, Cottrell stopped by with a chilling demand: "I want money, and money I will have," Brown recalled him as saying. According to his credit report, Cottrell, a saddler, was doing fine. But the slave market was undercutting the Browns' ability to parlay overwork into living as a family unit. The slave market had rebounded from its slump in the early 1840s and had risen dramatically between 1844 and 1848. Cotton and sugar masters in the Deep South were demanding young and able enslaved workers, which spurred a great forced migration of African-descended Americans to the punishing cotton fields and canebrakes.[36] Late summer was the start of the seasonal rise in the slave market, which heated up in winter months as enslavers plowed revenues into bound workers and deadly mosquito-

---

[34] Richmond, Vol. 43, pp. 247, 251, R. G. Dun & Co. Credit Report Volumes, Baker Library Historical Collections, Harvard Business School (quotations); Dew, *Ironmaker to the Confederacy*, chap. 2.

[35] John Majewski, *A House Dividing: Economic Development in Pennsylvania and Virginia before the Civil War* (New York, NY: Cambridge University Press, 2000); Dew, *Ironmaker to the Confederacy*, chap. 2.

[36] Brown, *Narrative of Henry Box Brown*, 39 (quotation); Walter Johnson, *River of Dark Dreams: Slavery and Empire in the Cotton Kingdom* (Cambridge, MA: Harvard University Press, 2013), chaps 9–10.

borne illnesses subsided in the slave markets of Natchez, Mississippi, and New Orleans, Louisiana. Brown's family became part of that human traffic.

After Henry went to work, Cottrell seized Nancy Brown and her children and consigned them for sale. After word reached Henry that his wife and children had been sold and were awaiting transport out of Virginia, he cast about frantically for some means of preventing their departure. Barret was unsympathetic. "He even told me that I could get another wife and so I need not trouble myself about that one," Brown recalled ruefully. Other putative allies also refused to intercede. When Cottrell discovered Brown was making overtures to reverse the sale, he had the sheriff raid Brown's house and confiscate his possessions, claiming that he was delinquent on a debt. And the following day the Browns were parted. Nancy was forced to walk and the children to ride in a wagon among a caravan of 350 African-descended people heading out of state. Nancy was pregnant, and Henry held her hand silently as they wept over the sudden separation, the children calling out in misery.[37] They would never meet again.

For most enslaved people facing the forced removals of loved ones, options were severely constricted. But Brown could not go on as before. Devastation gave rise to a risky scheme to escape. He grieved for months and could not return to church until December, but after a Christmas concert, he was introduced to a white Massachusetts-born shoemaker and shopkeeper, Samuel A. Smith. Brown continued saving money from over-work, and Smith was sympathetic to one so wronged. They hatched a plan.

Brown would hide in a shipping crate express-mailed to Pennsylvania. Smith traveled to Philadelphia and enlisted the support of two abolitionists there. In March 1849, just after the ice thawed on the Susquehanna River, Smith packed Brown into a custom-made wooden box fitted with air holes and sent it on the Adams Express to Philadelphia, freight charges due on arrival.

That was the start of a terrifying trip on a wagon, railroad cars, a steamboat, another railroad, a barge, a third railroad, and a delivery wagon. In transit, Adams agents mishandled the box. It was tumbled, dropped, sat upon, and generally treated roughly. Despite having a clear

---

[37] Brown, *Narrative of Henry Box Brown*, 44 (quotation); Calvin Schermerhorn, *Money over Mastery, Family over Freedom: Slavery in the Antebellum South* (Baltimore, MD: Johns Hopkins University Press, 2011), chap. 4.

sign, "this side up with care," Brown's box spent most of the twenty-four-hour ordeal head down. At one point he lost consciousness when dropped out of a wagon, the jolt of landing cracking his neck. North of Baltimore he may have passed out from exhaustion and took no more supplies than some dry crackers and a beef bladder full of water. When several abolitionists sawed open the box at their Philadelphia Anti-Slavery Office early the next morning, Brown saluted them and shook their hands, exhausted, drenched, aching, and depleted, but alive. And, for the moment, free.[38]

Brown went into activism. Following his escape, he moved to Boston, where he was sponsored by radical abolitionists. With editor Charles Stearns, he published an autobiography, known by the nickname Henry Box Brown. Word reached Richmond of his audacious escape, and other bondsmen tried mailing themselves to Philadelphia. Some died, and others were discovered. Security tightened, and authorities arrested Samuel Smith, who was held in jail in solitary confinement before trial. A Virginia court found him guilty of assisting Brown and another would-be fugitive. For assisting his friend, Smith spent six and a half years in the Virginia state penitentiary.

Brown kept clear of slave catchers and applied his diligence and creativity to agitating for the end of slavery. He created a moving panorama called *Mirror of Slavery*, which was a play with moving panes painted with scenes of slavery. He sold song sheets featuring his story and went on a book tour. Following enactment of the Fugitive Slave Act of 1850, Brown sailed for England, embarking on a British tour. He published another autobiography and staged box tours, thrilling audiences by arriving in a box and then bursting out, telling his story and making abolitionist appeals. Brown settled into a career as a showman, remarrying in England and returning to the United States in 1875, where he continued performing, though the historical record of his whereabouts ends in 1878.[39]

Brown was like a recruiting poster for an increase in slave security. Enslavers built an archipelago of jails, private and public, that housed a large population. In places like the Virginia Tidewater, enslavers sold off or removed above 20 percent of the enslaved population in the 1820s and 30 percent in the 1830s. One in seven African Americans was forcibly taken across state lines in the 1830s, slave traders managing two-thirds of

[38]　Brown, *Narrative of Henry Box Brown*, 61 (quotation); Ruggles, *The Unboxing of Henry Brown*, chap. 2.

[39]　Ruggles, *The Unboxing of Henry Brown*, chaps. 3–9.

that human traffic. Being sold meant being jailed, which means that about 5 percent of enslaved Americans were jailed in the 1830s, from young children to the elderly. Some were held for a few days; some were held for years at a time. Most who were jailed were incarcerated twice, once after sale and again before resale. Many faced a series of dark chambers. Solomon Northup saw the inside of four private jails between his kidnapping in Washington, DC, in April 1841 and his sale in New Orleans six weeks later. The author of *Twelve Years a Slave* in 1853 commented that the slave jail or "pen" was "a very common establishment, it appears, in the cities of the South."[40]

That understatement captures a hidden side of slavery's history, a decentralized network of jails built to house African Americans. One such establishment was on West Pratt Street in Baltimore, where the city's convention center stands today. A visitor in 1846 was struck by the sign outside, which read simply "Hope H. Slatter, from Clinton, Georgia." Inside was the fifty-six-year-old Georgian who obliged the visitor by showing him around. Slatter advertised that his jail cells "are both large, light and airy, and all above ground, with a fine large yard for exercise, with pure delightful water within doors." He boasted of the "health and cleanliness of the slaves, as well as the many other necessary conveniences," charging twenty-five cents a day, which bought "plenty of good and wholesome provisions." But Slatter's top priority was security. "I hold myself bound to make good all jail breaking, or escape from my establishment," he told readers of the Baltimore *Sun*. The visitor trod the forty-by-seventy-five-foot bring yard, toured "a small two story brick building with barred windows and all apparatus believed necessary to secure the presence so long as wanted of the guests, willing or unwilling, who were temporarily lodged there."

Slatter was among the more successful of Maryland's slave traders. His jail was his headquarters. Slatter paid agents to hunt up young, saleable African Americans, exchanging banknotes for title to their bodies. Those young people, whom he called "stock," were locked up in his Pratt Street jail until a sufficient cargo was assembled. The inmates were "allowed the range of the court yard by day and beguiled their time with cards, and dance, and fiddle and banjo, and every device that he could suggest or they

---

[40] Solomon Northup, *Twelve Years a Slave: Narrative of Solomon Northup, a Citizen of New-York, Kidnapped in Washington City in 1841, and Rescued in 1853, from a Cotton Plantation near the Red River in Louisiana* (New York, NY: Miller, Orton, and Mulligan, 1854), 66.

could devise to while away the time and banish memory and anticipation." Slatter had them dance for exercise, but "by night they were shut in the barred building back of the yard, which was known as 'Slatter's jail,' and which in summer weather when his stock was larger was only more tolerable than the famous black hole – for the inmates did survive though one of his assistants once informed me that it was 'hot as hell in there' at night."

Israel Jones found that out when he was incarcerated in the summer of 1847. There was no air conditioning, and the compound was quickly crowded with forlorn captives. Some were sick. All were disoriented. When not funneling some of his human purchases to Richmond for quick sale, Slatter "gathered slaves in this jail of his till its capacity was reached or a cargo was ready, then shipped to New Orleans or other [S]outhern market by sailing vessel, and there himself or by agents disposed of his goods according to the demands of the market to which he had sent them." Those were enslavers like Nancy Brown's owner who cashed in on robust slave prices. At the time, prices were two-thirds higher in New Orleans than in Maryland.

And so African Americans were processed through jails and conveyances under strict guard. In mid-September 1847, Slatter marched Jones and fifty-one other African Americans out from the jail compound and over Jones Falls to Flanagan's Wharf and embarked them in the belly of the *Pioneer*, a wooden merchant ship. It was already loaded with cargo when the captives were brought aboard. The shipmaster sailed around Florida and through the Bahamas shipping channel, landing in New Orleans in a respectable twenty-two days. There Jones was disembarked, jailed again, sold, and taken to the cotton frontier.

Shipping lines and railroad companies welcomed Slatter's business. One traveler encountered Slatter at the head of a coffle at the rail depot in Washington, DC, in 1848. He was embarking several captives aboard a rail car. Many were bidding loved ones a tearful farewell. Slatter's men beat down a black man who "clambered up to one of the windows of the car to see his wife," claiming that "she was free – that she had free papers, and was 'torn away from him and shut up in the jail.'" The trader "knocked him down from the car, and ordered him away."

All over the South and even in the borderlands of Pennsylvania and New York jails served the ends of white supremacy and black servitude. Bondspersons were warehoused in city and county jails, built at public expense, as well as slave traders' dungeons. Jailing African Americans on suspicion of being a fugitive from slavery was a sharp tool of white supremacy. Philadelphia bishop Richard Allen, founder of the African Methodist Episcopal Church, was accused of running away from a Southern plantation (he had long before purchased his legal freedom in Delaware). A slave hunter locked up perhaps the most powerful black man in America in a Philadelphia jail before Allen was identified and released. Such incarcerations chilled activism and even religious worship.

Instead of eroding an institution that had taken shape in the colonial tobacco economy, upper South factories took advantage of enslaved human resources while reinforcing chattel slavery. Hiring slave labor forced down wages for free workers like those at Tredegar Iron Works. And broker-allocated slave labor could fill a section gang or staff a factory. The resulting economies of scale among tobacconists, millers, and railroaders freed employers to focus on marketing and growth rather than labor discipline.

Slavery lent industrial employers exceptional flexibility when it came to increasing worker productivity through a combination of carrots and sticks. But the demands of commodity production, including a slave market pegged to commodity prices rather than industrial returns, favored the growth of the cotton complex at the expense of the slave factory system. The industrial North and England held too many comparative advantages by the 1850s to permit the Tredegar Iron Works model to be replicated elsewhere in the South. Tobacconists had advantages in Virginia because their product was so highly specialized, but the great hopes of industrialists to combine new technologies with slave labor foundered on the imperatives of "war capitalism" and the slave security state that frustrated creativity, innovation, and entrepreneurship among all but the wealthiest.[41]

Enslaved workers attempting to glean advantages – like Henry Box Brown – usually lost. The enslaved attempted to intervene in contract negotiations or manipulate sales, and the resulting labor deals were an intricate dance of commercial aspirations, financial demands, and desperate contests to keep intact families and networks. Enslaved people recovered some of the money that changed hands in the process, some conspicuously participating in a growing urban consumer culture. But whatever purchasing power bondspeople exercised, whatever ephemeral liberties enslaved workers seized, enslavers enforced discipline with a growing network of incarceration given teeth by a tough federal fugitive slave law.

---

[41] Sven Beckert, *Empire of Cotton: A Global History* (New York, NY: Knopf, 2014), 29, passim.

9

Narrative

Americans' understanding of slavery was wrapped in stories, but slavery's narrative was internally conflicted. Americans argued with one another about the true character of an institution dividing a political nation. And slavery more than any other issue needed narrative elaboration. Some of slavery's supporters insisted on upholding slavery in the abstract. But personal stories were more effective. Both slavery's defenders and opponents took up their pens, writing novels and publishing autobiographies that personalized enslavers and bondspersons. Both gave slavery plots and sequences, heroes and villains, dramatizing the institution and in the process making the South a battleground for Americans' literary self-understandings.

There were three main scripts in that national narrative, a proslavery script, an abolitionist script, and an antislavery script. And like political factions, each had its peculiar assumptions and arguments. Southern white writers developed a proslavery paternalist script contending that slavery was held together by bonds of affection between masters and slaves, bonds that were more durable than chattel slavery's property relations. By the 1830s, proslavery storytellers argued that black bondage was a positive good, not for the economic value of cotton, but for the supposedly organic society that slavery supported. In their telling, slavery's light yoke harnessed the bondsman to tradition, not toil. White Southern authors imagined a distinctive region in which the peculiar institution benefited enslavers and enslaved alike, claiming that the Slave South was the true offspring of the American Revolution. Slavery's opponents disagreed bitterly, arguing that plantations were slave labor camps and that slavery halted the progress of American freedom.

Ex-slave autobiographers crafted an abolitionist script exposing the horrors of racial, social, and sexual violence wherever slavery existed. They emphasized the chattel principle of absolute ownership of humans, whether they were mothers, spouses, or babies. That abolitionist script was given rhetorical structure by the radical activists who sponsored African-descended authors in the 1840s. Black writers in turn strove for authenticity while articulating African American demands for freedom and equality, framed through witnessing a landscape of cruel immorality. But not all dipped their pens in the same inkwell. The abolitionist script involved internal conflicts among authors who sought white assistance and others urging black revolution. But ex-slave autobiographers were the most effective abolitionists by the measure of their popular readership. Political abolitionism – a movement to abolish slavery in law – gained some victories in the 1840s as ex-slave autobiographers' voices became part of the national debate. But into that narrative struggle came a literary juggernaut in the 1850s, which threatened to eclipse black abolitionists even as it drew from both proslavery and abolitionist scripts.

Led by Harriet Beecher Stowe's *Uncle Tom's Cabin* (1852), the anti-slavery script held that slavery victimized black people who needed white guidance and, perhaps, a ticket out of the United States once free. Uncle Tom gave Northern antislavery political partisans a new character and plot by which to understand and condemn slavery while appeasing whites' belief in white racial exceptionalism. Free labor was honorable, Stowe and her imitators argued, but African Americans were not quite candidates for citizenship either. The antislavery script partly undermined the abolition-ist script by validating some of the key racial premises of the proslavery script. But it did so by infusing slavery with sentiment while evading questions of its political economy. There was no war capitalism in Uncle Tom's South, no political questions of interest, republicanism, or imperial expansion. Instead the main drama was human sentiment against enslaver cruelty. By the eve of disunion in 1860, slavery was at the center of American national literature, which would have seemed unlikely just two generations before.

Early nineteenth-century writers, novelists, and humorists developed a literature of national identity centered on white people. Slavery's narra-tive was an outgrowth of that project of imagining the American character in print. But in trying to portray the South as a distinctive region, white writers stumbled over slavery. South of the Ohio River lay a region increasingly ruled by wealthy property owners keeping their African-descended countrymen and women in bondage, stealing the fruits of their labors and repaying that toil with violence. Since the nation's founding, enslavers had apologized for slavery as an unfortunate vestige of colonial rule. In 1781, founder and enslaver Thomas Jefferson of Virginia contended that slavery was a "great political and moral evil" that had no rightful enduring place under republican government.[1] How Americans were to get rid of it was a national conundrum. The problem of slavery deepened in the 1810s as the nation expanded, and citizens drove enslaved people all the way to the Mississippi River Valley cotton frontier. And instead of a colonial hangover, slavery seemed to be an increasingly problematic part of American nationhood, localized in its southern regions.

The land of the free was also a land of unspeakable brutality to those in bondage. Travelers who toured the South told hair-raising stories of enslavers' cruelty, of lashings in parlors, and torture in the fields. Pennsylvanian Jesse Torrey interviewed a Maryland native named Anna in 1815, a mother whose husband was separated from her when enslavers sold her and her daughters to a slave trader "from Georgia," she testified. The slave trader took them to the nation's capital and imprisoned them in the attic of a tavern on F Street. To prevent the sale and dispersal of her children, Anna jumped from the third-story window, shattering her spine and breaking her arms. She survived but told Torrey that she was so distressed, "I didn't want to go, and I jumped out of the window," but still "they have carried my children off with [them] to Carolina."[2] Besides a valiant act of personal defiance, Anna's leap was a metaphor for the choiceless choices slavery imposed, a violation of what Americans imagined themselves to be. Exposed to such criticism, enslavers counterpunched.

Southern white regional writers reversed critics' moral indictments of slavery when they imagined plantations as landscapes of bucolic plenitude. They argued that the South was populated by extended families encompassing both white and black members who abided together in harmony. In Southern pastoral visions, enslaved people served and were in turn dependent upon whites who protected and provided for them. Virginian George Tucker's novel *The Valley of Shenandoah, or, Memories of the Graysons* (1824) depicted plantation life removed from economic activity. Slaves' "simple wants are abundantly supplied" on the

---

[1] Thomas Jefferson, *Notes on the State of Virginia*, ed. William Peden (Chapel Hill, NC: University of North Carolina Press, 1955), 87.

[2] Jesse Torrey, *American Slave Trade* (London: J. M. Cobbett, 1822), 67, 70.

plantation, and regarding "whatever of coercion there is on his will," Tucker explained, "it is so moderate and reasonable in itself, and, above all, he has been so habituated to it, that it appears to be all right, or rather he does not feel it to be wrong." Such a petted slave was "a member of a sort of patriarchal family: but when hoisted up to public sale, where every man has a right to purchase him, and he may be the property of one whom he never saw before, or of the worst man in the community, then the delusion vanishes." Only through sale would the slave perceive "the bitterness of his lot" and long for the plantation.[3] But slave trading was an aberration. The desperate actions of an enslaved mother like Anna were outside of the norm. Slave sales were forced on the enslaver rather than a consequence of cotton capitalism.

And when families were split on the auction block, proslavery writers shrugged and blamed black people themselves for the separations. In John Pendleton Kennedy's novel *Swallow Barn; or, A Sojourn in the Old Dominion* (1831), Abe was a young enslaved man whose "occasional bursts of passion" and a "habit of associating with the most profligate menials" in the neighborhood "had corrupted his character, and ... had rendered him offensive to the whole plantation." Abe injured himself with his short-sighted rebellion. Because his owner puts people over profits, however, the enslaver "could never bear the idea of disposing of any of his negroes," in Kennedy's telling, and sent him to sea instead.[4]

What began as a pastoral vision of Southern society became a patriotic proslavery argument in the books of some of the South's most gifted white authors. William Gilmore Simms wove a script of doting masters and dependent slaves into the history of the nation's founding. Like Kennedy, he argued that slavery was a positive good at the center of the republic rather than an unfortunate colonial vestige. He sketched variations within the South, characterizing Southern regional distinctiveness while softening slavery's features. Slavery in Alabama was different than slavery in his native South Carolina. Gone were auction blocks and the domestic slave trade. In *The Yemassee: A Romance of Carolina* (1835), *The Partisan* (1835), *Richard Hurdis, a Tale of Alabama* (1838), *Border Beagles, or, A Tale of Mississippi* (1840), *The Kinsmen* (1841), and *The Wigwam and*

---

[3] George Tucker, *The Valley of Shenandoah, or, Memories of the Graysons*, Vol. 3 (New York, NY: C. Wiley, 1824), 127–28.

[4] John Pendleton Kennedy, *Swallow Barn, or, A Sojourn in the Old Dominion* (Philadelphia, PA: Carey & Lea, 1832), 239–40 (quotations); Andrew R. Black, *John Pendleton Kennedy: Early American Novelist, Whig Statesman, and Ardent Nationalist* (Baton Rouge, LA: Louisiana State University Press, 2016), chap. 3.

the Cabin (1845), Simms imagined for readers a South in which enslavers were moral models and patriots who imposed order on a chaotic frontier, undermined criminal gangs of slave stealers, and stood up for white supremacist republicanism. Under such steady and manly guidance, enslaved people are unflinchingly loyal, grateful dependents.

African American authors vigorously disputed the proslavery script, arguing instead that enslavers were greedy, cruel victimizers. Their advantage over travel writers was their inside view of slavery. But instead of writing novels they chose autobiography in a bid to support their testimony with the authenticity of eyewitness accounts.

Ex-slave autobiographers in the 1820s characterized the South as a moral wasteland in which enslavers broke up families for profit, raped enslaved females to assert mastery, and punished anyone who stood between them and their human property. William Grimes's *Life of William Grimes, the Runaway Slave. Written by Himself* (1825) details his life growing up enslaved in Maryland, Virginia, and Georgia, being sold several times, and held in slavery by ten different men who put him to work in a variety of jobs including field hand, house servant, and coachman. One of his owners "came into the stable and seized me by the collar with his left hand, while with his right fist clenched, he beat me with that in my breast and face, until all in a gore of blood. I dared not say a word, but pretended to be very much hurt; he all the time exclaiming who wants to buy you? God dam[n] you, I say who wants to buy you? [Y]ou rascal." Such savage beatings continued under that owner, followed by being locked up in a filthy lice-infested dungeon, where his wounds festered.[5] After being subjected to a catalogue of such horrors, Grimes escaped by stowing away on a ship in 1814. In witnessing slavery's evils, African American authors like him birthed a genre of American literature – slave narratives – that crystallized the black experience. In doing so they called into question not only the benevolence of enslavers but American democracy and republican institutions.

Some African-descended authors concluded that black freedom was only available abroad. In *A Narrative of Some Remarkable Incidents in the Life of Solomon Bayley* (1825), the Delaware native sketches ordeals of family separation and cruelty at the hands of enslavers. Yet Bayley and

---

[5] William Grimes, *Life of William Grimes, the Runaway Slave, Written by Himself* (New York, NY: William Grimes, 1825), 46–47, quotations; William L. Andrews, *To Tell a Free Story: The First Century of Afro-American Autobiography* (Urbana, IL: University of Illinois Press, 1988), chap. 3.

his generation of ex-slave autobiographers lacked a political remedy. Slavery must end, African-descended authors insisted, but there did not seem to be much hope for black citizenship in the United States. After buying his freedom and that of his family members, Bayley became an expatriate, moving to Liberia in 1828 under the sponsorship of the Union Colonization Society of Wilmington, Delaware. There are notes of conciliation in Bayley's narrative, which he wrote as confessional Christian literature.[6] But conciliation turned to scathing criticism by 1830.

In the context of David Walker's *Appeal* (1830) and Nat Turner's Rebellion, the political stakes on black protest and slave uprisings rose considerably. *The Confessions of Nat Turner* (1831) showed no remorse for murders of whites. And after Turner suggested that it was part of his ministry to recruit rebels to slaughter them, enslavers sought to enforce illiteracy and silence black voices. At the same time, abolitionists were insisting that slavery was a moral wrong and in need of immediate termination. They brought the black abolitionist script to a broader reading public, infusing it with moralistic rhetoric borrowed from English abolitionists. William Lloyd Garrison began publishing the abolitionist *Liberator* in 1831, a newspaper subscribed to mainly by free black readers, vowing, "I will be as harsh as truth, and as uncompromising as justice. ... I am in earnest – I will not equivocate – I will not excuse – I will not retreat a single inch – AND I WILL BE HEARD."[7] And he was heard. Garrison's *Liberator* reprinted Walker's *Appeal*, endorsing black calls for revolution. An outraged Georgia legislature offered $5,000 ($143,000 in 2016 dollars) for anyone who brought Garrison there to face trial for inciting insurrection.[8] Belligerent with the pen, Garrison was nevertheless a committed pacifist, his Baptist faith informing his mission to rid the world of slavery through persuasion.

Activists like Garrison were effective communicators of the emerging abolitionist script. They were deeply unpopular but highly adept at drawing public attention to enslaved people's plight, rebuking Americans'

---

[6] Solomon Bayley, *A Narrative of Some Remarkable Incidents in the Life of Solomon Bayley, Formerly a Slave in the State of Delaware, North America; Written by Himself, and Published for His Benefit; to Which Are Prefixed, a Few Remarks by Robert Hurnard* (London: Harvey and Darton, 1825); Peter T. Dalleo, "'Persecuted but not forsaken; cut down, but not destroyed': Solomon and Thamar Bayley, Delawarean Emigrants to Liberia," *Delaware History* 31.3 (2006): 137–78.

[7] *The [Boston] Liberator*, January 1, 1831, 1.

[8] Ibram X. Kendi, *Stamped from the Beginning: The Definitive History of Racist Ideas in America* (New York, NY: Nation Books, 2016), chap. 13.

pretense of being freedom lovers in the process. Garrison and kindred abolitionists like New York businessman Arthur Tappan founded societies that were hubs of strategic communications networks. Tappan's American Anti-Slavery Society was founded in New York in 1833 and began its own newspaper the *National Anti-Slavery Standard* (1840–70). New printing technologies like steam-powered presses and stereotyping – which made printing books much more efficient – were among the reasons why slavery's narrative became so prominent. Americans had more printed materials available at the same time as literacy rates rose (outside of the South). Americans had more leisure time and money, and such things as indoor lamps and reading glasses became more common. Novels and other imaginative literature had a correspondingly important role in shaping national self-perceptions. In taverns, hotels, and coffeehouses, Americans became avid newspaper readers, a process aided by the rise of the penny press or large-circulation daily papers sold on street corners for one cent (or less).

The abolitionist script inflamed enslavers. The abolitionist publicity strategy of the 1830s culminated in the Great Postal Campaign in the spring of 1835. The New York Anti-Slavery Society mailed 175,000 tracts and pamphlets all over the country. It was the first direct-mail campaign in the country's history. And it shocked white Southerners. In Charleston, where Denmark Vesey and his insurgents had been hanged thirteen years before, a mob of about 2,000 South Carolinians turned up at the end of June to cheer the burning of a bag of abolitionist tracts stolen from the post office. And while abolitionists did not succeed in delivering many tracts to their list of 20,000 Southerners, they did stir up social reactions well beyond their numbers.[9] President Andrew Jackson called abolitionists "monsters" and demanded that Congress authorize the postmaster to censor the mails, "to prohibit, under severe penalties, the circulation in the Southern States, through the mail, of incendiary publications intended to instigate the slaves to insurrection." Beyond blocking delivery, local postmasters were to draw up lists of recipients. South Carolina senator John C. Calhoun proposed putting the federal post office under state law, forbidding delivery of abolitionist mail in states with laws banning literacy among African-descended people. But the plans backfired. Northerners

---

[9] Mark G. Schmeller, *Invisible Sovereign: Imagining Public Opinion from the Revolution to Reconstruction* (Baltimore, MD: Johns Hopkins University Press, 2016), chap. 6; Manisha Sinha, *The Slave's Cause: A History of Abolition* (New Haven, CT: Yale University Press, 2016), chaps. 8–9.

and members of the opposition Whig Party – even Southern Whigs – recoiled at the thought that a president could take away their constitutional rights to freedom of speech and freedom of the press. It seemed to confirm the abolitionist script that enslavers opposed democracy and slavery threatened republican government.[10]

In that volatile political atmosphere, African American authors emphasized nonviolent responses to slaveholder cruelty. Charles Ball's *Slavery in the United States: A Narrative of the Life and Adventures of Charles Ball* (1837) is a catalogue of horrors of family theft, kidnapping, violence, and cruelty, all without redemption. But Ball ran off rather than murder his enslavers. Some ex-slave autobiographies, like Richard Allen's *The Life, Experience, and Gospel Labours of the Rt. Rev. Richard Allen* (1833) emphasize Christian faith and African-descended people as suffering servants. Allen's autobiography is a spiritual journey and church history, and it touches on themes that would come into prominence in 1840s ex-slave autobiography.

African American autobiographers asserted their authenticity in part by becoming the heroes of their own narratives and by pitching them to a white audience. Beginning in the 1840s, black male ex-slave autobiographers condemned slavery but not all white people. They emphasized the cruelty done to enslaved people without promising bloody retribution. But they did so by celebrating masculinity and manliness in a society that was racist and sexist as well, all while demonstrating Christian restraint. A model of that strategy is Frederick Douglass's *Narrative of the Life of Frederick Douglass, an American Slave, Written by Himself* (1845).[11]

In recounting growing up enslaved in Maryland, Douglass took direct aim at enslavers' supposed family values, arguing that property always trumped paternalism. After the death of his first owner, Aaron Anthony, Douglass wrote: "We were all ranked together at the valuation. Men and women, old and young, married and single, were ranked with horses, sheep, and swine. ... At this moment, I saw more clearly than ever the brutalizing effects of slavery upon both slave and slaveholder."[12] Slavery also hurt white people, including one of his mistresses, Sophia Auld, who

---

[10] Daniel Walker Howe, *What Hath God Wrought: The Transformation of America, 1815–1848* (New York, NY: Oxford University Press, 2007), 429; James Brewer Stewart, *Holy Warriors: The Abolitionists and American Slavery*, rev. edn. (New York, NY: Hill and Wang, 1997).

[11] William S. McFeely, *Frederick Douglass* (New York, NY: Norton, 1991), chap. 10.

[12] Frederick Douglass, *Narrative of the Life of Frederick Douglass, an American Slave, Written by Himself* (Boston, MA: Anti-Slavery Office, 1845), 45.

taught Douglass to read as a child, only to receive a stern rebuke from her husband. By domesticating his autobiography and using stylized violence, Douglass positioned himself as a fugitive witness that put the lie to the romance of the plantation.

As fugitive slaves became abolitionist heroes, some Northern states passed laws to protect them. Personal liberty laws, called Latimer laws in honor of fugitive George Latimer, forbade state cooperation in fugitive slave recapture. Enslavers were legally entitled to their slave property under federal law, supporters said, but states need not help. Antislavery Northern citizens seemed to identify with heroic fugitives hunted by mercenaries who were no better than kidnappers. As Congress debated the question of whether slavery would be allowed in the lands ceded by Mexico in 1848, ex-slave autobiographers like Henry Bibb, James W. C. Pennington, and William Wells Brown argued that families would be ripped apart in a slave market that now stretched from the headwaters of the Chesapeake Bay to the Brazos River bottom in far-off Texas. Pennington called it "the chattel principle."[13]

The chattel principle was dangerous to the republic, abolitionists argued. Brown warned that slavery's westward expansion was especially ominous for the enslaved. *Narrative of William W. Brown, an American Slave. Written by Himself* (1847) told of the author's unwilling involvement in splitting up families when he was owned by a slave trader. Domestic slavery, he argued, was the domestic slave trade. Sojourner Truth and other female former bondspersons narrated another strand in the abolitionist script.

Departing from the heroic male fugitive script, Truth's *The Narrative of Sojourner Truth* was a searching and harrowing account of hardships overcome by faith and grit. Females faced particular challenges that could not be overcome by masculine resistance, she revealed, hinting at sexual abuse by owners and the separations of enslaved mothers from their own children. Unlike Douglass and so many other heroic fugitives, Truth did not receive instruction in reading or writing and, even when freed, relied on menial jobs such as housekeeping to earn a living. But Truth toured, spoke, raised funds, and participated in the abolitionists' project of thrusting their version of slavery's narrative into the nation's consciousness.

---

[13] James W. C. Pennington, *The Fugitive Blacksmith; or, Events in the History of James W. C. Pennington, Pastor of a Presbyterian Church, New York, Formerly a Slave in the State of Maryland, United States* (London: Charles Gilpin, 1849), iv–v; Andrews, *To Tell a Free Story*, 143–55.

Activists like Brown and Douglass also built a transatlantic network of sponsors, media outlets, and political activists stretching from London and Dublin to Philadelphia, New York, and Boston, and up into Canada West, as Ontario was then known, and hubs like St. Catharine's and in the settlements of Kent and Essex Counties. In so doing they created an African American diaspora, an extension of the African diaspora, with roots in the American South.[14]

As the Congressional Compromise of 1850 sought to bind up sectional differences over slavery extension, a literary juggernaut cracked the slavery debate open again. This was the antislavery script, which opposed slavery because it took unfair advantage of African-descended people rather than emphasizing black creativity and heroism. Harriet Beecher Stowe's *Uncle Tom's Cabin, or Life among the Lowly* (1851–52) brought a profound change in slavery's narrative. Sentiment pervaded the new antislavery script, and female writers led literary contests over slavery thereafter.

Uncle Tom's Cabin was a publishing sensation in the 1850s, as successful as it was unlikely. Stowe's novel of the emotional landscape of American slavery tugged at the hearts and touched the minds of readers, causing "Uncle Tom mania" and heating up debate over slavery while the political crisis of slavery extension deepened.[15] Slavery had always been a thorny issue, but in masterfully sentimental language, Stowe captured the human drama of families separated and enslaved refugees breaking their chains. The novel inflamed white Southerners and thrilled readers worldwide. Uncle Tom, "whose truly African features were characterized by an expression of grave and steady good sense," belongs to Arthur Shelby of Kentucky, who after a fit of moral hesitation sells him to a slave trader to pay a debt.[16] As Tom makes his way along the paths of the interstate slave trade, he surveys the human wreckage of a system of inhumane bondage, gently touching the lives of those he encounters with his Christian faith. Tom ends up on the Louisiana plantation of a transplanted Northerner, Simon Legree. There Tom makes one last heroic act of pious humanity before dying from the enslaver's violent reprisal. When the late Arthur Shelby's son George arrives to redeem the

---

[14] W. Caleb McDaniel, *The Problem of Democracy in the Age of Slavery: Garrisonian Abolitionists and Transatlantic Reform* (Baton Rouge, LA: Louisiana State University Press, 2013).

[15] Sarah Meer, *Uncle Tom Mania: Slavery, Minstrelsy, and Transatlantic Culture in the 1850s* (Athens, GA: University of Georgia Press, 2005).

[16] Harriet Beecher Stowe, *Uncle Tom's Cabin* (London: John Cassell, 1852), 18.

captive, it is too late. Slavery killed Tom, took unfair advantages of black Americans, and harmed all the whites involved in it.

Stowe had turned antislavery sentimentality into literary gold, and other authors were quick to follow. Emily Clemens Pearson capitalized on Stowe's success and amplified it with *Cousin Franck's Household; Or, Scenes in the Old Dominion* (1852), published under the pseudonym Pocahontas. The novel denounced slavery using the voices of nearly every character type in Southern fiction, the antislavery voices being as sympathetic, principled, and credible as the proslavery voices were vapid, stolid, and untrustworthy. Sarah J. Hale developed the theme of black colonization out of the United States in her antislavery novels *Northwood; or Life North and South* (1852) and *Liberia; or, Mr. Peyton's Experiment* (1853) featuring schemes by an enslaver who educated his slaves and protected them from sale so they could emigrate to Liberia.[17] Southern regionalists energetically responded to the flood of antislavery melodrama.

Proslavery Southerners became alarmed at the success of Stowe and other white antislavery authors. "The success of 'Uncle Tom's Cabin,'" screamed University of Virginia law professor James P. Holcombe, "is an evidence of the manner in which our enemies are employing literature for our overthrow." Enslavers better get busy rebutting the claims that were seducing a nation, Holcombe insisted. "Let Southern authors, men who see and know slavery as it is," he urged, "make it their duty to deluge all the realms of literature with a flood of light on this subject."[18] William Gilmore Simms had already responded to *Uncle Tom's Cabin* with a more muscular version of the proslavery script. Simms's *Woodcraft; or, the Hawks about Dovecote: A Story of the South at the Close of the Revolution* (1854) revived his most successful proslavery themes, including the proslavery romance of the American founding.[19]

---

[17] Emily Catharine Pearson, *Jamie Parker, The Fugitive* (Hartford, CT: Brockett, Fuller and Company, 1851); Emily Catharine Pearson, *Cousin Franck's Household; Or, Scenes in the Old Dominion, by Pocahontas* (Boston, MA: Upham, Ford and Olmstead; New York: L. Colby & Company, 1853); Sarah J. Hale, *Northwood; or Life North and South* (New York, NY: H. Long & Brother, 1852); Sarah J. Hale, *Liberia; or, Mr. Peyton's Experiment* (New York, NY: Harper and Brothers, 1853).

[18] *Southern Literary Messenger* 23.4 (1856): 242–43.

[19] William Gilmore Simms, *Woodcraft; or, the Hawks about Dovecote: A Story of the South at the Close of the Revolution* (New York, NY: Redfield, 1854); William Gilmore Simms, *Katharine Walton: or, the Rebel of Dorchester* (Philadelphia, PA: A. Hart, 1851; New York, NY: Redfield, 1854; New York, NY: W. J. Widdleton, 1854).

Anti-*Tom* novels reinvigorated the proslavery script, arguing that the real danger to African Americans was not enslavers but abolitionists. J. W. Page's *Uncle Robin in His Cabin in Virginia, and Tom without One in Boston* (1853) tells of an abolitionist-reared Northerner who learns the truth about slavery's goodness by witnessing the true workings of a Virginia plantation household. Anti-*Tom* novels reasserted enslaver paternalism, seeking to refute Stowe point by point. Charles Jacobs Peterson's pseudonymously published *The Cabin and Parlor, or Slaves and Masters* (1852) argued that slavery was framed by paternalistic duties of masters to slaves in sharp contrast to the North's loathsome commercial society. In a concluding scene, a Tom-like Peter and his family are offered freedom, but the old slave responds, "No, God bless yer, I'd rather be a slave here, under a good masser, dan a free colored man [in the] North."[20]

Female proslavery authors artfully domesticated the anti-*Tom* genre, sentimentalizing it in ways that mirrored *Uncle Tom's Cabin*. Caroline Gilman's *Recollections of a New England Bride and of a Southern Matron* (1852) featured Jacques, a slave who "died, breathing a prayer for his master's family."[21] Gilman was born in New England but spent most of her life in Charleston. Other female authors upheld proslavery patriarchy, including Mary Henderson Eastman's *Aunt Phillis's Cabin; or, Southern Life As It Is* (1852), which dramatizes a Virginia plantation society while arguing that abolitionists were rank hypocrites. Caroline Lee Hentz was one of the most successful novelists of her age. Her eleventh novel, *The Planter's Northern Bride* (1854), dramatizes the conversion of an abolitionist to proslavery after witnessing the harm done to black people by Yankees, hopeful in spite of all that political attempts at compromise could restore national unity.[22] But as the proslavery script became more strident, Southern regionalists rehearsed disunion themes.

[20] J. Thornton Randolph, *The Cabin and Parlor, or Slaves and Masters* (Philadelphia, PA: T. B. Peterson, 1852), 324 (quotation); Joy Jordan-Lake, *Whitewashing Uncle Tom's Cabin: Nineteenth-Century Women Novelists Respond to Stowe* (Nashville, TN: Vanderbilt University Press, 2005).

[21] Caroline Howard Gilman, *Recollections of a New England Bride and of a Southern Matron* (New York, NY: G. B. Putnam & Company, 1852), 89 (quotation).

[22] Mary Henderson Eastman, *Aunt Phillis's Cabin; or, Southern Life As It Is* (Philadelphia, PA: Lippincott, Grambo, and Company, 1852); Caroline Lee Hentz, *The Planter's Northern Bride*, 2 vols. (Philadelphia, PA: T. B. Peterson; A. Hart, 1854); Susan K. Harris, *19th-Century American Women's Novels: Interpretative Strategies* (Cambridge: Cambridge University Press, 1990).

Proslavery literary voices were making arguments for secession from the Union. James M. Smythe's anonymously published *Ethel Somers; or, The Fate of the Union* (1857) features a romance between the daughter of a Mississippi planter and a New York City bachelor in which affection cannot quite overcome sectional divisions. In that allegory of national disunity, the Southern belle remains true to her roots, which is the Yankee's loss. By decade's end, proslavery authors unfolded a sexualized critique of abolitionism that reflected the fever pitch of slavery debates. G. M. Flanders's *The Ebony Idol* (1860) features black male sexuality as a threat that abolitionism maliciously conceals. Flanders set her novel in a fictional all-white New England town whose minister attempts an abolitionist social experiment by sheltering Caesar, a fugitive slave. Caesar plunges the town into chaos capped by his plans to marry a white girl, a theme shared by V. G. Cowdin's *Ellen; or, The Fanatic's Daughter* (1860), which elaborates the theme of abolitionists' aggressive and subversive sexuality.[23]

Both proslavery and antislavery responses to *Uncle Tom's Cabin* presented a challenge to abolitionists since they shared a belief in black inferiority. And so in the 1850s, African American abolitionists struggled to reclaim their voices and re-argue that African Americans were Americans first. To do so, black autobiographers wove in novelistic dialogue and blurred the lines between reconstructed memory and historical fiction. Solomon Northup's *Twelve Years a Slave: Narrative of Solomon Northup, a Citizen of New-York, Kidnapped in Washington City in 1841, and Rescued in 1853* (1853) is an odyssey of captivity and a panorama of slavery's evils. Northup was born free but was kidnapped into unremitting toil on the cotton frontier of the Red River in Louisiana. Because he was black, he was presumed a slave until he was rescued twelve years later. Such anti-heroism contrasts with the morality play of Uncle Tom's final days and the heroic aspects of 1840s male ex-slave autobiography.[24] But Northup was reliant on white sponsors, depending

---

[23] G. M. Flanders, *The Ebony Idol* (New York, NY: D. Appleton and Company, 1860); V. G. Cowdin, *Ellen; or, The Fanatic's Daughter* (Mobile, AL: S. H. Goetzel and Company, 1860); Paul Quigley, *Shifting Grounds: Nationalism and the American South, 1848–1865* (New York, NY: Oxford University Press, 2012).

[24] Solomon Northup, *Twelve Years a Slave: Narrative of Solomon Northup, a Citizen of New-York, Kidnapped in Washington City in 1841, and Rescued in 1853, from a Cotton Plantation near the Red River in Louisiana* (New York, NY: Miller, Orton, and Mulligan, 1854); R. J. M. Blackett, "Dispossessing Massa: Fugitive Slaves and the Politics of Slavery after 1850," *American Nineteenth Century History* 10.2 (2009): 119–36.

on Stowe to get *Twelve Years a Slave* published. Frederick Douglass revised his autobiography in *My Bondage and My Freedom* (1855), novelizing the dialogue and denouncing Northern racism as well as Southern slavery. But in denouncing racism, Douglass and other abolitionists were contending with powerful forces that were gaining momentum.

Scientific racism took hold in the 1850s, and some of the country's leading biologists theorized African-descended people as inherently inferior to Caucasians. Louis Agassiz at Harvard and Samuel George Morton at the Pennsylvania Medical College were two pillars of what became known as the American School of Ethnology. Agassiz argued that different climates produced different human attributes. Like crocodiles and finches, which flourished according to climate, humans too were inherently different, the northern peoples having superior intellect and the southern – and darker skinned – a slavish and subservient nature, able to work in hot climates. These findings were published before Charles Darwin's *Origins of Species* (1859) argued that adaptive mutations were random. Agassiz even studied photographs taken of African American subjects as part of his research, treating them like specimens rather than humans. George R. Glidden and Josiah C. Nott published *Types of Mankind* (1854) which was a theological-scientific odyssey into the separate creation of supposedly different races along with an assessment of darker-skinned people's intellectual and moral inferiority. Nott, who was for many years a professor at the University of Alabama, claimed to practice "niggerology."[25] Others medicalized racist assumptions.

Dr. Samuel A. Cartwright, practicing in Louisiana and Mississippi, claimed to have discovered certain diseases peculiar to African-descended people. One was *Dysaesthesia Aethiopica*, which caused "mischievous behavior" in bondspersons, also called "Rascality." The disease, he argued, "attacks only such slaves as live like free negroes in regard to diet, exercise, etc.," the cure for which was a regimen of hard labor, warmth, and a good diet, all meant to stimulate the liver and kidneys. This would turn the infected subject from an "arrant rascal [into] a good negro that can hoe or plow, and handles things with as much care as his fellow servants." It was a doctor's prescription for sale to the cotton frontier. Cartwright also purported to diagnose *Drapetomania*, which

[25] Josiah Nott, cited in George M. Fredrickson, *The Black Image in the White Mind: The Debate on Afro-American Character and Destiny, 1817–1914* (New York, NY: Harper & Row, 1971), 78.

was a "disease causing negroes to run away." Severe cases caused enslaved people to disregard the property and even the lives of whites.[26] Such a powerful set of contentions bolstered both the proslavery paternalist narrative and the white antislavery script that shared such racist assumptions.

Abolitionists were again on the defensive, pushing back against pseudoscience.[27] Refuting the contentions of Agassiz, Cartwright, Morton, and Nott, Frederick Douglass argued that "the very crimes of slavery become slavery's best defence," when apologists for the institution "overthrow the instinctive consciousness of the common brotherhood of man." Instead, Douglass contended that diversity was strength. Prejudice and not evidence led to scientific racism, he argued, which did nothing but give enslavers intellectual cover for brutality and seek to run African Americans out of their own country. "All the facts in his history mark out for him a destiny," Douglass argued, "united to America and all Americans."[28] African American novelists agreed.

Black-authored fiction rehearsed a revolution. The first African American novels departed from appealing to white readers' moral and emotional sensibilities. William Wells Brown's *Clotel; or, The President's Daughter* (1853) was a fictional account of Thomas Jefferson's enslaved children of an African-descended bondswoman. The subject was so explosive that Brown had to publish it in England. Harriet E. Wilson's *Our Nig; or, Sketches from the Life of a Free Black* (1859) condemns Northern antislavery racism and the chauvinism of male autobiography. Arguably the first African American novel, *Our Nig* was published in Boston but was little read outside of New Hampshire, white booksellers refusing to stock it. Martin R. Delany's *Blake; or The Huts of America* (published serially, 1859–62) developed the theme of violent uprisings against American enslavers, reviving the anger of Nat Turner's *Confessions* and denying the Christianity of Uncle Tom. *Blake* opens with the separation of an enslaved family caused by the sexual advances of an owner (who was also the biological father of the wife of title character, Henry Blake). Delany elegantly denounces antislavery sentimentalism and proslavery romanticism through Blake's sojourn in the South to foment rebellion,

---

[26] Katherine Kemi Bankole, *Slavery and Medicine: Enslavement and Medical Practice in Antebellum Louisiana* (New York, NY: Garland Publishing, 1998), 227, 114.

[27] Kendi, *Stamped from the Beginning*, chap. 14.

[28] Frederick Douglass, *The Claims of the Negro, Ethnologically Considered* (Rochester, NY: Lea, Mann & Company, 1854), 32–33, 36, 15 (quotations).

threatening enslavers with violence that could emerge from within the neighborhoods of African Americans held in slavery. By the time the last six chapters were published in May 1862, *Blake* had become prophecy.

Slavery's narrative was a creative proxy for a destructive process. By the end of the 1850s, it was a tangle of antagonistic scripts at war with one another yet each using a literary tactic borrowed from an adversary. Proslavery novelists did not hesitate to put into the mouths of black subjects affection for their owners and satisfaction with their enslavement. Antislavery novelists too imagined a South bound together by sentiment yet torn apart by greedy slave owners who took unfair advantages of naïve African-descended people. Black abolitionists fought both antislavery denials that they were Americans and proslavery contentions that enslavement was benevolent. But African American authors also borrowed from white fiction writers, novelizing arguments against slavery and the racism it generated. Ultimately they met white novelists on the ground of the latter's choosing, artfully manipulating the sentimentality that swayed readers of *Uncle Tom's Cabin*, its imitators, and the anti-*Tom* flood of protests. In the process they hybridized genres and incubated realism of subsequent African American literature. And like the American republic itself, African American authors traveled a road from the heroic fugitive's appeal to white sponsorship to Henry Blake's revolutionary fury.

10

Geopolitics

Slavery caused disunion and civil war, but it did so at a slant. The future of slavery was the fulcrum of national political divisions in the United States from the 1810s to the Civil War. Rather than dividing over slavery in the South, where most bondspersons lived, that political crisis deepened over slavery in North America west of the Mississippi River, where comparatively few African Americans resided. Rather than what slavery did to African-descended people, the most divisive national political issue was what slavery did to or for white citizens. Enslavers argued that banning slavery in western territory threatened their property in people in the South, and that prohibiting slavery's expansion threatened their rights. Non-enslavers disagreed, contending that the American West should be free of both slavery and African-descended people. As migration from Britain, Ireland, and Europe brought millions of citizens to states that prohibited slavery, non-enslavers held supermajorities in the House of Representatives. And increasingly, Northerners suspected that enslavers trampled on the rights and democratic entitlements of free people to protect a regional and undemocratic interest in slavery. As the republic added more territory, the two visions of the future clashed. But a series of compromises allowed enslavers to exercise outsized political power while granting small concessions to non-enslavers. Congress arrested political disunion by placing limits on slavery's expansion while the national political parties channeled sectional disagreements over slavery into policy disagreements and ideological divisions over banks, tariffs, and the role of the federal government in such things as internal improvement projects. That national political party system directed disagreement away from armed conflict until the late 1850s.

Americans avoided disunion for two generations between the Missouri crisis of 1820 and the winter of 1860–61 through a series of political compromises. Some were statesmanlike concessions balancing interests, and others were partisan gambits averting short-term crises yet exacerbating tensions in the long run. But all endorsed the perpetuation of slavery in some way. The republic's first major crisis of union developed over the movement to the west of enslaved people and the cotton interest enslavers planted there. When Missouri residents petitioned for statehood in 1819, the territory was 16 percent enslaved. Northerners worried about the political ramifications of Missouri entering the Union as a state that permitted slavery. Opponents of Missouri statehood contended that enslavers were breaking up families for profit and – more importantly – they were grabbing political power unfairly. At the time, the republic's twenty-two states were evenly divided between those permitting slavery and those restricting it. Missouri was a middle ground between the plantation complex of the lower South and the northern plains where free farmers flourished. Since Missouri was also a western gateway, it seemed to point to the future of westward expansion.

Defenders of slavery argued that Missouri slavery was no one's business but Missouri citizens', who deserved the same rights in slaves as their Kentucky neighbors. The major problem of slavery extension in the 1810s and 1820s, then, was the harm done to white democracy and American republicanism. The Constitution's Three-Fifths Clause gave slave owners disproportional representation, antislavery voices shouted, and slavery therefore undermined the republican idea of civic equality among whites. In Congress, a New York representative introduced an amendment to the Missouri statehood measure that provided for gradual abolition in that state. It failed in the House but passed in the Senate, the members voting along sectional lines. From his retirement in Virginia, former president Thomas Jefferson wrote that the Missouri crisis was "like a fire bell in the night, [which] awakened and filled me with terror. I considered it at once as the knell of the Union."[1] He saw the issue as an existential threat to the republic.

And then Congress compromised and avoided disunion in 1820. There would be no gradual abolition in Missouri, but Congress banned slavery from the rest of the Louisiana Purchase north of Missouri's southern

---

[1] Jefferson to John Holmes, April 22, 1820, in *The Life and Writings of Thomas Jefferson*, ed. Adrienne Koch and William Peden (New York, NY: Modern Library, 1998), 637.

border of 36° 30' latitude, just as the Confederation Congress had banned slavery in the Northwest Territory in 1787. The Missouri Compromise included the admission of Maine (carved out of Massachusetts) as a state in which slavery was not permitted. Since each state sent two US senators to Washington, DC, both enslavers and their opponents could rely on a balance of sectional interests in the Senate, which would be the legislative check on any measure to encroach on enslavers' property rights in people.

Still, Jefferson feared that divisions would grow on either side of the Missouri Compromise line as a deepening slavery interest in the South confronted a rising population of free Americans in the North. "A geographical line," he wrote, "coinciding with a marked principle, moral and political, once conceived and held up to the angry passions of men, will never be obliterated; and every new irritation will mark it deeper and deeper." Slavery seemed to be an indissoluble problem. "But as it is, we have the wolf by the ears," Jefferson shrugged, "and we can neither hold him, nor safely let him go. Justice is in one scale, and self-preservation in the other."[2]

Jefferson noted the problem but failed to acknowledge the irony that his administration had acquired Missouri as part of the Louisiana Purchase. And the Missouri Compromise signaled a profound political transformation along a new axis. From the time of the Constitution in the 1780s to the 1810s, the most pronounced political divisions had been between East and West, between Federalists in coastal cities and Democratic-Republicans whose constituents increasingly populated the trans-Appalachian West. Federalists favored an active federal government including a central bank, protections to grow manufacturing, and a broad reading of the Constitution. Democratic-Republican support came from agriculturalists, including cotton planters, and they backed rapid westward migration. Partial to free trade and suspicious of bankers, they lacked enthusiasm for an active central government, except when it came to promoting their party's interests. But Federalist declines after the War of 1812 and the expansion of slavery in the Southwest reoriented American political fault lines along a North–South divide. As Jefferson predicted, the Missouri Compromise did not appease Northerners wary of the growth of a slaving interest. And it did not placate white Southerners

---

[2] Jefferson to Holmes, April 22, 1820, in Koch and Peden, *The Life and Writings of Thomas Jefferson*, 637.

who suspected their Northern countrymen of harboring schemes to erode or even terminate slavery.[3]

Fifteen years passed between Missouri's admission and that of the next state, Arkansas, which joined the Union in 1836, and in the meantime uprisings and abolitionist activism accentuated divisions over slavery. Denmark Vesey's plot and the Nat Turner Rebellion sent white Southerners into panics over security. Ex-slave autobiographies and urgent political manifestos like David Walker's 1830 *Appeal* provoked defensiveness and legislation imposing severe restrictions on African-descended people. Abolitionists forced Americans to confront their beliefs about slavery through strategies and tactics that put African American bodies in white spaces and abolitionist speech in public places, stirring up social reactions. One of the most provocative was the Great Post Office Campaign of 1835. The New York Anti-Slavery Society organized the distribution of 175,000 pieces of antislavery literature all over the country. A portion of that direct mail campaign went to recipients in the South. The campaign provoked hostility from the Andrew Jackson administration and horror from enslavers in places like Charleston, South Carolina, where bags of mail containing abolitionist materials were stolen from the post office and burned by an angry proslavery mob. Abolitionists also inundated Congress with petitions to ban or restrict slavery. So many petitions flooded Congress in 1836 that the republic's great deliberative body moved to censor itself by passing the Gag Rule. Southerners in Congress insisted that any petition touching slavery be tabled without consideration. Silencing a vocal minority became the issue. Southerners' burning bags of mail, Jackson's support of it, and Congress's Gag Rule convinced many Northerners that enslavers were threatening democracy and undermining republican government – everywhere, not just in the South. Enslavers started to appear like an organized threat to the rights of free white people.

And Congress took no steps to regulate slavery as interstate commerce. As the domestic slave trade from the upper South to the lower South crested in the late 1830s, abolitionists pointed out that Congress was abetting an undemocratic force by failing to ban transporting enslaved people across state lines for sale. If Congress could ban the transatlantic slave trade to America's shore, as it did in 1808, it could certainly exercise its commerce power to end an immoral traffic among states. In 1838,

---

[3] William W. Freehling, *Road to Disunion, Vol. 1: Secessionists at Bay, 1776–1854* (New York, NY: Oxford University Press, 1990), 121–43.

abolitionist Henry Stanton argued, "the internal slave trade is the great jugular vein of slavery; and if Congress will take the same weapon with which they cut off the foreign trade, and cut this vein, slavery would die of starvation in the southern, and of apoplexy in the northern slave states."[4] Congress would do no such thing, and the Gag Rule prevented discussion of the matter. And many Northerners began to see an arrogant Slave Power at work against American liberty. Meanwhile another powerful force was gathering on the side of free labor and antislavery expansion.

Immigrants tended to settle in places free from chattel slavery, and they came in unexpectedly high numbers. States were dropping property requirements for voting, and men recently arrived from countries like Ireland and the German states could vote upon establishing residency. Most did not approve of slavery. Architects of the Missouri Compromise could not have foreseen the massive immigration that gave states with slavery exclusions an overwhelming superiority in the House of Representatives. Nearly 600,000 foreign immigrants arrived in the United States in the 1830s, followed by 1.7 million in the 1840s, and nearly 2.6 million more would arrive in the 1850s. By 1860, the 4.1 million foreign-born Americans made up 13.2 percent of the population.[5] Most entered through big eastern cities and traveled as far west as their means would take them. Northern and mid-western regions of the country were populated by Germans and Scandinavians who had little interest in slavery's perpetuation, settling among transplanted Yankees. The South attracted fewer foreign immigrants even though pockets of German and Irish immigrants were scattered from North Carolina to Texas. It was not that immigrants were abolitionists. Many arrivals were refugees from famine or political upheavals who competed with African Americans for menial jobs in cities like New York.

But because of immigration patterns, Southern congressional representation declined even though the South's slave population grew. For slavery's supporters to keep their political power, they believed, they needed to add new slave states in order to send US senators to Washington, DC. Problem was, only two states joined the Union between 1821 and 1840,

---

[4] Stanton cited in David L. Lightner, *Slavery and the Commerce Power: How the Struggle against the Interstate Slave Trade Led to the Civil War* (New Haven, CT: Yale University Press, 2006), 102 (quotation).

[5] US Census Bureau, "The Foreign-Born Population in the United States," online: www .census.gov/newsroom/pdf/cspan_fb_slides.pdf, accessed: July 21, 2016; US Immigration Commission, *Statistical Review of Migration, 1820–1910: Distribution of Immigrants, 1850–1900*, 5.

Arkansas – permitting slavery – in 1836, and Michigan – prohibiting slavery – in 1837. The United States still claimed vast non-state territories, including what was left of the Louisiana Purchase and the Northwest Territory, and including the Florida territory, which Spain had ceded under the 1819 Adams–Onís Treaty. But proslavery expansionists set their eyes on a breakaway republic populated by American expatriates, Mexicans, Native Americans, and African-descended Americans, many forced across the US border after the 1837 financial panic.

Texas became the flashpoint of political arguments over slavery extension by the 1840s. It had won independence from Mexico in 1836, though Mexico contested that fact. It was also an enslavers' republic. President Andrew Jackson wanted to annex it but failed. In 1842, the John Tyler administration tried to annex Texas, hoping to build a constituency, but Congress prevented the deal going through before the 1844 presidential election. In 1844, Democrats nominated James K. Polk of Tennessee, an ardent proslavery expansionist. President Polk invited Texas to join the federal Union on favorable terms, including extending the border to the Rio Grande rather than the Nueces River. Antislavery members of the rival Whig Party in the North and even proslavery Whigs in the South moved to stop Texas annexation.

In 1845, political opposition to slavery expansion came from members of opposing parties, not opposing sections. Whether they were from Northern or Southern states, Whigs overwhelmingly argued that annexing Texas would bring war with Mexico, roil markets, and inflame sectional tension. Northern Whigs did not want more slave territory. Southern Whigs did not want competitors in Texas. Not only that, Whigs argued, Texas was populated by would-be Democrats who were against banks and internal improvements – which Whigs supported. Polk's Democrats favored Texas annexation, regardless of whether they were from New York or Mississippi. Proslavery Democrats wanted increased political representation and an extension of the cotton frontier. Northern Democrats considered territorial growth a measure of American robustness and an extension of a national "Manifest Destiny" to extend the republic over a continental empire.[6] It was an issue of prestige, cultural superiority, and expanding democracy.

Polk and fellow Democrats in Congress annexed Texas over strong Whig objection in 1845. One historian terms Texas a "Pandora's box" of

---

[6] Daniel Walker Howe, *What Hath God Wrought: The Transformation of America, 1815–1848* (New York, NY: Oxford University Press, 2007), chaps. 15, 17.

political disunion because it disrupted sectional parity and moved the United States and Mexico into direct confrontation.[7] The Texas economy was built on cotton and cattle, staffed with slave labor. One annexation scheme would have divided Texas into five states, which might have sent ten proslavery US senators to Washington, DC. That plan was dropped, but all understood that Texas statehood would extend the cotton kingdom and the domestic slave trade. And then President Polk sent US forces into a disputed area between the Nueces and Rio Grande, provoking armed conflict.

As Whigs warned, annexing Texas led to war with Mexico. There were not many Texans or Mexicans in between the rivers, an area that was home to peoples of the Lipan Apache confederacy. When US troops under the command of General Zachary Taylor confronted Mexican troops along the Rio Grande in April 1846, they were fired on. After the report reached Washington, DC, President Polk addressed Congress: "Mexico has passed the boundary of the United States, has invaded our territory and shed American blood upon the American soil. She has proclaimed that hostilities have commenced, and that the two nations are now at war." While such rhetoric whipped the country into a war frenzy, and Congress declared war on Mexico, abolitionists and many antislavery Northerners argued it was a war for Manifest Destiny and slavery extension.

In August 1846, a Pennsylvania Democrat dropped a political explosive into that debate. Congressman David Wilmot introduced a rider called a proviso on a war funding measure, which stipulated "[t]hat, as an express and fundamental condition to the acquisition of any territory from the Republic of Mexico by the United States, by virtue of any treaty which may be negotiated between them . . . neither slavery nor involuntary servitude shall ever exist in any part of said territory, except for crime, whereof the party shall first be duly convicted." Borrowing language from the 1787 Northwest Ordinance, the Wilmot Proviso forced Congress to confront the issue of slavery in any territory conquered from Mexico in war.[8]

In the space of a year, political divisions shifted from partisan to sectional. In 1845, nearly all the congressional votes for or against

[7] Michael F. Holt, *The Fate of Their Country: Politicians, Slavery Extension, and the Coming of the Civil War* (New York, NY: Hill and Wang, 2004), chap. 1.

[8] Don E. Fehrenbacher, *The Slaveholding Republic: An Account of the United States Government's Relations to Slavery* (New York, NY: Oxford University Press, 2001), 267.

Texas annexation were partisan. Whigs, whether Northern or Southern, antislavery or proslavery, had opposed Texas annexation. Democrats almost universally supported it, regardless of section. But in 1846, sectional sympathies overwhelmed party loyalties in the furor over the Wilmot Proviso. Nearly all Northern congressmen, regardless of party, supported the Wilmot Proviso. All Southern congressmen opposed the Wilmot Proviso. It was killed in the Senate, but each time it came up in the subsequent decade, it hammered a wedge between sections of the country. The political party system was failing to contain sectional disagreements over slavery extension.

The geopolitics of slavery seemed to push the country to the brink of disunion. When the US–Mexican War ended in 1848, Mexico ceded 529,189 square miles of land to the United States, including the territory that became California, Nevada, and Utah, as well as parts of Arizona, New Mexico, Colorado, and Wyoming. Debt peonage and Indian captivity were long-standing slaveries of the desert Southwest, though the political blinders of race would prevent many officials from seeing them until after the Civil War.[9] After the Mexican Cession, however, disagreement over the future of African American slavery reached a crisis point. President Polk stepped aside in the 1848 election. He had promised to serve a single term as president and honored that commitment. Having acquired more territory than any president since Jefferson, Polk left it to his successors to sort out the political crisis it caused.

The two national political parties, the Whigs and Democrats, were dividing North from South over the issue of whether slavery would be permitted in the territory won from Mexico in the recent war. In the 1848 presidential election, the Whigs ran a disingenuous Janus-faced campaign, persuading Southern voters that General Zachary Taylor, a Louisiana enslaver, represented their interests. Northern voters were told that Taylor was a nationalist, an opponent of slavery expansion who would defuse sectional tensions, and a unifier who opposed the Mexican War he helped win. The forty-year army veteran won the presidency having never held public office or even voted.[10] In New England, Conscience Whigs left the party, some joining the Free Soil Party. Democrats witnessed defections too. In New York State, Barnburners left the Democratic Party for

---

[9] William J. Kiser, *Borderlands of Slavery: The Struggle over Captivity and Peonage in the American Southwest* (Philadelphia, PA: University of Pennsylvania Press, 2017).

[10] Michael F. Holt, *The Rise and Fall of the American Whig Party: Jacksonian Politics and the Onset of the Civil War* (New York, NY: Oxford University Press, 1999), chap. 19.

the Free Soil Party, joining others disaffected by the two-party system. Whigs won the 1848 presidential contest but lost their House majority, the Democrats taking over leadership of Congress. And the crisis deepened as proslavery Southerners practiced political brinksmanship, threatening to secede if their demands for slavery in the territories were not met. While the future of slavery in the West was plunging the republic into crisis, the politics of fugitive slaves was becoming a divisive regional issue in the East.

Rebecca and George Latimer did not set out to start a sanctuary state movement when they escaped slavery in Virginia in early October 1842. She was nineteen and pregnant, posing as his servant. He was twenty-three, had light skin, and booked passage on a Philadelphia-bound ship, fleeing abuse and the auction block in Norfolk. They had been married just nine months, and now expecting a family, George Latimer could no longer take an owner's abuse. He had been subject to a dozen masters. But owner James B. Gray had a flair for cruelty, beating him with cowhide, fists, and sticks.[11]

But there was no safe harbor from slavery, even in a free state. The Latimers fled from Philadelphia to Boston and the help of abolitionists. Even on free soil, they were still on the run. Earlier that year, the US Supreme Court affirmed federal supremacy in fugitive slave cases in *Prigg* v. *Pennsylvania*. The case overturned states' personal liberty laws forbidding bounty hunters and slave catchers from kidnapping African Americans claimed as fugitive slaves.[12] *Prigg* was also a stern rebuke to state decisions like Massachusetts's *Commonwealth* v. *Aves* (1836). That case, decided by Judge Lemuel Shaw of the Massachusetts Supreme Judicial Court, held that a fugitive from slavery could sojourn in Massachusetts because the state had no law of slavery to restrain her or him. In other words, slavery was a local condition and freedom was a general one, even though the legal status of an enslaved person who reached Massachusetts did not change. *Prigg* asserted that the bonds of slavery followed the fugitive out of a slave state in the person of a fugitive hunter or slave catcher. It affirmed federal supremacy in the recapture of enslaved people fleeing across state lines. Latimer's case was a test of the extent to which such federal protections for slave property went.

---

[11] Stephen Kantrowitz, *More than Freedom: Fighting for Black Citizenship in a White Republic, 1829–1889* (New York, NY: Penguin, 2013), 70–76.
[12] John Coughlin, "*Prigg* v. *Pennsylvania* and the Rising Sectional Tension of the 1840s" (MA thesis, Arizona State University, 2010).

Three weeks after George Latimer left Virginia, he was discovered in Boston and arrested. Authorities charged him with stealing from his Virginia owner back in Norfolk. A group of African American abolitionists tried rescuing Latimer before trial but failed. Judge Lemuel Shaw issued a writ of habeas corpus requiring James Gray to prove Latimer was his fugitive property. Shaw had presided over *Commonwealth* v. *Aves* and was not unsympathetic to fugitives from slavery. But Gray petitioned US Supreme Court Justice Joseph Story, a Massachusetts native who authored the *Prigg* majority decision. Story was in Boston at the time and ruled that Latimer must remain in jail until his owner could present evidence. The presumption of innocence did not apply to African Americans accused of being fugitives.

While George Latimer waited for his trial, Rebecca entered a Boston safe house run by abolitionists. From there she embarked on the Underground Railroad, giving birth to a son, George Jr., in Lynn, Massachusetts. And as word of the Latimers' ordeals circulated through an antislavery network, Latimer committees sprung up in protest. They were citizens' groups that raised awareness and gathered the resources to protect the fugitives from a return to slavery. And they used the Latimer case to contest the laws of slavery.

Massachusetts antislavery activists argued it was wrong to uphold slavery in a free state. Abolitionist Liberty Party leader Samuel Sewell took Latimer's case. Sewell had argued the *Aves* case and many like it. And while he prepared Latimer's defense, activists like William Lloyd Garrison spread the word. African American abolitionists including Charles Lenox Remond and Frederick Douglass took Latimer's case to the public. "Men, husbands, and fathers of Massachusetts," Douglass pleaded, "put yourselves in the place of George Latimer; feel his pain and anxiety of mind. . . . Now make up your minds what your duty is to George Latimer, and when you have made your minds up, prepare to do it and take the consequences."[13]

Despite public outcry, the law seemed clear on Latimer's status as a slave. Gray won back his human property in court. Judge Story ruled that Latimer was held lawfully under the Fugitive Slave Act of 1793 and the Fugitive Slave Clause of the Constitution. Story also held that federal law trumped an 1837 Massachusetts personal liberty law requiring a jury trial in fugitive slave cases. Latimer's case seemed closed.

[13] *The [Boston] Liberator*, November 18, 1842, 182.

If the law was against Latimer, Boston's abolitionists argued, then the laws needed to change. They began agitating for a new state law to free Latimer and other refugees from slavery. In support, they published the *Latimer Journal and North Star* accusing authorities of abetting kidnapping. It went viral, gaining 20,000 subscribers in a month. Outrage spread, and volunteers raised money, collecting 64,527 signatures – starting with Latimer's – petitioning the state legislature. And to make sure Latimer was not returned to Virginia, abolitionists paid James Gray $400 for Latimer and freed him.

The freedom campaign was a success. In March 1843, Massachusetts passed a tough new sanctuary state act. The Personal Liberty Act, nicknamed the Latimer law, forbade state cooperation in the capture and detention of accused fugitive slaves. With few federal detention centers or marshals, it undercut federal enforcement. And it sent a clear message to enslavers that federal law was on their side, but Massachusetts was not.

The Latimer law was a bold assertion of states' rights against federal slavery protections. Sensing history was on their side, abolitionists protested against President John Tyler when he came to Boston that spring to dedicate the Bunker Hill Memorial. Tyler was a Virginia slave owner. And abolitionist William Lloyd Garrison howled that "descendants of those, who, in 1776, threw off the British yoke, and for seven years waged war against a despotic power," were now shown to be "hypocrites and liars" for supporting slavery.[14]

Antislavery sanctuary state laws spread across the North as citizens refused to aid slave catchers. Vermont and Ohio passed Latimer laws in 1843. Connecticut passed one in 1844, New Hampshire in 1846, Pennsylvania in 1847, and Rhode Island in 1848. To supporters, it was a victory of democracy against distant federal coercion. Some state courts agreed. In 1847, a Missouri court ruled that Dred Scott, who lived for many years in free states and territories, could no longer be held in slavery. His owner appealed to the Supreme Court. Yet freedom seemed to be on the march.

And Southern slave owners were outraged. Virginia legislators protested antislavery states' rights, calling it clear contrary to founding principles. One fumed that Massachusetts, Rhode Island, and Vermont's sanctuary laws were a "disgusting and revolting exhibition of faithless

---

[14] William Lloyd Garrison, "'The Address to the Slaves of the United States,' May, 1843," in *The Rise of Aggressive Abolitionism: Addresses to the Slaves*, ed. Stanley Harrold (Lexington, KY: University of Kentucky Press, 2004), 172–73.

and unconstitutional legislation."[15] "Our slave property is utterly inse-
cure," screamed a Virginia state representative to South Carolina senator
John C. Calhoun in 1847, adding that Pennsylvania's law was "a deliberate insult to the whole Southern people." If unchecked it was "a just
cause of war."[16]

To placate enslaver interests, Congress passed the Fugitive Slave Act of
1850 as part of a congressional compromise over slavery extension in
territories ceded by Mexico after the US–Mexican War. The Fugitive Slave
Act chilled state resistance to slavery. It gutted sanctuary state laws by
requiring any citizen of any state to help recapture accused fugitive slaves
under penalty of law. The Act treated anyone accused of being a fugitive
from slavery as guilty unless proved innocent, while forbidding African
Americans from giving evidence. Black parents could not testify on behalf
of children snatched away and libeled as fugitives. Obstructing enforcement was punishable with six months in jail and a $1,000 fine. (The price
equivalent of that fine in 2017 was $31,700.) Attorneys found to defend
guilty subjects were sanctioned. Officials were incentivized to enforce it.
Deputies received $5 if an accused fugitive was indeed free but $10 if an
accused fugitive was convicted and returned. Under the Act, African
American suspects were arrested in Detroit, Michigan and jailed in
Milwaukee, Wisconsin, and Boston. Reverend Charles Beecher spoke
for outraged abolitionists and antislavery citizens when he preached that
the Act "is an unexampled climax of sin. It is the monster iniquity of the
present age, and it will stand forever on the page of history, as the vilest
monument of infamy of the nineteenth century."[17]

The power of the federal government was turning sharply against state
and local efforts to provide safe haven to fugitives. In *Strader* v. *Graham*
(1851), the US Supreme Court again ruled against state sanctuaries.
The case arose when three professional – yet enslaved – musicians,
George, Henry, and Reuben, fled their owner in Harrodsburg,
Kentucky, aboard an Ohio River steamboat, escaping to Canada in

---

[15] "Extracts from [a] Report of Virginia on the Rendition of Fugitive Slaves, February 7,
1849," in *State Documents on Federal Relations: The States and the United States*, ed.
Herman V. Ames (Philadelphia, PA: University of Pennsylvania History Department,
1911), 252.

[16] Charles J. Faulkner to John C. Calhoun, July 15, 1847, in *Correspondence Addressed to
John C. Calhoun, 1837–1849*, ed. Chauncey C. Boucher and Robert P. Brooks
(Washington, DC: US Government Printing Office, 1930), 385–87.

[17] Beecher quoted in Stanley W. Campbell, *The Slave Catchers: Enforcement of the Fugitive
Slave Law, 1850–1860* (Chapel Hill, NC: University of North Carolina Press, 1968), 50.

1841. The owner, Christopher Graham, sued the steamboat owners and captain claiming they were responsible for his loss of property. The defendants argued that the laws of Ohio set them free once across the river. The Supreme Court disagreed. Writing for the majority, Chief Justice Roger B. Taney held that "it was exclusively in the power of Kentucky to determine for itself whether their employment in another state should or should not make them free on their return."[18] Taney also held that the Northwest Ordinance excluding slavery from Ohio under the Articles of Confederation was superseded by the laws of slavery under the federal Constitution. Opposed by the Fugitive Slave Act and federal courts, abolitionists had few legal options.

So they practiced civil disobedience. The Anthony Burns case in 1854 was the most theatrical resistance to the new Fugitive Slave Act. Like Latimer, Burns was enslaved in Virginia. Early in 1854, the nineteen-year-old preacher stowed away on a ship, arriving in Boston, where he took a job in a clothing store. Burns could read and write and posted a letter to his brother telling of his whereabouts – a letter that fell into the hands of his owner. The owner traveled from Virginia to recapture him in Boston, where a court ruled he was in fact a fugitive. While Burns was held in jail awaiting transport, abolitionists organized and marched to the courthouse to release the prisoner, gathering a crowd of about 2,000. They led a short siege on the jail in which a Boston deputy was shot and killed. The Franklin Pierce administration intervened, sending an armed guard and a federal warship, and Burns's return to Virginia cost taxpayers $40,000 ($1.18 million in 2017 dollars).[19] It was a pyrrhic victory. Some states tried passing sanctuary laws after the Fugitive Slave Act, but they were ineffective. Massachusetts reaffirmed its personal liberty law in 1855. Wisconsin and Ohio followed suit with sanctuary laws in 1857. But those fleeing slavery now had to make it all the way to Canada for safety.

The politics of slavery reached a crisis in the 1850s. The Fugitive Slave Act of 1850 was part of a broader federal effort to preserve and extend slavery, or at least placate proslavery interests. The Compromise of 1850 provided that states organized out of the Mexican Cession (land ceded by Mexico in 1848) would decide themselves whether to permit or prohibit slavery. The Compromise admitted California as a free state, according to

---

[18] *Strader v. Graham*, 51 U.S. (10 How.) 82 (1851), online: https://supreme.justia.com/cas es/federal/us/51/82/case.html, accessed: November 15, 2017.

[19] Charles Emery Stevens, *Anthony Burns: A History* (Boston, MA: John P. Jewett, 1856).

its 1850 constitution. Texas's boundaries were set at their current limits, and slave trading (though not slavery) was banned in the District of Columbia. Whig President Zachary Taylor rejected the Compromise, arguing that it conceded too much to proslavery interests. Southern Democrats were not satisfied either, screeching that the Compromise did not go far enough to protect slavery. Northern Whigs generally agreed with their president and opposed the Compromise. But President Zachary Taylor died suddenly on July 9, 1850, and the new president, Millard Fillmore of New York, sided with Northern Democrats and Southern Whigs in pushing the measures through Congress that September. He argued that this "armistice," as one historian called it, was preferable to risking slave-state secession.[20] The cornerstone of the Compromise of 1850 in the East was the Fugitive Slave Act, while in the West it was popular sovereignty. Both exacerbated political divisions.

Popular sovereignty pushed out to the far ends of the American empire the decision whether to permit slavery. Few expected cotton plantations in far-off New Mexico. African American slavery was seen as an "improbable" institution there, but there was no assurance of its "physical impossibility."[21] The push to open western territories to African American slavery was not so that cotton and sugar would flourish there, but so that proslavery representatives would propagate and proslavery US senators would be sent back to Washington, DC. The 1850 Compromise left that work unfinished. After California entered the Union as a free state, none of the territories organized permitting slavery. The 1820 Missouri Compromise seemed to take the possibility of a Northern slavery state off the table.

But the Kansas-Nebraska Act of 1854 deepened the political crisis over slavery extension by getting rid of the Missouri Compromise line in favor of popular sovereignty. Kansas sat north of the line, which was Missouri's southern border. To curry favor with Southern Democrats and help build a transcontinental railroad line through his own state, Illinois Democrat Stephen Douglas sponsored the legislation providing that Kansas citizens would decide whether slavery would be permitted when the territory became a state. Douglas straddled slavery's fence, giving assurances to Southerners that slavery could spread to the Kansas prairie while arguing

---

[20] David M. Potter, *The Impending Crisis: America before the Civil War, 1848–1861* (New York, NY: Harper & Row, 1976), 90, passim.

[21] *Horace Mann's Letters on the Extension of Slavery into California and New Mexico* (1850), 27.

to his own Northern constituents that geography would keep Kansas clear of enslaved people. Only a handful of actual bondspersons resided in Kansas. But there was furious reaction from many antislavery Northerners who considered the Missouri Compromise sacred.

And opposition to Douglas's proslavery compromise caused political realignment along sectional lines. Eight years after the Wilmot Proviso, the Republican Party formed in response to the Kansas-Nebraska Act and the political controversy it inflamed over slavery's expansion. Emerging leaders like Abraham Lincoln sought to protect freedom in the North, including the northwestern frontier. Republicans favored free soil and free labor, but they did not welcome African Americans. Republican Party organizations sprang up in states like Ohio and Illinois, which required black residents to post a bond, promise to keep the peace, and carry a residency permit. Such anti-black sentiment was pervasive. Outside of New England, no state permitted African Americans to vote by 1855.[22] But at least in principle, Republicans were antislavery.

In the South, the political middle ground was collapsing as sectional divisions became more pronounced. After losing the 1852 presidential election, the national Whig Party disintegrated. Democrats held a supermajority in the South as Southern Whigs melted into a loose opposition party with no Northern wing. Cotton planters like James Henry Hammond of South Carolina and Jefferson Davis of Mississippi set the Southern Democratic Party agenda. Without a viable opposition, proslavery expansionists ruled the South.

Vigorous political debate was declining in the Slave South. Large portions had become increasingly unequal, undiversified, and undemocratic. Whereas a third of white families in the South owned bondspeople in 1830, that proportion was reduced to a quarter by 1850. In plantation regions, little wealth trickled down to poorer whites. There were many jobs for patrollers and slave catchers, but like the path to ownership, the road to a diversified economy was blocked by King Cotton.[23] Subregions like Appalachia did not develop the extreme stratification of wealth that took hold in cotton country, but neither did the kind of economic vitality that was transforming Chicago and Cincinnati into major urban

[22] Holt, *Rise and Fall of the American Whig Party*, chap. 22; Alexander Keyssar, *The Right to Vote: The Contested History of Democracy in the United States*, rev. edn. (New York, NY: Basic Books, 2009), chap. 3.
[23] Keri Leigh Merritt, *Masterless Men: Poor Whites and Slavery in the Antebellum South* (New York, NY: Cambridge University Press, 2017).

manufacturing hubs, developing their hinterlands along the way.[24]
Enslavers tended to own larger assemblages of enslaved people working
in larger fields. Slave prices rose dramatically after 1855, becoming
unmoored from cotton prices. That put slave ownership out of reach of
most white Southerners and also made slave property a speculative investment. Prices became so high, in fact, that there was a push to reopen the
transatlantic slave trade to ease labor costs in cotton and sugar fields.
While some Southern editors and extreme proslavery politicians favored
doing so, leaders slammed the door on any such policy. President James
Buchanan warned Congress that "the introduction of wild, heathen, and
ignorant barbarians among the sober, orderly, and quiet slaves, whose
ancestors have been on the soil for several generations . . . might tend to
barbarize, demoralize, and exasperate the whole mass, and produce the
most deplorable circumstances."[25] If more slaves could not be brought
into the country, proslavery expansionists argued, the United States could
annex more slave territory.

As enslavers considered seceding from the federal Union, they imagined
a proslavery empire stretching from the Chesapeake to tropical Latin
America.[26] One scheme to realize that vision involved capturing Cuba
from Spain and annexing it as a slave territory. Cuban sugar masters were
still importing African captives of the transatlantic slave trade.
Democratic expansionists had eyed Cuba since the 1840s, arguing that
if the United States did not capture it, the British would swoop in and
abolish slavery there, leading to another Haitian Revolution. By the early
1850s, Americans were supporting Narciso López in his attempts to incite
a revolution in Cuba. López, a Venezuelan revolutionary, was caught and
executed in Cuba in 1851. Early in his term, President Franklin Pierce
directed James Buchanan, then US ambassador to Great Britain, and
Pierre Soulé, ambassador to Spain, to come up with a scheme to annex
Cuba, buying it if necessary, for up to $130 million. Spain refused to
negotiate, and instead Soulé coauthored the 1854 Ostend Manifesto

---

[24] Wilma A. Dunaway, *Slavery in the American Mountain South* (New York, NY:
Cambridge University Press, 2003); Damian Alan Pargas, *The Quarters and the Fields:
Slave Families in the Non-Cotton South* (Gainesville, FL: University Press of Florida,
2010).

[25] James Buchanan, message to Congress, December 27, 1857, cited in *A Compilation of the
Messages and Papers of the Presidents, 1789–1897, Vol. 5*, ed. James D. Richardson
(Washington, DC, 1897), 557.

[26] Matthew J. Karp, *This Vast Southern Empire: Slaveholders at the Helm of American
Foreign Policy* (Cambridge, MA: Harvard University Press, 2016).

declaring that the United States must annex Cuba by any means necessary.[27] There were other schemes to take Nicaragua and parts of Mexico not ceded in 1848, but events in Kansas arrested the nation's attention.

The Kansas territory erupted in what were known as the Border Wars or "Bleeding Kansas" in disputes over whether slavery would be permitted there. Proslavery Missourians and other Southern whites crossed into Kansas during political canvases and conventions, gathered in squatter encampments, and menaced or attacked free-soil citizens. And incursions were not confined to proslavery partisans. New England abolitionist societies sent arms and cash, and sponsored emigrants moving to Kansas in order to tilt the territory toward a free-state constitution.

And while partisans skirmished on the distant prairie, political violence broke out in Washington, DC. In May 1856, Massachusetts senator Charles Sumner gave a speech in Congress called "The Crime against Kansas." An outspoken abolitionist, Sumner argued that proslavery agitation in Kansas amounted to "the rape of a virgin Territory, compelling it to the hateful embrace of slavery; and it may be clearly traced to a depraved desire for a new Slave State, hideous offspring of such a crime, in the hope of adding to the power of slavery in the National Government." He singled out Illinois senator Stephen Douglas, whom he called "Sancho Panza," an insulting allusion to the abject enabler in Miguel de Cervantes's *Don Quixote*. Sumner called South Carolina senator Andrew Butler "Don Quixote," and accused him of "[having] chosen a mistress to whom he has made his vows, and who, though ugly to others, is always lovely to him … I mean the harlot, Slavery."[28] To avenge the insult, Butler's nephew Preston Brooks, a congressman from South Carolina, attacked Sumner while Sumner was seated at his desk on the Senate floor. Brooks beat Sumner senseless with a gutta-percha cane until it broke. Sumner suffered severe head injuries and would not return to the Senate for years. Southern Democrats raised a howl of approval. Fans sent Brooks new canes. The *Richmond Enquirer* cheered the attack, arguing that abolitionists "must be lashed into submission." Its editor insisted,

[27] Walter Johnson, *River of Dark Dreams: Slavery and Empire in the Cotton Kingdom* (Cambridge, MA: Harvard University Press, 2013), chap. 12.
[28] Charles Sumner, *The Works of Charles Sumner*, Vol. 4 (Boston, MA: Lea and Shepard, 1871), 140–49.

"Sumner, in particular, ought to have nine-and-thirty [whippings] early every morning."[29]

And violence begat violence. When word reached Kansas of Brooks's assault on Sumner, Connecticut abolitionist John Brown and several of his sons avenged Bleeding Sumner and a proslavery attack on Lawrence, Kansas, earlier in the week. Brown and his men attacked a settlement of proslavery men at Pottawatomie Creek south of Lawrence, dragging several from their cabins, cutting them down with broadswords, and shooting the bodies. The Pottawatomie Massacre and Bleeding Sumner showed the nation the dark side of popular sovereignty. Instead of arguing about slavery's extension, Americans were fighting over it.[30]

By 1856, political realignment along sectional lines was nearly complete, thanks to popular sovereignty and the rise of the Republicans. The national Democratic Party was dividing along sectional lines, and a third party, the American or Know-Nothing Party, formed in opposition to Catholicism and immigrants. Republicans thundered against an arrogant Slave Power. Know-Nothings feared an insurgency of Catholic foreigners. And as immigration surged to the North and West, Southern Democrats became frenzied about Republicans' antislavery stances. In the presidential election of 1856, Republicans – who had not existed until two years before – won a third of the popular vote and eleven states, including all of New England plus New York, Ohio, Michigan, Wisconsin, and Iowa. The party had just a handful of members south of the Ohio River, and the Democrats won a narrow victory.[31] The new president, James Buchanan, vowed unity, but instead meddled in a court decision, further exacerbating tensions over slavery.

The political system was failing to contain sectional differences, and so the Supreme Court stepped in to settle a source of political disagreement. *Dred Scott* v. *Sandford*, decided just two days after Buchanan was inaugurated president, was superficially about the freedom of one man, Dred Scott. Born in Virginia in 1795, Scott had traveled with his owner to the

---

[29] Richmond *Enquirer*, June 3, 1856, 2 (quotations); Williamjames Hull Hoffer, *The Caning of Charles Sumner: Honor, Idealism, and the Origins of the Civil War* (Baltimore, MD: Johns Hopkins University Press, 2010).

[30] Manish Sinha, *The Slave's Cause: A History of Abolition* (New Haven, CT: Yale University Press, 2016), chap. 16.

[31] Patrick Rael, *Black Identity and Black Protest in the Antebellum North* (Chapel Hill, NC: University of North Carolina Press, 2002); William W. Freehling, *Road to Disunion, Vol. 2: Secessionists Triumphant, 1854–1861* (New York, NY: Oxford University Press, 2007), chap. 9; Jay P. Dolan, *The Irish Americans: A History* (New York, NY: Bloomsbury Press, 2008), chap. 4.

free state of Illinois and the free Wisconsin territory (in what is now Minnesota). There the Northwest Ordinance and Missouri Compromise had banned slavery. With the help of abolitionists, Dred Scott and his wife, Harriet, filed suit for their freedom in 1846. The cases were part of a flood of freedom suits brought in Saint Louis as part of a grassroots legal struggle against slavery.[32] A Missouri court freed Scott in 1850, ruling that his time in free states and territories changed his status (a year before the Supreme Court ruled the opposite in *Strader v. Graham*). But the owner appealed, and in 1852, the Missouri Supreme Court reversed the lower court's ruling. Scott sued again, this time against his new owner, John Sanford (misspelled Sandford in court documents). Sanford lived in New York, so Scott filed suit in federal court. The federal court held that Scott was still enslaved and had no standing to sue.

Scott appealed to the US Supreme Court, asking the narrow question of whether he had standing to sue. Implicit in the question was whether he was owed his freedom. Chief Justice Roger Taney heard the case, and before the decision was handed down, President-elect James Buchanan contacted justices John Catron of Tennessee and Robert Grier of Pennsylvania, fellow Democrats, building consensus for a proslavery ruling. Buchanan announced an upcoming Supreme Court decision in his inaugural address on Wednesday, March 4, 1857. And on that Friday, the Supreme Court handed down a 7–2 ruling, all Democrats on the court voting together, to deny Scott's freedom. But the ruling went much farther.

Instead of applying law and precedent, Chief Justice Taney's decision read more like a proslavery political stump speech. He ruled that that the nation's founders considered African-descended people "beings of an inferior order, and altogether unfit to associate with the white race either in social or political relations, and so far inferior that they had no rights which the white man was bound to respect, and that the negro might justly and lawfully be reduced to slavery for his benefit."[33] It was an originalist argument that purported to peer into the minds of the framers of the Declaration of Independence and infer that they intended no black people to be citizens of the United States. Taney admitted that the ruling did not

---

[32] Kelly M. Kennington, *In the Shadow of Dred Scott: St. Louis Freedom Suits and the Legal Culture of Slavery in Antebellum America* (Athens, GA: University of Georgia Press, 2017).

[33] *A Report of the Decision of the Supreme Court of the United States ... Dred Scott versus John F. A. Sandford* (New York, NY: D. Appleton, 1857), 407.

overturn state citizenship for African Americans but ruled that Scott had no standing to sue in federal court. In fact, Taney argued, Scott was never free, and in reaching the 1820 Missouri Compromise, Congress had exceeded its constitutional authority. The Missouri Compromise had been repealed by the Kansas-Nebraska Act, but the *Dred Scott* decision nailed its coffin. A slave in any state was a slave in every state or territory of the United States.

The *Dred Scott* decision provoked outrage in much of the country. Two associate justices, John McLean of Ohio and Benjamin R. Curtis of Massachusetts, wrote scathing dissents, arguing that Taney's history was wrong and his originalism was a fig leaf over proslavery politics. McLean argued that the exclusion of African Americans from national citizenship "is more a matter of taste than of law," pointing out that "several of the States have admitted persons of color to the right of suffrage, and in this view have recognized them as citizens; and this has been done in the slave as well as the free States." In fact, Justice McLean pointed out, "[u]nder the late treaty with Mexico, we have made citizens of all grades, combinations, and colors. ... They have exercised all the rights of citizens, without being naturalized under the acts of Congress." As for slavery, he argued, "the principle laid down will enable the people of a slave State to introduce slavery into a free State, for a longer or shorter time, as may suit their convenience; and by returning the slave to the State whence he was brought, by force or otherwise, the status of slavery attaches, and protects the rights of the master, and defies the sovereignty of the free State."[34] A Vermont editor put it more bluntly. Under the *Dred Scott* ruling, "slave labor is legalized and protected in every state of the Union."[35] State court rulings like *Mitchell* v. *Wells* (1859) extended the *Dred Scott* decision. *Mitchell* v. *Wells* involved Nancy Wells, born enslaved in Mississippi to a white father and an enslaved mother. The father – her owner – sent her to Ohio and freed her. He died, leaving her property. But in her attempt to inherit her father's property the Mississippi court held that she had never been manumitted because Mississippi's law of slavery superseded Ohio's law of manumission.[36] Besides affirming slavery, such court decisions were attacks on white democracy in the North and majority rule.

[34] *Dred Scott* v. *Sandford* (1857), 553, 559.
[35] *St. Albans [Vermont] Messenger*, March 19, 1857, 2.
[36] Paul D. Finkelman, *An Imperfect Union: Slavery, Federalism, and Comity* (Chapel Hill, NC: University of North Carolina Press, 1981), 285–93.

The Republican Party rallied around the cause of protecting free labor and free soil. Abraham Lincoln hammered that message in his bid for a US Senate seat from Illinois in 1858. He ran against Democratic Kansas-Nebraska Act author Stephen Douglas. In a series of debates, Lincoln articulated a core contention of the Republican Party. "A house divided against itself cannot stand," Lincoln told a 1,000-member audience in Springfield. "I believe this government cannot endure, permanently half slave and half free. I do not expect the Union to be dissolved," he explained, "I do not expect the house to fall – but I do expect it will cease to be divided. It will become all one thing or all the other." Lincoln framed the political crisis in biblical terms, paraphrasing the Gospel of Mark 3:25.[37] Either Republicans would protect freedom or Democrats would transform the entire republic into slave country. He was not alone in framing the political crisis. US senator William H. Seward of New York also warned of an "irrepressible conflict" in 1858.[38] Lincoln lost narrowly to the more well-known Democrat, but had gained national attention as an eloquent spokesman for Republican principles.

And then an abolitionist raid on Harper's Ferry provoked a frenzy. On the night of October 16, John Brown led twenty-one men to the Virginia town at the confluence of the Shenandoah and Potomac Rivers with the aim of capturing the federal arsenal there. His strategy was to free enslaved people, arm them, and lead a spontaneous uprising into the heart of slave country. The plan had been years in the making, and Brown had abolitionist sponsorship and a wide network from which to recruit. His paramilitary organization planned to seize Harper's Ferry, take hostages, and free bondspersons, who would form the heart of an army that would spread throughout Virginia and then the South. Recruits included veterans of the Kansas Border Wars, his youngest sons Oliver and Watson, and former bondsmen and fugitives from Virginia and South Carolina, among many white recruits from Connecticut, Indiana, New York, and Virginia. Brown had tried to recruit Frederick Douglass, a longtime acquaintance and ally. Douglass refused. But Shields Green, a former bondsman, signed on.[39]

---

[37] Abraham Lincoln, "House Divided Speech," Springfield, Illinois, June 16, 1858, Abraham Lincoln Online, www.abrahamlincolnonline.org/lincoln/speeches/house.htm, accessed: July 21, 2016.

[38] Holt, *The Fate of Their Country*, 124.

[39] Tony Horwitz, *Midnight Rising: John Brown and the Raid That Sparked the Civil War* (New York, NY: Henry Holt, 2011); Edward L. Ayers, *In the Presence of Mine Enemies:*

John Brown's raid unraveled soon after it began. Alarmed citizens banded together to fight off Brown's men. Dangerfield Newby, a formerly enslaved man, was the first killed. Brown's force took hostages and fought off locals as it fell back and barricaded itself in a fire engine house. Some raiders tried to escape but were killed, their bodies mutilated, including Shields Green. After the alarm reached Washington, DC, President Buchanan ordered marines led by Colonel Robert E. Lee to Harper's Ferry to secure the town and halt the insurrection. Lee ordered Lieutenant J. E. B. Stuart to negotiate surrender. Stuart recognized one of Brown's sons from Kansas, but Brown refused to give up. Stuart then gave the order to batter down the engine house doors. In the siege, John Brown was stabbed. But he was captured alive along with several others. His staging area outside town was raided, and authorities uncovered his network including sponsors in New England. Several allies – including Frederick Douglass – fled to Canada.

Virginia tried John Brown for murder, treason, and inciting a slave uprising, all three crimes punishable by death. Southern whites blamed abolitionists, Republicans, and even Northerners in general, insisting that in the shadow of each stood an abolitionist. Many Northerners were outraged at what they considered a terrorist attack. And white Southerners were frenzied that other abolitionists would try to arm bondsmen and ignite a rebellion. Brown used his trial to plead his cause, writing letters arguing for the justice of emancipation. The jury found him guilty. And as the mastermind of the Harper's Ferry raid was led to the gallows to be hanged, he handed off a note reading, "I John Brown am now quite certain that the crimes of this guilty, land: will never be purged away; but with Blood."[40] He was hanged on December 2, 1859, and many abolitionists celebrated him as a martyr.

By the spring of 1860, the political ties keeping the republic together were unraveling. The national Whig Party had dissolved, and the Republicans were an antislavery party with few Southern members. And the last national party was coming apart too. The 1860 Democratic Party Convention met in Charleston, South Carolina, but delegates could not agree on a presidential candidate. The likely nominee – and Kansas-Nebraska Act author – Senator Stephen Douglas of Illinois did not seem

The Civil War in the Heart of America, 1859–1863 (New York, NY: W. W. Norton, 2003), 5–36.

[40] Franny Nudelman, *John Brown's Body: Slavery, Violence, and the Culture of War* (Chapel Hill, NC: University of North Carolina Press, 2004), 35.

proslavery enough for Southern Democrats. The Charleston convention closed without a party nomination. Northern Democrats nominated Douglas six weeks later at their convention in Baltimore. Proslavery Democrats stayed home in protest, nominating instead the sitting vice president, John C. Breckinridge of Kentucky, for president. Breckinridge would appear on Democratic ballots in much of the South while Douglas would appear on Democratic ballots in much of the North. The party split ensured each a loss in the November election.[41]

In the face of Democratic disunity, the Republicans rallied around a dark horse candidate whom few knew. At their national convention in Chicago, Republicans nominated Abraham Lincoln of Illinois. Unlike party leaders William H. Seward of New York and Salmon P. Chase of Ohio, Lincoln had a thin political record and became instead a candidate voters could pin hopes – or fears – on. He had been a lawyer in private practice since losing reelection to the US House of Representatives in 1848 but had attracted attention for his unsuccessful 1858 campaign against Stephen Douglas. Lincoln was a moderate. He pledged to stop slavery's expansion in the West but promised not to interfere with slavery in the South.[42] And there was a third party candidate running against both Democrats and the Republican nominee. The Constitutional Union Party formed on a platform of preserving the Union but set forth no policy specifics.

Slavery expansion and the question of fugitive slaves divided the country in 1860. Sectional political realignment was complete by November. Lincoln won the presidency with just under 40 percent of the popular vote in a four-way race. The Democratic vote split along sectional lines with Douglas capturing just one state – Missouri – and the southern Breckenridge ticket winning all of the Deep South states plus Arkansas and North Carolina. One of those Deep South states did not even wait for the Electoral College to meet before holding a secession convention. Just weeks after Lincoln became the first Republican president-elect, South Carolina exited the Union, beckoning others to follow. Yet even then it was far from clear there would be a civil war, let alone a war against slavery.[43]

[41] Eric H. Walther, *The Fire-Eaters* (Baton Rouge, LA: Louisiana State University Press, 1992), 3, passim.

[42] Eric Foner, *The Fiery Trial: Abraham Lincoln and American Slavery* (New York, NY: W. W. Norton, 2010), chap. 5.

[43] William J. Cooper, *We Have the War upon Us: The Onset of the Civil War, November 1860–April 1861* (New York, NY: Knopf, 2012).

The US republic withstood forty years of slavery's divisive geopolitics before disuniting in the winter of 1860–61, and during that time a proslavery minority managed to win nearly every one of its political demands. Most Northerners tolerated slavery so long as it did not conflict with their democratic entitlements. The Missouri Crisis over slavery's extension was resolved in 1820 by compromise legislation that did not seem to fatally disadvantage either enslavers or those suspicious of slavery's expansion. But it predicated compromise on the possibility of slavery's expansion. In the 1830s, national political parties – Whig and Democrat – developed contrasting principles and policies yet neither was antislavery. Both the Democratic and Whig Parties had proslavery and antislavery wings. In 1845, disagreement over whether to annex Texas was partisan rather than sectional. Whigs opposed it and Democrats supported it. But in 1846, the US–Mexican War disrupted the parties' abilities to diffuse sectional tensions over slavery extension. The question of whether to permit chattel slavery in the Mexican Cession was sectional, Whigs and Democrats being themselves divided North from South. The solution seemed to be to leave the question of slavery extension to new state governments.

In the East, fugitives from slavery inspired a states' rights reaction against slavery. States like Massachusetts pushed back thanks to organizing by and on behalf of fugitives like George and Rebecca Latimer. But the Compromise of 1850 incubated a political crisis greater than the one it solved. The sweeping Fugitive Slave Act roiled Northerners as it curtailed local and state efforts to combat slavery.

And the political Compromise of 1850 pushed the question of slavery's expansion into the future, based on the principle of popular sovereignty. The timing of secession was caused by a political realignment on sectional lines featuring the rise of the Republican Party. The geopolitics of slavery extension created divisions that political organizations worked against until the national Democratic Party disunited in 1860 and the Republicans gained enough support to win the presidency. Rather than wait for the election of 1864, South Carolina exited the federal republic. The other cotton states soon followed. All expected war.

Abolition War

The American Civil War was a conflict with massive unintended consequences. When the United States fought to keep thirteen Southern states
from forming an independent Confederacy, they fought for political
Union – some Republicans demanding an end to slavery and other
Unionists indifferent or opposed to freeing 4 million bondspersons. And
when Deep South states seceded from the federal Union in the winter of
1860–61, they did so based on the false assumption that a newly elected
Republican president would move to abolish slavery. Enslaved people
listened to whites' talk about Republicans' ambitions to free them from
bondage. And many believed.[1] "In the year 1860," Virginian Thomas
Johnson recalled, "there was great excitement in Richmond over the
election of Mr. Abraham Lincoln as [p]resident of the United States.
The slaves prayed to God for his success, and they prayed very especially
the night before the election. We knew he was in sympathy with the
abolition of [s]lavery."[2] In Georgia, Levi Branham recalled, "one of my
young masters came home and said that Breckenridge, Douglas and Abe
Lincoln were running for president, and that if Mr. Abe Lincoln was
elected that the negroes would be free. Then he asked me if I wanted to
be free and I told him 'yes.'"[3] But neither Johnson nor Branham got it

---

[1] James Oakes, *Freedom National: The Destruction of Slavery in the United States,
1861–1865* (New York, NY: W. W. Norton, 2014).
[2] Thomas L. Johnson, *Twenty-Eight Years a Slave* (Bournemouth: W. Mate and Sons, 1909),
27, online: http://docsouth.unc.edu/neh/johnson1/menu.html, accessed: August 31, 2016.
[3] Levi Branham, *My Life and Travels* (Dalton, GA: A. J. Showalter Company Printers and
Publishers, 1929), 45, online: http://docsouth.unc.edu/neh/branham/branham.html,
accessed: August 31, 2016.

completely right. Lincoln was neither an abolitionist nor a revolutionary. The Republicans in 1860 promised to let slavery expand no farther than current borders. Yet they also vowed not to prohibit property in people in Virginia, Georgia, and everywhere else in the United States where slavery was legal. Would-be secessionists listened to their fears instead of Republican promises.

Cotton states seceded to protect slavery. After Lincoln won the presidency in a four-way election, South Carolina's secession convention met and voted 169–0 to leave the federal Union. "A geographical line has been drawn across the Union," South Carolina declared in its December 1860 secession declaration, "and all the [s]tates north of that line have united in the election of a man to the high office of [p]resident of the United States, whose opinions and purposes are hostile to slavery." Rather than to wait until the next election, South Carolina dissolved political ties, fearing that "the South shall be excluded from the common territory, that the judicial tribunals shall be made sectional, and that a war must be waged against slavery until it shall cease throughout the United States."[4] Secession was a no-confidence vote in their constitutional guarantees of slave property rights.

Abolitionists like Frederick Douglass were mystified. He had reached the opposite conclusion, contending that Republicans were uninterested in the fight against slavery. Lincoln's "victory threatens and may be the death of the modern Abolition movement," he warned in the waning days of 1860. "The Republican [P]arty does not propose to abolish slavery anywhere," Douglass argued. The Deep South therefore had no reason to secede. "If Mr. Lincoln were really an [a]bolition [p]resident, which he is not; if he were a friend to the [a]bolition movement, instead of being, as he is, its most powerful enemy, the dissolution of the Union might be the only effective mode of perpetuating slavery in the Southern [s]tates – since if it could succeed, it would place slavery beyond the power of the [p]resident and his [g]overnment."[5] Secession was madness, in other words.

Even some South Carolinians agreed. Former state attorney general James L. Petigru gasped that a seceding "South Carolina is too small for a republic and too large for an insane asylum." But leaders of the other

---

[4] "Declaration of the Immediate Causes Which Induce and Justify the Secession of South Carolina from the Federal Union," December 24, 1860, online: http://avalon.law.yale.edu/19th_century/csa_scarsec.asp, accessed: August 31, 2016.

[5] Frederick Douglass, "The Late Election," *Douglass' Monthly* 3.7 (December 1860): 370–71.

cotton states followed South Carolina's lead. And before Lincoln was inaugurated in March 1861, Alabama, Florida, Georgia, Louisiana, Mississippi, and Texas seceded from the Union and formed their own republic.

The Confederate States of America was an experiment in white male republicanism and a robust defense of both slavery and patriarchy. Confederate Vice President Alexander Stephens insisted in March 1861 that "[o]ur new government is founded upon ... its foundations are laid, its corner-stone rests, upon the great truth that the negro is not equal to the white man; that slavery subordination to the superior race is his natural and normal condition. This, our new government, is the first, in the history of the world, based upon this great physical, philosophical, and moral truth."[6] Stephens's "Corner-Stone" speech was a bold endorsement of scientific racism and proslavery imperialism. Shorn of a backward, protectionist North, teeming with abolitionists, he argued, the Southern Confederacy was free to expand slavery into Latin America and reap the benefits of global trade in cotton unencumbered by protections for domestic manufacturers and other obstacles to free trade Republicans promised to throw in the way. But at the Confederacy's moment of creation not all slave states were aboard.

Southern states were disunited. The upper South did not immediately follow the lower South out of the Union and into the Confederacy. White Southerners of the non-cotton states knew that their constitutional rights were not rolled back just because a Republican was elected president. States like Arkansas and Virginia held secession conventions, but delegates were not convinced by overheated secessionist rhetoric. In March, Arkansas voted 39–35 to remain in the Union. Virginia decided in early April to stay loyal, by a 2–1 margin. And in Washington, DC, leaders frantically bargained with Southern states to stall disunion and reverse secession.

Congressional leaders attempted a final compromise to reverse secession. Kentucky senator John J. Crittenden proposed six new constitutional amendments protecting slavery, including one prohibiting any future amendment from interfering with it. But Lincoln rejected the Crittenden Compromise. Another constitutional amendment, the

---

[6] Alexander Stephens, "Corner Stone," March 21, 1861, Savannah, Georgia, online: http://teachingamericanhistory.org/library/document/cornerstone-speech/, accessed: August 31, 2016 (quotations); Stephanie McCurry, *Confederate Reckoning: Power and Politics in the Civil War South* (Cambridge, MA: Harvard University Press, 2010).

Corbin Amendment, proposed in March 1861 and ratified by Maryland, Illinois, and Ohio, forbade "Congress the power to abolish or interfere, within any [s]tate, with the domestic institutions thereof, including that of persons held to labor or service by the laws of said [s]tate."[7] That would-be Thirteenth Amendment failed ratification. Armed conflict intervened.

When forced to choose sides in a civil war beginning in April 1861, Arkansas and Virginia threw their loyalty to the proslavery Confederacy. On April 12, just eight days after Virginia's secession convention voted to remain in the Union, Confederates attacked Fort Sumter off the coast of Charleston, South Carolina. The Lincoln administration called it an act of war and on April 15, President Lincoln called for 75,000 volunteers to put down the rebellion. And secessionists' fears seemed to be coming to pass after Fort Sumter that Lincoln would send an army to invade the Confederacy.[8] Weighing whether to side with fellow enslavers or fellow Unionists, Virginia's delegates to the secession convention staked slavery's future on the Confederate States, which was calling for 100,000 volunteers to join its ranks. On April 17, Virginia's secession convention voted 88–55 to secede from the federal Union. Virginia was the state with the largest slave population. Birthplace of seven out of sixteen presidents, it was the home of George Washington, James Madison, and Thomas Jefferson. And Virginia's secession led Arkansas, North Carolina, and Tennessee out of the Union and into the Confederacy as both sides prepared for a deepening conflict.

The Civil War began as a political conflict for or against the federal Union. But in the months following Fort Sumter, the object of the Civil War was as conflicted as the motivations on all sides. In the North, the political Union quickly became a sacred cause. "The Union feeling," read a widely circulated report from New York in May 1861, "is spreading with an impetus and a rapidity that is overwhelming all opposing sentiment. All party names and party strifes are sunk."[9] They would quickly reemerge, but most white Unionists mobilizing for war in 1861 were fighting to restore political ties, leaving slavery untouched. As former bondsman Sam Ward remembered years later, a Union solider entered his dwelling and made off with his mother's quilts. She pursued the soldier

---

[7] Michael Vorenberg, *Final Freedom: The Civil War, the Abolition of Slavery, and the Thirteenth Amendment* (New York, NY: Cambridge University Press, 2001), chap. 1.

[8] Daniel W. Crofts, *Reluctant Confederates: Upper South Unionists in the Secession Crisis* (Chapel Hill, NC: University of North Carolina Press, 1989).

[9] *San Francisco Bulletin*, May 8, 1861, 1.

screaming, "[y]ou say you come down here to fight for the niggers, and now you're stealing from 'em," to which the solider responded, "[y]ou're a god-damn liar. I'm fighting for $14 a month and the Union."[10] White soldiers who fought for the Union may have understood that slavery was the cause of the war, but they did not necessarily fight to end it.[11] In 1861, the Lincoln administration did not discourage that attitude.

Slavery remained alive and well in the Union. Constitutional protections for slavery remained, as did the Fugitive Slave Act of 1850, which the Lincoln administration enforced. More than 429,000 enslaved people counted in the 1860 census lived in the loyal border states of Delaware, Maryland, Missouri, and Kentucky, many owned by loyal enslavers.[12] To put down the rebellion and restore the Union, the Lincoln administration refused to make slavery an issue. "I hope to have God on my side," Lincoln reportedly said when the war broke out, "but I must have Kentucky," with its strategic access to the Cumberland and Tennessee Rivers draining into the heart of the Confederacy.[13] Thousands of soldiers, including officers whose leadership the Union desperately needed, supported slavery.

But African Americans seized on the divisive issue, arguing that slavery must be eliminated in order for the republic to be permanently united. "Any union which can possibly be patched up while slavery exists," Douglass argued in February 1861, "must either completely demoralize the whole nation, or remain a heartless form, disguising, under the smiles of friendship, a vital, active and ever-increasing hate, sure to explode in violence. It is a matter of life and death. Slavery must be all in the Union, or it can be nothing."[14] Douglass's words echoed Lincoln's 1858 "House Divided" speech, but the abolitionist saw clearly, even before the war, that the political crisis must be resolved by removing chattel slavery from the federal Union.

With orders to avoid making war on slavery, Union armies nevertheless became beacons to the enslaved. Each who learned – mistakenly or not –

---

[10] Testimony of Sam Ward in *Lay My Burden Down: A Folk History of Slavery*, ed. B. A. Botkin (Chicago, IL: University of Chicago Press, 1945), 206.

[11] Chandra Manning, *What This Cruel War Was Over: Soldiers, Slavery, and the Civil War* (New York, NY: Alfred A. Knopf, 2007).

[12] James M. McPherson, *The Negro's Civil War* (New York, NY: Pantheon Books, 1965), Appendix A.

[13] Eric Foner, *The Fiery Trial: Abraham Lincoln and American Slavery* (New York, NY: W. W. Norton, 2010), 169 (quotation).

[14] Frederick Douglass, "The Union and How to Save It," *Douglass' Monthly* 3.9 (February 1861): 401.

that Republicans were plotting slavery's overthrow had reason to greet Union soldiers as liberators. On the night of May 24, 1861, three black Hampton residents arrived at Fort Monroe, Virginia, across a narrow causeway from Old Point Comfort, asking for Union protection from their enslavers. The war had started just six weeks earlier. But on that night, Shepard Mallory, Frank Baker, and James Townshend escaped from Confederate Colonel Charles Mallory, seeking protection in the fort. The next morning, Confederate Major John Cary tracked them down, demanding that the federals deliver up the men under the Fugitive Slave Act of 1850. The Union commander, General Benjamin Butler, had no orders to receive fugitives from slavery in Virginia and none to deliver them up.

So Butler made an ad hoc policy that accommodated both political and military objectives. Mallory, Baker, and Townshend remained property, he declared, and so did the thousands who were escaping from disloyal owners. But they were confiscated property, Butler argued, like guns or horses captured from the enemy. He called them contraband of war, arguing that "the fugitive-slave act did not affect a foreign country, which Virginia claimed to be, and that she must reckon it one of the infelicities of her position that in so far at least she was taken at her word; that in Maryland, a loyal [s]tate, fugitives from service had been returned."[15] Butler had no problem returning the bondspersons of loyal owners. But federal "contrabands" became wards of the government, and the army put them to work. Mallory, Baker, and Townshend built a bakery. Three dozen who followed their steps to Fort Monroe were sent to Hampton to build breastworks, toiling in the hot Virginia sun for the protection of Union soldiers. Some hired themselves out and earned wages. And the Lincoln administration endorsed Butler's contraband policy as a way to punish disloyal enslavers while postponing the issue of freedom while the war was fought.[16]

Contraband policy made the US War Department the largest enslaver in the country during the year or so between the policy's implementation and Congress's Second Confiscation Act. More importantly, officers like

---

[15] Robert Francis Engs, *Freedom's First Generation: Black Hampton, Virginia, 1861–1890* (New York, NY: Fordham University Press, 2004), chap. 1; *The War of the Rebellion: Official Records of the Union and Confederate Armies*, Series 1, vol. 2 (Washington, DC, 1880), 650 (quotation).

[16] William W. Freehling, *The South vs. the South: How Anti-Confederate Southerners Shaped the Course of the Civil War* (New York, NY: Oxford University Press, 2001), chap. 6.

General Butler used the policy to goad the administration into recognizing self-freedom as steps toward emancipation and transferring bondspersons' individual aspirations to the policy-making apparatus of a nation at war. As the enslaved freed themselves in places like Hampton and the South Carolina Lowcountry, they presented themselves, as individuals, as families, as groups, and in some places by the hundred, to army commanders, who then put the issue of their status before the secretary of war, President Lincoln, and congressional leaders. Union military leaders did not generally welcome fugitives from Confederate slavery. But so many African Americans voting with their feet pressured congressional Republicans to weave slavery's abolition into military policy.[17] It did not take the army long to realize that contrabands were useful to the cause.

John Washington was one of them. Escaping from slavery, he decided to aid the cause of freedom for those left behind in bondage. In doing so, he helped force a new moral economy on the war. When the war began, Washington was twenty-one and had been enslaved in Richmond, Virginia. In August 1861, Congress passed the First Confiscation Act declaring that any enslaved person who fought for the Confederacy or who labored for it were freed from serving their owners. Confederates howled that this was an emancipation act, which had the effect of attracting defectors like Washington. "Already the [s]laves had been [e]scaping into the Union army[']s lines and [m]any thereby getting off to the [f]ree [s] tates," Washington recalled. "I could read the papers and eagerly [w] atched them for tidings of the [w]ar [w]hich had beg[u]n in earnest [and] almost every day brought news of [b]attles." None were decisive, but "[i]t had now become a well known fact that [s]laves was [*sic*] daily [m]aking their escape into the Union lines. So at Christmas 1861, I left Richmond, having been provided with a pass and fare to Fredericksburg Va."[18] Washington's owners were wary of his running off, but he found employment at a hotel in Fredericksburg, about fifty miles north of the Confederate capital.

Washington was more fortunate than most. He was young, fit, and could read. Those who could not read newspapers listened for news of the war's progress. And many like Washington kept an eye out for an opportunity to escape. They slowed the pace of work when and where they

---

[17] Oakes, *Freedom National*.
[18] John Washington, *John Washington's Civil War: A Slave Narrative*, ed. Crandall Shifflett (Baton Rouge, LA: Louisiana State University Press, 2008), 36.

could, testing the limits of a slave regime in which so many owners, overseers, and patrollers were joining the fight for Confederate independence. Late in 1861, a report from Beaufort, South Carolina, carried word that self-freed black residents were "playing masters where they were formerly slaves."[19] Some owners fled, but other enslavers marched their bondspersons inland and away from Union forces. One self-freed African American man reported to General William Tecumseh Sherman that "all the slaves who refused to go into the interior with their fugitive owners, were shot, having seen several shot for this reason alone."[20] The stakes were rising on all sides.

The war was becoming deadlier than expected, and hopes for a quick resolution were dimming. A February 1862 Union victory at Fort Donelson, Tennessee, on the Cumberland River resulted in 17,398 soldiers killed, wounded, or missing. The victor, General Ulysses S. Grant, moved his Army of the Tennessee south by southwest, pursuing Confederates. In April, Confederates under Albert Sidney Johnston attacked Grant's army on the Tennessee River. The resulting Battle of Shiloh claimed 23,000 killed, wounded, or missing. That one battle caused more casualties than all the American battlefield losses of the Revolution, the War of 1812, and the US–Mexican War combined. Two determined enemies, each using similar infantry tactics developed in the late eighteenth century, were causing unanticipated death and horror.[21] But by the spring of 1862, the Lincoln administration refused to fully endorse the new reality that a war for Union had become a war against slavery.

But it was increasingly difficult to separate civil war from the question of slavery's continuance. Both Union and Confederate armies enrolled able-bodied workers as the deepening conflict strained human resources on all sides. "A great many [s]lave [m]en were [s]ent to the Rebel army as [d]rivers, [c]ooks, [h]ostlers and any thing [e]lse they could do," Washington recalled.[22] Enslaved men and women were put to work in nearly every industry, accelerating the antebellum trend of industrial hiring. They made iron and salt and staffed and repaired railroads. And besides agricultural work, enslaved people staffed hospitals as nurses,

---

[19] *Cape Ann Light and Gloucester [Mass.] Telegraph*, November 23, 1861, 2.

[20] *The [Baltimore] South*, November 20, 1861, 1.

[21] Jack H. Lepa, *Grant's River Campaign: Fort Henry to Shiloh* (Jefferson, NC: MacFarland & Company, 2014); Earl J. Hess, *Civil War Infantry Tactics: Training, Combat, and Small-Unit Effectiveness* (Baton Rouge, LA: Louisiana State University Press, 2015).

[22] Washington, *John Washington's Civil War*, 38.

cooks, launderers, and cleaners. Virginia and North Carolina passed impressment laws in 1862, the Confederate government following suit in 1863, requiring enslavers to turn over able-bodied workers to the Confederate Army for labor.[23]

In the commotion, John Washington saw his chance to free himself. In April 1862, the Union Army of the Potomac advanced up Virginia's Lower Peninsula in the direction of Richmond. To the north and west, in Fredericksburg, Confederates withdrew. Washington's enslavers told him they were evacuating and would travel to Salisbury, North Carolina, some 300 miles to the south and west. On Good Friday, 1862, Union forces stormed Fredericksburg. Washington was working in the dining room of the Shakespeare Hotel when the news of the invasion came. "Every body was on their feet at once, [n]o-body finished but [s]ome ran to their rooms to get a few things." The owner "came running back[,] called me out in the [h]all[,] and thrust a roll of [b]ank notes in my hand and hurriedly told me to pay off all the [s]ervants, and [s]hut up the house and take charge of every thing. 'If the Yankees catch [m]e they will kill me So I can't stay here,'" Washington recalled him saying, "and [he]was off at full speed like the [w]ind."[24]

Enslaved people fled in the opposite direction as their former enslavers. "In less time than it takes me to [w]rite these lines, every [w]hite [m]an was out [of] the house," Washington averred. "Every [m]an [s]ervant was out on the house top looking over the [r]iver at the Yankees for their glistening bayonets could easily be [s]een[.] I could not begin to [e]xpress [m]y [n]ew born hopes[,] for I felt already like I was certain of my freedom now."[25] Washington's jubilee came when he crossed the Rappahannock River in a boat commanded by federal soldiers. He ran off with a cousin and another man. Washington was among Union soldiers, but he was not yet free. The First Confiscation Act held that fugitives from rebel owners were contraband of war.

By the summer of 1862, the Lincoln administration's refusal to make emancipation a war aim gave an opening to Radical Republicans in Congress to punish Confederates and commence the process of emancipating African American loyalists. Congress banned slavery in the territories, fulfilling Republicans' campaign promise and countering the

---

[23] Jaime Amanda Martinez, *Confederate Slave Impressment in the Upper South* (Chapel Hill, NC: University of North Carolina Press, 2013).

[24] Washington, *John Washington's Civil War*, 39, 45.

[25] Washington, *John Washington's Civil War*, 45.

Supreme Court's decision in *Dred Scott* v. *Sandford* (1857). In August, Congress passed the Second Confiscation Act, which set free any enslaved person who reached Union lines as captives of war.

Congress forced Abraham Lincoln to reconsider whether the war begun for Union could be a war to restore it with slavery. He wrote a public letter to *New York Tribune* editor Horace Greeley late in August 1862, contending that "[m]y paramount object in this struggle is to save the Union, and is not either to save or to destroy slavery. If I could save the Union without freeing any slave I would do it, and if I could save it by freeing all the slaves I would do it; and if I could save it by freeing some and leaving others alone I would also do that."[26] But events were overtaking the president's political strategy. In May 1862, General David Hunter issued General Order 11, declaring that "[s]lavery and martial law in a free country are altogether incompatible; the persons in these three [s]tates – Georgia, Florida and South Carolina – heretofore held as slaves, are therefore declared forever free."[27] Lincoln countermanded it. He also overrode similar orders by General John C. Frémont. Privately, he worried that making emancipation a war aim would cause the border slave states to secede, saying to his secretary of state, William Seward, "it would be construed our last shriek on the retreat."[28] Yet over that bloody summer Lincoln was being persuaded that African American bondspersons could fill the ranks of fallen Union soldiers, if freedom became a war aim.

The Lincoln administration stepped decisively toward making emancipation a war aim in the late summer of 1862. The Battle of Antietam, Maryland, on September 17 was the single bloodiest day of the war. Union losses numbered more than 12,000. The Confederacy lost more than 10,000 soldiers, retreating across the Potomac River back into Virginia. Antietam came less than a month after the staggering Union defeat at the Second Battle of Bull Run or Second Manassas, where nearly as many soldiers were killed, wounded, or went missing. Five days after Antietam, Lincoln issued a battlefield ultimatum.

[26] Abraham Lincoln to Horace Greeley, August 22, 1862, in *The Collected Works of Abraham Lincoln*, Vol. 5, ed. Roy P. Basler (New Brunswick, NJ: Rutgers University Press, 1953), 388.

[27] Abraham Lincoln, "Proclamation Revoking General Hunter's Order of Military Emancipation of May 9, 1862," in *The Collected Works of Abraham Lincoln*, Vol. 5, ed. Roy P. Basler (New Brunswick, NJ: Rutgers University Press, 1953), 222–23.

[28] Francis B. Carpenter, *Six Months at the White House with Abraham Lincoln* (New York, NY: Hurd and Houghton, 1866), 22.

The Preliminary Emancipation Proclamation of September 22, 1862 promised slavery's abolition if Confederates did not start laying down arms and sending loyal congressional delegations to Washington, DC. The deadline was January 1, 1863. If Confederates made no effort at political reunification, the president as commander in chief would proclaim "all persons held as slaves within any [s]tate, or designated part of a [s]tate, the people whereof shall then be in rebellion against the United States shall be then, thenceforward, and forever free." For loyal states still permitting slavery, Lincoln promised to recommend to Congress compensated gradual abolition legislation coupled with colonization schemes including continuing "the effort to colonize persons of African descent, with their consent, upon this continent, or elsewhere, with the previously obtained consent of the [g]overnments existing there."[29] Self-freed African Americans and spiraling war costs had forced a new moral politics of the war.

But long-time abolitionists were skeptical. Slavery had been entrenched for nearly 250 years, and an executive order – even a wartime proclamation – could not end it at a stroke. "Verily," Frederick Douglass argued in November 1862, "the work does not end with the abolition of slavery but only begins." Freedom without civil rights was no freedom at all. "Slavery," Douglass explained just days before the Emancipation Proclamation was signed, "has stamped its character too deeply and indelibly to be blotted out in a day or a year, or even in a generation. The slave will remain in some sense a slave, long after the chains are taken from his limbs and the master will retain much of the pride, the arrogance ... and love of power, acquired by his former relation[s]."[30] Slavery would end through armed conflict and force of law, but equality would have to be achieved over time, with education, and with cooperation on all sides.

During the final months of 1862, Lincoln searched desperately for cracks in Confederate political resistance, beckoning rebels with an assurance that should elections be held and loyal congressional delegations return to Washington, DC, the country might "have peace again upon the old terms under the Constitution."[31] But in mid-December, generals

[29] Abraham Lincoln, "Preliminary Emancipation Proclamation," *The Collected Works of Abraham Lincoln, Vol. 5*, ed. Roy P. Basler (New Brunswick, NJ: Rutgers University Press, 1953), 434.

[30] Douglass quoted in David Blight, *Frederick Douglass' Civil War: Keeping Faith in Jubilee* (Baton Rouge, LA: Louisiana State University Press, 1991), 177, n. 4.

[31] Abraham Lincoln to Frederick Steele et al., November 18, 1862, *The Collected Works of Abraham Lincoln, Vol. 5*, ed. Roy P. Basler (New Brunswick, NJ: Rutgers University Press, 1953), 500.

Robert E. Lee and Thomas "Stonewall" Jackson inflicted a costly defeat on Union forces at Fredericksburg. Federals lost 13,300 soldiers dead, wounded, or missing, to Confederates' 4,500 casualties. The Confederacy seemed to be winning the war, and there was no incentive to lay down arms and rejoin the Union.

The Civil War entered a new phase on January 1, 1863, when Lincoln signed the Emancipation Proclamation. It freed all those bondspersons in Confederate-held states, cities, and counties as a war measure. It did not touch the enslaved people in the Union or Union-held areas, in effect freeing solely those bondspersons beyond the reach of the government. Lincoln had no authority to interfere with slavery in the Union since enslavers' human property was constitutionally protected. But the Emancipation Proclamation did change the war for Union into a war for emancipation within the territory held by the Confederate States of America. A Union victory would make all slaves in rebel-held areas "thenceforth and forever free." And the Lincoln administration sought to win by enrolling African American combat troops. The Proclamation reversed military policy, decreeing that "such persons of suitable condition, will be received into the armed service of the United States to garrison forts, positions, stations, and other places, and to man vessels of all sorts in said service."[32] African Americans would be enlisted in the army and navy, not merely as laborers, nurses, and in other supporting roles – but as soldiers.

Confederates howled that emancipation was an atrocity and that the use of black soldiers was a massive crime. "Our own detestation of those who have attempted the most execrable measure recorded in the history of guilty man is tempered by profound contempt for the impotent rage which it discloses," President Jefferson Davis thundered that January, promising that any officer taken in command of African American troops would be treated as if "exciting servile insurrection" or encouraging slaves to rebel, the punishment for which was death.[33] Many white Northerners were outraged as well. The Democratic *Cincinnati Inquirer* yelped that Lincoln's proclamation amounted to "a complete overthrow of the Constitution he swore to protect and defend."[34] Political divisions had

---

[32] Abraham Lincoln, "Emancipation Proclamation," in *The Collected Works of Abraham Lincoln*, *Vol. 6*, ed. Roy P. Basler (New Brunswick, NJ: Rutgers University Press, 1953), 29–30.

[33] Jefferson Davis, "Message of Jefferson Davis," January 12, 1863, in *Rebellion Record: A Diary of American Events*, ed. Frank Moore (New York, NY: G. P. Putnam, 1863), 380.

[34] Michael Burlingame, *Abraham Lincoln: A Life*, *Vol. 2* (Baltimore, MD: Johns Hopkins University Press, 2008), 471.

reemerged, and Lincoln's most fiery opposition in the North came from Peace Democrats or Copperheads who opposed emancipation and urged a negotiated end to the war, recognizing the Confederacy if necessary.

African Americans greeted the Emancipation Proclamation with joy not unmixed with trepidation. Speaking to a crowd at New York's Cooper Union, Reverend Henry Highland Garnet praised President Lincoln, saying that the proclamation was the fulfillment of a promise made "with his eyes set on the God of Justice, and determined to disenthral[l] an injured race and glorify God." Slavery was not gone, Garnet warned, but it had "lost its power." Garnet urged his audience "never to mind what Jeff. Davis says about hanging." The Confederate president "must know that the black man, when he joins the army, goes in to win."[35] Veteran of the Underground Railroad Harriet Tubman took a steely-eyed view of the Emancipation Proclamation. "I can't rejoice no more," she said, contemplating the hard work of making good on freedom's promise.[36]

Black soldiers, scouts, and spies soon became the Union's most intrepid allies on Southern soil. Tubman was serving in Beaufort, South Carolina, nursing sick refugees and assisting both the army and aid workers helping thousands of formerly enslaved people when the Emancipation Proclamation was issued. There one of the first black regiments, the 1st South Carolina Volunteer Infantry, was in camp. Abolitionist officers had recruited black volunteers in the area early in 1862, but had trouble retaining them since the army refused to pay them. Soldiering was open solely to males, but female recruits like Tubman served in pivotal roles. She helped recruit the 2nd South Carolina Volunteer Infantry.

Tubman soon became a scout, a spy, and a military leader. African Americans knew Tubman as Moses for her work freeing bondspeople from Maryland's Eastern Shore. John Brown had called her General Tubman, and in South Carolina, she worked closely with one of Brown's comrades in the Kansas struggle, Colonel James Montgomery. She recruited soldiers, gathered intelligence from among formerly enslaved refugees, moved about freely, and bought provisions for the army. From a network of black watermen and other African-descended informants, she learned of Confederate positions, troop strengths, rebel traps, and stores of supplies such as rice and cotton.

[35] *The [Boston] Liberator*, January 16, 1863, 9.
[36] Sarah H. Bradford, *Harriet: The Moses of Her People* (New York, NY: George R. Lockwood and Son, 1886), 93.

In June 1863, Montgomery relied on Tubman to plan and lead an armed raid up the Combahee River, undertaken by the 2nd South Carolina. There they captured supplies, burned or flooded rebel plantations, and raised a call for all the enslaved people in the area to flee to the Union forces – while terrified whites threatened to whip or shoot any black defector. Hundreds arrived off of plantations. "They came down every road, across every field," Tubman later recalled, "just as they had left their work and their cabins; women with children clinging around their necks, hanging to their dresses, running behind, all making at full speed for 'Lincoln's gun-boats.'" Some 800 self-emancipated people swarmed a riverbank near Union steamers, some with livestock such as pigs and others with baskets of belongings. Enslavers had spread rumors that Union soldiers were devils. "Mas'r said de Yankees had horns and tails," Tubman recalled one man saying as he boarded a Union steamboat. But word was passed along that "Lincoln's gun-boats come to set them free."[37]

In the spring of 1863, African American leaders like Frederick Douglass traveled thousands of miles recruiting volunteers for all-black regiments being raised in states like Massachusetts. "By every consideration which binds you to your enslaved fellow-countrymen, and the peace and welfare of your country," Douglass told potential black soldiers in New York, "by every aspiration which you cherish for the freedom and equality of yourselves and your children; by all the ties of blood and identity which make us one with the brave black men now fighting our battles in Louisiana and in South Carolina, I urge you to fly to arms, and smite with death the power that would bury the government and your liberty in the same hopeless grave."[38] Douglass was instrumental in raising the 54th and 55th Massachusetts Volunteer Regiments, his sons Charles and Lewis serving in the 54th. Other prominent leaders like Martin R. Delany recruited from a network of African American expatriates and free black Northerners.

Yet Union resistance to black soldiers was institutional and political. The army refused to pay bounties or recruitment bonuses to African American volunteers, paid black soldiers less than whites, and both military and civilian leaders dug in their heels against them. But the new recruits were animated by a higher purpose. "We are determined to act

---

[37] Sarah H. Bradford, *Scenes in the Life of Harriet Tubman* (Auburn, NY: W. J. Moses, 1869), 40 (quotations).

[38] Frederick Douglass, "Men of Color, to Arms!" *Douglass' Monthly* (March 21, 1863): 1.

like men, and fight, money or not," James Henry Gooding wrote from camp in Readville, Massachusetts, where the 54th was training, but the army needed to hold up its end. "Colored men generally, as a class," Gooding argued, "hav[e] nothing to depend upon but their daily labor; so, consequently, when they leave their labors and take up arms in defense of their country, their homes are left destitute of those little necessities which their families must enjoy as well as those of white men."[39] Most black volunteers passionately believed in the cause of freedom and Union, but they could not feed their families with it. Meanwhile, Abraham Lincoln tried persuading opponents of black soldiers to relent and cast aside prejudice. "The colored population is the great available and yet unavailed of, force for restoring the Union," the president wrote Senator Andrew Johnson of Tennessee. "The bare sight of fifty thousand armed, and drilled black soldiers on the banks of the Mississippi, would end the rebellion at once."[40] Like many Southern Unionists, however, Johnson was not easily convinced of the virtues of African-descended troops.

Grim tests for African American soldiers arrived that summer. In the dark early morning hours of June 7, 1863, at Milliken's Bend, Louisiana, Confederate regiments from Texas surprised and attacked federal soldiers of the 8th, 9th, 11th, and 13th Louisiana Infantry Regiments and the 1st Mississippi Infantry, along with the 23rd Iowa Infantry. The Union position on the west bank of the Mississippi River was fifteen miles north of Vicksburg. The Louisiana and Mississippi units were recently recruited African American regiments. Poorly armed and in some cases poorly led, they were overwhelmed by Confederates. The 9th Louisiana lost more than two-thirds of its men. Reports on both sides concurred that the black soldiers fought valiantly. But the Texas Confederates exacted revenge. After capturing nearly eighty federals and murdering two Union officers and perhaps some African-descended soldiers, Confederates sent the rest to slavery in Texas.[41] Soldiers in all-white regiments could expect rough treatment and deprivation as prisoners of war, but African American

[39] James Henry Gooding, *On the Altar of Freedom: A Black Soldier's Civil War Letters from the Front*, ed. Virginia Matzke Adams (Amherst, MA: University of Massachusetts Press, 1991), 7.

[40] Abraham Lincoln to Andrew Johnson, March 26, 1863, in *The Collected Works of Abraham Lincoln*, Vol. 6, ed. Roy P. Basler (New Brunswick, NJ: Rutgers University Press, 1953), 149–50.

[41] Bob Luke and John David Smith, *Soldiering for Freedom: How the Union Army Recruited, Trained, and Deployed the U.S. Colored Troops* (Baltimore, MD: Johns Hopkins University Press, 2014), chap. 5.

soldiers faced summary execution and enslavement, which included bondage for freeborn black soldiers.[42]

Later that month, the 54th Massachusetts showed the nation that African-descended soldiers lacked nothing in bravery and determination. It let a frontal assault on Fort Wagner on Morris Island, South Carolina, which protected Charleston Harbor. The Confederates fired from fortified positions, and the 54th advanced southward on an open beach booby-trapped with palmetto spikes, struggling across a ten-foot-wide moat, and scrambling up fortifications. Confederates furious at the sight of black soldiers fought ferociously. The risky assault failed. The 54th lost 281 men that night killed, wounded, or missing. Two captains were killed, as was the colonel, Robert Gould Shaw. Sergeant-Major Lewis Douglass had his sword shot off his body by canister artillery fire. During the assault, Sergeant William Carney witnessed the flagbearer fall. Throwing his musket down, he picked up the flag and scrambled up to the fort, raising the colors to rally his comrades. Miraculously, he survived. For his bravery, he was awarded the Congressional Medal of Honor – but had to wait until 1900 for it to be awarded. In the wake of the unsuccessful assault, Confederates stripped the bodies of the slain and buried them in a ditch.[43]

The combat service of African-descended soldiers was a down payment on civil and political rights. "Once let the black man get upon his person the brass letter, U.S.," Frederick Douglass argued in July 1863, "let him get an eagle on his button, and a musket on his shoulder and bullets in his pocket, and there is no power on earth or under the earth which can deny that he has earned the right of citizenship in the United States."[44] That was a pious hope. But the 54th's heroism in South Carolina was overshadowed by two momentous yet costly Union victories, the fall of Vicksburg, Mississippi, on July 4 and the Battle of Gettysburg, which ended on July 3, sending the Confederate Army of Northern Virginia retreating south into Virginia's Shenandoah Valley. The Confederate armies'

[42] William A. Dobak, *Freedom by the Sword: The U.S. Colored Troops. 1862–1867* (Washington, DC: US Army Center of Military History, 2011); *Black Soldiers in Blue African American Troops in the Civil War Era*, ed. John David Smith (Chapel Hill, NC: University of North Carolina Press, 2002).

[43] George S. Burkhardt, *Confederate Rage, Yankee Wrath: No Quarter in the Civil War* (Carbondale, IL: Southern Illinois University Press, 2007), chap. 5.

[44] Douglass quoted in Christopher B. Booker, *"I Will Wear No Chain!" A Social History of African-American Males* (Westport, CT: Praeger, 2000), 69 (quotation); Douglas R. Egerton, *The Wars of Reconstruction: The Brief, Violent History of America's Most Progressive Era* (New York, NY: Bloomsbury Press, 2014).

offensive strategy had failed, but a defensive strategy would prolong the life of the proslavery republic for another twenty-one months.

Freedpeople faced many hardships even if they did not join Union forces. For most of the enslaved, freedom came contingently and haltingly, and for many, sickness and death arrived close on its heels. Of the 4 million African-descended people in slavery in 1860, about 500,000 sickened or died in wartime and its immediate aftermath. Waves of epidemics of smallpox and other communicable diseases afflicted people exposed to rough conditions in refugee camps.[45] Hundreds of thousands of those like John Washington had fled their homes and old neighborhoods to the Union lines, only to find conditions that could be more perilous than slavery. The army wanted able-bodied adults, not the full complement of old and young, sick and crippled.

Those without options ended up in refugee camps like those outside Washington, DC. Harriet Jacobs arrived in the District of Columbia in the summer of 1862, to "where the shackles had just fallen," she wrote. At "[g]overnment head-quarters for the contrabands here," Jacobs recalled, "I found men, women and children all huddled together, without any distinction or regard to age or sex. Some of them were in the most pitiable condition. Many were sick with measles, diptheria [*sic*], scarlet and typhoid fever. Some had a few filthy rags to lie on; others had nothing but the bare floor for a couch." Employers showed up to hire the refugees and pay slaves' wages of $4 per month for "[s]ingle women," $2.50 to $3 per month for "a woman with one child." Men earned $10. Confined in sickly contraband camps, "[t]he little children pine like prison birds for their native element." And, she sighed, "[e]ach day brings its fresh additions of the hungry, naked and sick." Many were dying alone. "Men, women and children lie here together, without a shadow of those rites which we give to our poorest dead," she reported. "There they lie, in the filthy rags they wore from the plantation. Nobody seems to give it a thought." As the overwhelmed camp superintendents processed new arrivals, refugees took ill and died. One morning, Jacobs recalled, "I saw lying there five children. By the side of them lay a young man. He escaped, was taken back to Virginia, whipped nearly to death, escaped again the next night, dragged his body to Washington, and died, literally cut to pieces. Around his feet I saw a rope; I could not see that put into the grave

---

[45] Chandra Manning, *Troubled Refuge: Struggling for Freedom in the Civil War* (New York, NY: Knopf, 2016).

with him."[46] Much of that hardship and suffering came about because of poor war planning.

Union armies were strained by the unexpectedly high casualties, two-thirds from disease, and they were unable or unwilling to perform refugee resettlement during wartime. Freedpeople faced desperate alternatives. Army officers seldom welcomed refugees, and erstwhile enslavers – often bitter at their sudden loss of slave property – suddenly demanded rent and work should the formerly enslaved seek to stay in their homes. Uncertainties multiplied and, in the words of one historian, "[w]hen slaves ran away from Southern plantations, they ran towards a war."[47] Less than 15 percent of those enslaved in the Confederacy were freed during the war, but they included hundreds of thousands who fled to the Union army or Union-controlled areas. Between 1862 and 1868, waves of epidemics of smallpox and other communicable diseases afflicted people exposed to rough conditions in refugee camps. About 60,000 died.[48] To the young and able, like John Washington and his family, freedom held shimmering possibilities. But the march to freedom quickly got bogged down for thousands like the formerly enslaved Miller family of Lincoln County, Kentucky.

Joseph Miller fled to Camp Nelson, Kentucky, with his wife and four children in the bitterly cold November of 1864. Joseph wanted to enlist and fight for the Union cause, but worried "that if I enlisted he would not maintain them and I knew they would be abused by him when I left." The Millers – Joseph, his wife, and four children aged four, seven, nine, and ten – were seeking freedom and refuge, and the camp – about twenty miles south of Lexington – was a beacon. The fort there housed between 3,000 and 8,000 US soldiers, and the camp provisioned parts of the Army of Ohio. But the Union commanders there did not see themselves as liberators.[49]

The Millers arrived along with about 500 former bondspersons. Some took months to arrive, and others died on the way. But at the gates the Millers were allowed entry on one condition. Joseph Miller must enlist in

[46] Harriet A. Jacobs, "Life among the Contrabands," *The [Boston] Liberator* September 5, 1862, 3, online: http://docsouth.unc.edu/fpn/jacobs/support5.html, accessed: August 31, 2016.

[47] Jim Downs, *Sick from Freedom: African-American Illness and Suffering during the Civil War and Reconstruction* (New York, NY: Oxford University Press, 2012), 22.

[48] Downs, *Sick from Freedom*, chap. 4.

[49] "Affidavit of Joseph Miller, 26 Nov. 1864, filed with H-8 1865, Registered Letters Received, er. 3379, TN Asst. Comr. RG 105 [A-6148]," in *Freedom: A Documentary*

the US Army before his family would be fed and sheltered. He did, becoming one of 179,000 able-bodied black men to join the army. The deal was in keeping with the army's need for soldiers and laborers and implied a transaction: service in exchange for security and support. But Miller's deal was quickly broken.

Army officials had their own priorities. On November 22, 1864, the commander of Camp Nelson decided it was time for freedpeople to leave and ordered the refugee village on the camp's outskirts to be broken up and the refugees dispersed. Early the next "bitter cold" morning, Joseph Miller recalled, a guard on horseback ordered them to leave at once. Mrs. Miller protested, saying her seven-year-old boy was gravely sick and might not survive the cold. The guard said that did not matter. He had his orders. "He told my wife and family," Miller later testified, "that if they did not get up into the wagon which he had he would shoot the last one of them." And so they fled, leaving clothes and most of their belongings, to a drafty church meetinghouse six miles from camp.

Miller, now in the army, was not given leave to find his family until after dark that Wednesday night. "I found my wife and children shivering with cold and famished with hunger." None had had anything to eat all day. "My boy was dead," he recalled, and the rest of the family was huddled with hundreds of other African American refuges likewise evicted.[50] And the process was repeated at other camps throughout the South as military demands for able-bodied laborers and soldiers conflicted with the desperate strategies of formerly enslaved people to forge a new life in freedom.

The expectations of soldiers like Joseph Miller were at odds with the practical imperatives of the army. After 1862, the Union fought for emancipation as a war aim, but officials wanted work out of black freedpeople. To that end, the army and the Freedmen's Bureau, created in March 1865 as the Bureau of Freedmen, Refugees, and Abandoned Lands, insisted that freedpeople work if they were able. Officers and agents sought able-bodied laborers, primarily men. There was little space in that vision of Reconstruction for the family integrity of those forced to flee with little beyond the tattered clothes on their back. Agents sent able-bodied workers off to work, sometimes at great distance from

History of Emancipation, 1861–1867, Series 2, Book 1: The Black Military Experience, ed. Ira Berlin (Cambridge: Cambridge University Press, 1982), 270 (quotations); Downs, *Sick from Freedom,* chap. 1.
50 "Affidavit of Joseph Miller," 270 (quotations).

loved ones, while sequestering the ill or disabled in places where disease spread. And like the Millers, the army tended to move refugees in and out of camps, splitting families in the process. For those needing medical care, there was little nimbleness in the system that delivered aid to refugees, resulting in widespread illness that might have been contained and treated.

Emancipation or what bondspersons called Jubilee became a massive public health crisis in many parts of the South. The smallpox epidemic of the 1860s took an unusually heavy toll on African Americans, and so much so that health officials tended to identify the virus with black victims. Measles and other infectious diseases tore through camps and displaced populations. Blackness became so associated with disease that public health threats to whites were ignored at their peril. Dead bodies of African Americans were routinely buried without coffins, many without family or a funeral, and in a time and place where a "Good Death" approached the importance of baptism or marriage, the solitary, miserable, and anguished ordeal of dying among strangers visited untold thousands of refugees.[51] During wartime, in places, bodies of freedpeople killed by disease were dumped into trenches with dead horses. Some Union officials adopted the position of ex-enslavers that freedom actually made black people sick and that they were unsuited to it. That reinforced a racist stereotype of African-descended people as incapable of freedom and, by extension, citizenship or civil rights.

Even so, freedpeople went looking for scattered family members in heroic attempts to reverse generations of family separations. Charity Moss wanted information on "my two boys, James and Horace, one of whom was sold in Nashville and the other was sold in Rutherford [C]ounty," Tennessee. Moss was sold to Alabama and returned to Nashville in 1865, looking for her children.[52] Thornton Copeland wanted information "of my mother, whom I left in Fauquier [C]ounty, Va., in 1844, and I was sold in Richmond, Va." It had been twenty-one years since their parting when Copeland told readers of the *Colored Tennessean*, "I am very anxious to hear from my mother ... Betty [who] was sold by Col. Briggs to James French."[53] Some families did reunite, though the years had made siblings into strangers. Frederick Douglass reunited with his sister Eliza in 1864, twenty-six years after he ran off from slavery on

---

[51] Drew Gilpin Faust, *This Republic of Suffering: Death and the American Civil War* (New York, NY: Knopf, 2008), 7, passim.
[52] *The [Nashville] Colored Tennessean*, October 14, 1865, 3.
[53] *The [Nashville] Colored Tennessean*, October 7, 1865, 4.

Maryland's Eastern Shore, where she lived. A year later, Douglass received a message from a long-lost brother, who in 1867 went by the name Perry Downs. Douglass had changed names too. Forty years before, Frederick Bailey and Perry Bailey were separated when older brother Perry was bound away. But when they reunited in Rochester, New York, the Downs family – just up from slavery – had little in common with Douglass's middle-class children, who had been educated. The Downs family nevertheless stayed with the Douglasses for two years, living in a cabin built for them, before returning to the Eastern Shore, where Perry died in 1880.

The Civil War's emancipation struggle was led by African Americans, beginning with the pairs, families, and later scores who fled disloyal owners and pledged allegiance to the cause of Union and freedom. Freedpeople's power came primarily from their capacity to work, serve, and fight, and yet leaders like Douglass developed the struggles of millions of enslaved people into a freedom narrative that became a new way to frame the Civil War. A conflict Confederates began over the false assumption that the Lincoln administration was an abolitionist force turned into an abolition war. "Neither party expected for the war the magnitude or the duration which it has already attained," Lincoln declared in March 1865. "Neither anticipated that the cause of the conflict might cease with or even before the conflict itself should cease," and although enslavers' interest in human property "was somehow the cause of the war," Lincoln argued, the Civil War failed to decide what form freedom would take.[54] Radicals envisioned black freedom as full citizenship and equal protection of the law. But Confederate surrender in the spring of 1865 left open whether African Americans were on the road to citizenship or whether emancipation's fullest extent had been reached and with peace would come an erosion of freedom purchased ay such a great price. Begun in war, emancipation became a political process.

---

[54] Abraham Lincoln, "'Second Inaugural Address,' March 4, 1865," in *The Collected Works of Abraham Lincoln, Vol. 8*, ed. Roy P. Basler (New Brunswick, NJ: Rutgers University Press, 1953), 332–33.

12

No Justice, No Peace

War did not make slaves into citizens. Enslaved people's self-freedom and federal emancipation did away with chattel slavery, or legal property in people. But rather than ending suddenly, slavery transformed in the midst of civil war, and while emancipation wiped slave wealth off of enslavers' balance sheets, it did not completely end forced labor. Victory in war did not change hearts. And constitutional amendments did not change minds. Not by themselves. Federal Reconstruction, beginning in wartime and extending until the late 1870s, was a halting, incremental, and incomplete process of working out what freedom meant for African Americans. For most freedpeople, it was an agonizing transition from a form of chattel slavery to quasi-free labor in a new political and social order. Some achieved citizenship. African Americans for the first time served in the US Congress, in state legislatures, and in state executive offices.[1] But others fell into slavery by another name, in convict labor, forced labor, and debt bondage. And that resulted in large part from Reconstruction policies embodying a contradiction between justice and peace. The US Civil War was won on the promise of black freedom. But peace in a restored Union depended on drawing ex-rebels back into the political order. The latter imperative wavered in the face of black political activism but ultimately emerged triumphant.

When the Abraham Lincoln administration commenced Reconstruction during wartime, the president sought a middle course. It was a titanic gamble that an unexpectedly costly and terrible war would be resolved

---

[1] Ira Berlin, *The Long Emancipation: The Demise of Slavery in the United States* (Cambridge, MA: Harvard University Press, 2015).

and the nation healed by an accommodation with the forces of change. After 1862, a return to chattel slavery was not an option. But the Lincoln administration was not prepared to push for citizenship rights for formerly enslaved people either. That ambiguous policy set the tone for Reconstruction, giving victories to white supremacist Unionists and betraying the promises of emancipation.

Like many white Americans, Lincoln was ambivalent about African Americans as citizens. He told a delegation of African Americans visiting the White House in the summer of 1862, "You and we are different races," the differences being so great that "I think your race suffer very greatly, many of them by living among us, while ours suffer greatly from your presence." Even after slavery, the president predicted, "you are yet far removed from being placed on an equality with the white race." He proposed colonizing them out of their country, to a place in Central America where – if as few as twenty-five went – "I could make a successful commencement." Two thousand African Americans had emigrated to Haiti in 1861–62, but many returned.[2] Colonization had always been more political than practical. And Lincoln sighed that the moral imperative of emancipation carried a heavy political liability when it came to the question of black civil rights.

At first Lincoln decided that building goodwill with ex-Confederates would lead to peace, and justice would follow gradually as former rebels accepted the verdict of the war. Louisiana was a test of that policy. It was the most urban state in the South, and New Orleans had a vibrant African-descended middle class. Union forces had captured most of the state early in the war. Lincoln's vision for Louisiana Republicans was broad and inclusive, a middle position between Radicals' civil rights program and conservatives' resistance to emancipation. Late in 1863, Lincoln ordered Louisiana's new military governor – and former US House Speaker – General Nathaniel P. Banks to "give us a free-state re-organization of Louisiana, in the shortest possible time."[3] Early in 1864, Banks ordered new elections for state offices and constitutional convention delegates. Louisiana's 1852 constitution, amended in 1861 to pledge allegiance to the Confederacy, needed to be scrapped. But Banks did not enlist African

[2] Lincoln, quoted in Louis P. Masur, *Lincoln's Hundred Days: The Emancipation Proclamation and the War for the Union* (Cambridge, MA: Harvard University Press, 2012), 88.
[3] Abraham Lincoln to Nathaniel A. Banks, December 24, 1863, *The Collected Works of Abraham Lincoln, Vol. 7*, ed. Roy P. Basler (New Brunswick, NJ: Rutgers University Press, 1953), 90.

American support in Louisiana, instead focusing on Unionist whites and
even former enslavers.

And in a bid to draw in white support all over the occupied South,
Lincoln offered the Ten Percent Plan, under which a Confederate state
might reenter the Union should 10 percent of its electorate or white male
population swear allegiance to the US government and repudiate the
Confederacy. That low bar was meant to start the reunification process
in states like Virginia, a small fraction of which was Union-occupied. Ex-
Confederates swearing allegiance had to accept that slavery was over, but
Lincoln's amnesty proclamation of December 1863, set a tone that the
war would end with a peaceable reunion rather than treason trials and
executions of traitors.

But under such policies African Americans gained nothing but freedom. And even that legal freedom was often a mask for coercive labor
practices aimed at preserving slave-like conditions. In Louisiana, as elsewhere in the South, formerly enslaved people were often forced to
sign year-long labor contracts with former owners. Supposedly protected
from whippings, they nevertheless returned to work for ex-enslavers who
wielded all the enforcement power in the contracts. And when elections
were held in 1864, voting was restricted to white males who swore
a loyalty oath. Ex-Confederates could vote so long as they took the
oath; black Unionists and even veterans could not.

Moderate Republican Michael Hahn was elected Louisiana's first
Reconstruction governor in February 1864. Lincoln asked Hahn for
some concessions on black voting rights. "I barely suggest for your private
consideration," the president wrote, "whether some of the colored people
may not be let in – as, for instance, the very intelligent, and especially those
who have fought gallantly in our ranks. They would ... help ... keep the
jewel of liberty within the family of freedom."[4] But Hahn refused, deciding that African Americans would be excluded no matter their intelligence, loyalty, or service.

Reconstruction in Louisiana seemed to be a victory for moderates.
It abolished slavery with no compensation to owners (or reparations to
those enslaved). It provided for free public education for all Louisianans
ages six to eighteen, set minimum wages of public employees, and established the state capital at New Orleans. But it also denied black men the
ballot box, leaving it open to future legislators to decide the issue. White

---

[4] Abraham Lincoln to Michael A. Hahn, March 13, 1864, Basler, *Collected Works of
Abraham Lincoln*, Vol. 7, 243.

Louisiana voters adopted it by more than a four-to-one margin in July, and General Banks took it to Congress, returning to Washington, DC, to lobby for its passage. Meanwhile, Louisiana's fourteen delegates to the 1864 Republican National Convention in Baltimore voted unanimously for Lincoln's re-nomination for president (and ultimately supported Andrew Johnson of Tennessee for vice president). Lincoln supported the compromise Louisiana constitution, but it alarmed Radicals in Congress.

Congressional Republicans in Washington, DC, were divided on the issue of black civil rights and the role ex-Confederates were to play in Reconstruction. Radicals worried that sacrificing a chance at African American civil rights would hollow out any Union victory. Deaths numbered in the hundreds of thousands, and Radicals feared a quick return to white rule would waste the sacrifice, punish black veterans who risked all for the Union cause, and undermine emancipation itself. Radicals did not trust ex-Confederates whom many considered traitors and argued that the most staunchly loyal Unionists in the South were African-descended. African American patriots – not ex-Rebels – should be rewarded, Radicals argued, deciding that Lincoln's plan relied too much on ex-Confederates' goodwill while penalizing formerly enslaved people.

African American abolitionists were growing frustrated by Lincoln's moderation in the face of the war's towering costs and a moment they knew might easily slip away. Frederick Douglass thundered that the war needed to be "no war but an [a]bolition war; no peace but an [a]bolition peace; liberty for all, chains for none; the black man a soldier in war, a laborer in peace; a voter at the South as well as at the North; America his permanent home, and all Americans his fellow countrymen."[5] Douglass spoke for a political constituency that was largely disenfranchised but also for a moral constituency of nearly 200,000 African Americans in Union uniforms or who worked as loyal scouts and laborers supporting the war effort. He spoke for 4 million would-be citizens. And Douglass kept up pressure on the administration to change its policy from colonization to civil rights while he lobbied for equal pay for black soldiers for most of 1864.

Worried that Lincoln's détente with moderates like Hahn would sacrifice victory, Radicals in Congress opposed the Ten Percent Plan. Henry Winter Davis of Maryland and Benjamin Wade of Ohio proposed the

---

[5] Frederick Douglass, "'The Mission of the War,' January 13, 1864," in *The Frederick Douglass Papers, Series 1: Speeches, Debates, and Interviews, Vol. 4, 1864–80*, ed. John W. Blassingame (New Haven, CT: Yale University Press, 1991), 11–13.

Wade-Davis Bill in 1864, which required a majority in each ex-Confederate state to swear that they had never supported the Confederacy. It set an impossible standard meant to thrust control over Reconstruction into the hands of Congress rather than the president and state conventions. Lincoln refused to sign the Wade-Davis Bill in the summer of 1864, and it never became law. Conflict between Lincoln's moderates and Radical Republicans grew when House leaders refused to accept the 1864 Louisiana constitution or seat representatives elected under it. In the Senate, abolitionist Charles Sumner of Massachusetts threatened to filibuster the question of Louisiana's readmission under Banks's constitution. What abolitionist Wendell Phillips called "Mr. Lincoln's model" of Reconstruction was jammed up in intraparty disagreement over black civil rights. Lincoln admitted defeat but turned his attention to winning reelection and with it a costly strategy to win the Civil War.[6]

The presidential election of 1864 was less a contest between Lincoln and the Radicals than one between Lincoln's moderation and Democratic conservatism. Republicans campaigned that summer and fall on Lincoln's moderate vision of emancipation and reunification following Confederate surrender. Democrats nominated former Army of the Potomac commander General George B. McClellan. McClellan's Democratic Party was divided as well. War Democrats like McClellan favored ending the war and restoring the Union but welcoming back ex-Confederates as fellow citizens, without penalties and without African American civil rights. Peace Democrats like McClellan's vice presidential running mate, George H. Pendleton of Ohio, favored a negotiated settlement with the Confederacy that included reversing the Emancipation Proclamation. Peace Democrats, sometimes called Copperheads, were a vocal minority within the party and included Confederate sympathizers who wrote the 1864 national Democratic Party platform. Both Democratic and Republican campaigns featured nasty and acrimonious caricatures and accusations, Democrats arguing that Republicans favored black equality in social and political contexts. Lincoln, Democrats insisted, secretly wanted freed black men to marry and father children with white women. They introduced "miscegenation" into American politics. It was

---

[6] Wendell Phillips to Edward Gilbert, May 27, 1864, cited in Peyton McCrary, *Abraham Lincoln and Reconstruction: The Louisiana Experiment* (Princeton, NJ: Princeton University Press, 1978), 5.

a disingenuous revival of an old charge that Lincoln favored social equality for African Americans.[7]

Republicans insisted that Union – not black equality – was the sacred object of the war. Some charged Democrats with being traitors, urging voters to keep the Lincoln administration and allow it to lead the Union to victory. Republicans even changed their name for the 1864 election to the National Union Party, which downplayed the implications of emancipation. The War Department encouraged voting among soldiers and veterans, most of whom supported their commander in chief and a platform of winning the war. Lincoln won by a landslide in the Electoral College, 212–12, including Louisiana's seven electoral votes for Lincoln and Johnson.

After the presidential election, the political question shifted from whether emancipation was final to what kind of freedom African Americans would enjoy. Reconstruction policies were paramount in that debate, and Congress's top priority became the passage of a constitutional amendment abolishing chattel slavery in the United States. Lincoln had promised to do that in his second term, and he did not wait on military victory. The war was not yet over by the winter of 1864–65, but the Confederacy was faltering. Union forces controlled the Mississippi River, effectively dividing Arkansas, Louisiana, and Texas from the East. And General William Tecumseh Sherman's devastating 1864 March to the Sea, featuring the burning of Atlanta and Columbia, South Carolina, cut a swath of ruin through the center of the eastern Confederacy. In that climate, moderate Republicans brought about the crowning achievement of the Lincoln administration.

In January 1865, Congress passed the Thirteenth Amendment to the Constitution outlawing slavery. It was a daunting undertaking. The US Constitution had not been amended since 1804, and the first fight concerned whether it needed to be amended at all. Passing the Thirteenth Amendment took nearly eleven months and involved a series of compromises, including outright bribes. Radicals Thaddeus Stephens in the House and Sumner in the Senate proposed an amendment early in 1864 that outlawed slavery while guaranteeing legal equality to all citizens

---

[7] Jean H. Baker, *Affairs of Party: The Political Culture of Northern Democrats in the Mid-Nineteenth Century* (Ithaca, NY: Cornell University Press, 1983); Elise Lemire, *"Miscegenation": Making Race in America* (Philadelphia, PA: University of Pennsylvania Press, 2002), chap 5; John C. Waugh, *Reelecting Lincoln: The Battle for the 1864 Presidency* (New York, NY: Da Capo Press, 1997).

regardless of race, color, or previous condition of slavery. Sumner borrowed language from the 1789 French Declaration of the Rights of Man. Moderate Republicans outmaneuvered Sumner and the Radicals, putting the process in the hands of moderate members and using instead the Northwest Ordinance of 1787 as a model, adopting language that made no declarations about civil rights, ducking the question of both African American rights and women's rights. The proposed amendment was modified to attract moderate Republicans and even some Democrats. Timing of the Thirteenth Amendment was critical. Most Southern states were not represented in Congress, so the old proslavery argument was off the table. And the final push for the amendment came between the 1864 elections and the seating of a new Congress in 1865, during the so-called lame duck session. It was nevertheless a controversial measure.

Emancipation was bitter medicine for enslavers who had lost so much else in a devastating war. The aggregate value of slave property in 1860 equaled nearly 19 percent of total US wealth, and as property enslaved people exceeded all other kinds except land itself. That value disappeared incrementally as enslaved people freed themselves. And it vanished finally when the Thirteenth Amendment was ratified. Enslavers lost a little more than $3 billion in property. Not all were Confederates. The Lincoln administration contemplated owner-compensated emancipation in the border slave states in 1862. There was historical precedent for the scheme. When Britain's parliament freed bondspersons in the West Indies in 1833, it had set up a £20 million fund to compensate enslavers for the loss of their human property. Despite some interest in compensated emancipation, Congress never passed it. The sole compensated enslavers were the owners of nearly 3,000 Washington, DC, bondspersons whom the government paid up to $300 per person. A supplemental act recognized the freedom of hundreds more as emancipation became a fact in the national capital. But enslaved people were given no compensation.[8]

The Thirteenth Amendment was a moderate victory, baked in an intensely hot political furnace. The final version was passed on January 31, 1865, in a narrow House vote in which a handful of Democrats crossed over to side with the vast majority of Republicans. The Senate followed, approving an amendment that was elegantly terse and deliberately limited. "Neither slavery nor involuntary servitude, except as a punishment for crime whereof the party shall have been duly

---

[8] Edward E. Baptist, *The Half Has Never Been Told: Slavery and the Making of American Capitalism* (New York, NY: Basic Books, 2014), 246.

convicted, shall exist within the United States, or any place subject to their jurisdiction." Congress had the power to enforce it. The amendment prevented states from reestablishing chattel slavery. It solved the problem of the Emancipation Proclamation because it wrote emancipation into the fundamental law – the Constitution. No president or Congress could reinstate chattel slavery. Nothing but freedom appeased civil rights opponents North and South, while leaving enough room for civil rights proponents to hope to build on it. But between passage in January 1865 and ratification ten months later, the ramifications of "nothing but freedom" became brutally clear.[9]

By the close of 1865, it was clear that the Civil War was not a matrix of moral decision-making. The contest of arms did not win arguments concerning race or the wrongness of a white supremacist vision of a Confederate republic. Overwhelming Union force did not win hearts or allegiances among the defeated. War did not establish the rightness of causes, just the deadness of those whose loss compelled provisional submission in the survivors. And Confederates surrendered armies, not ideas. The massive task left for the victors was to reconstruct the devastated former Confederacy according to the principles of freedom the Union proclaimed when it made emancipation a war aim.

Reconstruction's principal flaw in 1865 was in sacrificing the moral meanings leaders like Abraham Lincoln attached to military victory for the sake of economic recovery and swift political reunification. That crystallized in the seeming imperative to have black people in the South producing cotton again, which led white Northerners to turn away from bringing slavery to a true end, the amendment notwithstanding. And that was an opening ex-Confederates seized, taking by foul means what they had failed to win on the battlefield. It need not have turned out that way. When Congress passed the Thirteenth Amendment outlawing slavery, freedom looked bountiful.

In parts of the old Confederacy, it seemed like enslaved people would get freedom and land on which to establish themselves as independent citizens. The two were intimately connected since most freedpeople were mainly farmers who needed land in order to support economic independence. Freedom and resources could establish the basis for citizenship, strengthening their claim to equal rights. General William T. Sherman issued Special Field Order 15 in January 1865, promising "respectable"

---

[9] Eric Foner, *Nothing but Freedom: Emancipation and Its Legacy* (Baton Rouge, LA: Louisiana State University Press, 1983).

heads of African-descended families forty acres of confiscated land and a mule to work it.[10] Although the land subject to the order was just a thin strip of seacoast in South Carolina, Georgia, and Florida, news of Sherman's proclamation electrified African Americans, hinting at reparations for slavery and rewards for loyalty to black Unionists who helped win the war.[11]

But in actual practice, wartime land confiscation was a policy meant to punish Confederate disloyalty and shift the burden of maintenance to the formerly enslaved themselves. Called the Port Royal Experiment, it was a policy designed to get African-descended freedpeople back to work and came with no promise of citizenship. Sherman was an army general, not a social engineer or a Radical. He had predicted in 1864 that "[s]lavery will exist in the South after the conclusion of peace, let the war terminate as it may."[12] Under the Special Field Order, freedpeople's settlements were segregated from whites to prevent violence. As if to underscore the message, the Union commander at Charleston urged freedpeople to return to the fields, saying, "the Union army brought you the right to be free, but not to be idle. ... Remember that the hoe, the spade and the plough, are the true remedies for idleness, wrong and misery."[13] That paternalistic attitude toward freedpeople soon became institutionalized.

The Freedman's Bureau, officially known as the Bureau of Freedmen, Refugees, and Abandoned Lands, was formed early in 1865 by the Lincoln administration and run as an agency of the War Department. In practice, it assisted those displaced by war, black or white. Led by General Oliver Otis Howard, its mandate was to provide emergency services to refugees and help to allocate the labor of able-bodied workers. It directed resources from benevolent organizations, setting up schools for both freedpeople and displaced whites and allocating medical care, however disastrously meager the resources. Agents lectured freedpeople on the necessity of work. Soldiers worked as security forces, and officers arbitrated disputes arising over work contracts. As the war reached its final months, it looked

---

[10] William T. Sherman, "Special Field Order 15, January 16, 1865," in *Milestone Documents in African American History: Exploring Primary Sources, Volume 2, 1853–1900*, ed. Paul Finkelman (Dallas, TX: Schlager Group, 2010), 607.

[11] Steven Hahn, *A Nation under Our Feet: Black Political Struggles in the Rural South from Slavery to the Great Migration* (Cambridge, MA: Harvard University Press, 2003), chaps. 2–3.

[12] *Camden [NJ] Democrat*, January 7, 1865, 2.

[13] *Daily National Republican* (Washington, DC), April 14, 1865, 1.

like emancipation would be coupled with returning to fields with no political rights.

At his second inauguration in March 1865, President Abraham Lincoln struck a conciliatory tone with a prostrated Confederacy, calling for peace with "malice toward none, with charity for all," in hopes of rebuilding the republic with ex-Confederates' help. It was his most eloquent plea for moderation and goodwill. A return to slavery was impossible, he contended. "Fondly do we hope, fervently do we pray, that this mighty scourge of war may speedily pass away. Yet, if God wills that it continue until all the wealth piled by the bondsman's two hundred and fifty years of unrequited toil shall be sunk, and until every drop of blood drawn with the lash shall be paid by another drawn with the sword, as was said three thousand years ago, so still it must be said 'the judgments of the Lord are true and righteous altogether.'" Frederick Douglass endorsed Lincoln's words as "a sacred effort." But the president was assassinated on April 14, the day Arkansas ratified the Thirteenth Amendment.[14]

Moderates' optimism was sunk soon after Lincoln's assassination. Radicals despaired. The new president, Andrew Johnson, had been put on the 1864 presidential ticket because he was the last remaining loyal Southern US senator. But the Tennessean was staunchly opposed to African American civil rights and sympathized with the Confederate soldiers whom he held were tricked into fighting a treasonous secession war. When Johnson became president, the war was over, Confederate armies had surrendered, and the Thirteenth Amendment abolishing slavery was undergoing ratification. But instead of capitalizing on victory, President Johnson conciliated the vanquished.

Black freedom took four years of civil war and 750,000 deaths to win but was nearly lost before it was even constitutionally enshrined.[15] The Confederacy died in April and May 1865 as its eastern armies stacked their arms. Emancipation seemed an accomplished fact. But the Andrew Johnson administration showed clemency to rank-and-file rebels, offering amnesty to all but the Confederate leadership. That amounted to permission to form white supremacist state governments, doubling down on Lincoln's strategy of quick political reunion with ex-Confederates. But unlike Lincoln,

---

[14] Frederick Douglass, *Life and Times of Frederick Douglass, Written by Himself. His Early Life as a Slave, His Escape from Bondage, and His Complete History to the Present Time* (Boston, MA: De Wolfe and Fiske Company, 1892), 445.

[15] J. David Hacker, "A Census-Based Count of the Civil War Dead," *Civil War History* 57.4 (2011): 306–47.

Johnson was unwilling to consider former bondspersons as potential constituents. He was the former Tennessee governor and the sole US senator from a Confederate state to stay loyal. Republicans picked Johnson for vice president in 1864 as a gesture of amity to southern Unionists. And in 1865, Johnson did not stop ex-Confederate officers from returning to Southern state capitals, some in Rebel uniforms, where they set up governments by, of, and for themselves. As South Carolina's provisional governor, Benjamin Perry, explained, "[t]his is a white man's government and intended for white men only" in that majority black state.[16]

South Carolina ratified the Thirteenth Amendment in November 1865, but it also declared that Congress had no power to enforce its provisions. Instead, legislators added a warning "that any attempt by Congress towards legislating upon the political status of the former slaves, or their civil relations, would be contrary to the Constitution."[17] Alabama followed suit three weeks later, declaring, "that [the Thirteenth Amendment] does not confer upon Congress the power to legislate upon the political status of freedmen in this state."[18] Black civil rights were a state matter, legislators insisted. Former slaves would get nothing but freedom. Eager to accomplish political reunification, Secretary of State William H. Seward failed to comment on such signing statements as he certified the constitutional ratification. Meanwhile, President Johnson rescinded Sherman's Special Field Order 15 and with it the principle of redistributing ex-Confederate property.

Moderation gave way to a resurgent white supremacy. As Johnson pardoned ex-Confederates, the Democratic Party in former rebel states came roaring back, electing conservative white legislatures in 1865. The Louisiana Democratic convention pledged allegiance to the Union but resolved: "we hold this to be a [g]overnment of white people, made and to be perpetuated for the exclusive benefit of the white race; and ... that people of African descent cannot be considered as citizens of the United States."[19] That language was taken from the 1857 *Dred Scott*

---

[16] Benjamin F. Perry, cited in Eric L. McKitrick, *Andrew Johnson and Reconstruction* (New York, NY: Oxford University Press, 1960), 167.

[17] *A Political Manual for 1866 ... April 15, 1865 to July 4, 1866*, ed. Edward McPherson (Washington, DC: Philip and Solomons, 1866), 23.

[18] W. E. B. Du Bois, *Black Reconstruction in America: Toward a History of the Part Which Black Folk Played in the Attempt to Reconstruct Democracy in America, 1860–1880* (New Brunswick, NJ: Transaction Publishers, [1935] 2013), 185.

[19] *Appletons' Annual Cyclopædia and Register of Important Events of the Year 1865*, Volume V (New York, NY: Appleton and Company, 1866), 512.

ruling, affirming that slavery may be gone, but African Americans had no hope of citizenship either.

In the face of such a turnaround, black leaders argued with renewed insistence that nothing but freedom amounted to no freedom at all. "Slavery is not abolished until the black man has the ballot," Douglass argued in May 1865. "While the [l]egislatures of the South retain the right to pass laws making any discrimination between black and white, slavery still lives there."[20] Douglass and other leaders argued that the gains won by nearly 200,000 black veterans were being suddenly lost by a Johnson administration that oversaw Reconstruction for the seeming benefit of rank-and-file ex-Confederates. Lincoln's gamble on ex-Confederate cooperation had lost.

Even border slave states that had stayed loyal to the Union coupled emancipation with denial of black civil rights. Maryland, where Douglass was born and from where he escaped slavery, adopted a constitution in 1864 that ended slavery there but also confined citizenship to white men. Maryland punished rebels but also bound out some of the black children of poor parents under indentures that approximated slavery. At the same time, former enslavers cast off those too old to work. A "great number of aged and decrepit colored people [were] thrown upon the [g]overnment by their former masters," came a report that summer.[21] Maryland had ratified the Thirteenth Amendment almost immediately, on February 3, 1865. But Maryland legislators' attitudes reflected an undercurrent of white racism that saw black freedom and African American citizenship as two separate things. There, Douglass argued: "If the negro knows enough to pay taxes, he knows enough to vote; if the negro can form an opinion respecting the claims of rival candidates and parties, and knows good from evil, as all [Maryland's] laws concerning his conduct apply, he knows enough to vote."[22]

Freedmen did not wait for white legislators to come around on the issue. In Norfolk, Virginia, more than 1,000 African American men went to the polls in May 1865 to vote. But polling officials refused to count them, citing Virginia's 1864 constitution, which – like Louisiana's and Maryland's – abolished slavery but restricted voting to white men twenty-

---

[20] Frederick Douglass, "In What New Skin Will the Old Snake Come Forth?" May 10, 1865, *The Frederick Douglass Papers, Series 1*, Vol. 4, 83.

[21] *Baltimore Sun*, July 24, 1865, 4.

[22] Frederick Douglass, "A Friendly Word to Maryland," November 17, 1864, in *The Frederick Douglass Papers, Series 1*, Vol. 4, 49–50.

one and over. (Although Virginia was the Confederate capital, Union-occupied Virginia adopted a Reconstruction constitution in 1864 pledging loyalty to the United States.) Undeterred, the African American voters marched from polling places to churches, recording their votes in order to contest the election later. Massachusetts senator Charles Sumner, writing to the Colored Union League in Wilmington, North Carolina, in May 1865, urged them to "insist on all the rights and privileges of a citizen." "They belong to you," he assured them. "They are yours; and whoever undertakes to rob you of them is a usurper and imposter."[23]

Radical Republicans like Sumner – those who supported African American civil rights – were alarmed that the Johnson administration seemed to be siding with ex-Confederates over black loyalists and African American Union veterans. The forces of reaction were gathering again in Southern statehouses, and the opposition Democratic Party was returning with potentially more power than before. The Constitution's Three-Fifths Clause had been invalidated by the Thirteenth Amendment. Now African Americans were counted as five-fifths of a person for congressional representation. But in places where they were prevented from voting, conservative white Democrats were quickly shaping Reconstruction in their own image. Radicals realized by the end of 1865 that they needed a robust extension of civil rights to African Americans to safeguard the wartime victory against slavery. The sole hope of a continued Republican majority in Congress required black Republicans voting in the South. And while Radicals responded to presidential Reconstruction by developing a legislative civil rights program, African Americans struggled to build institutions promoting uplift and opportunity.

Freedpeople kept faith in Jubilee, building networks of support. In Charleston, South Carolina, Denmark Vesey's son Robert Vesey constructed a new African Methodist Episcopal Church.[24] African Americans migrated to black-led congregations near instantaneously, while white Southern churches became hubs of charitable societies for returning Confederate veterans. Free of white supervision, African American churches sponsored schools and served as centers of community life and

---

[23] Charles Sumner to Colored Citizens of North Carolina, May 13, 1865, in Charles Sumner, *The Works of Charles Sumner*, Vol. IX (Boston, MA: Lee and Shepherd, 1875), 364.

[24] Douglas R. Egerton, *He Shall Go Out Free: The Lives of Denmark Vesey* (Madison, WI: Madison House, 1999), xxiii–xxiv.

neighborhood protection. Christians who had never joined churches before flocked to them. Along with autonomy in religion, African-descended people sought opportunities for a better life on many fronts.[25]

Freedmen's schools were founded out of alliances with Northern charitable organizations, the Freedman's Bureau, and local residents. Many were set up by Bureau agents, recruiting Northern teachers instructing African-descended students. Most focused on reading, writing, and practical mathematics. Some Northern volunteers treated black students as subjects of homilies on thrift and hard work, but schools founded by philanthropic Northerners were overseen in many cases by local African Americans with their own priorities. By the time the Freedmen's Bureau expired in 1870, more than 4,300 schools had been founded with 9,500 teachers serving nearly 250,000 students. Many students attended for a short time, and schools tended to be clustered in places with resources, such as cities and towns. Some locations were well served, others were underserved, and many were bypassed because of geography or lack of transportation. After the Bureau closed, African American leaders took over. In Texas, African American teachers organized in 1884. Their attitudes and efforts had profound effects on African American literacy in the state. More than 60 percent of African American Texans over ten years old were literate by 1900, up from 25 percent in 1880, and as white Northern teachers returned home in the face of increasing violence, African American teachers took their places.[26]

Work followed a similar pattern of transition. Rather than looking to whites for guidance, many self-freed African Americans earned high wages in a tight wartime market despite having no clear legal rights. Those who could avoid punishing labor contracts moved to where labor was in demand, along with their skills. In some places, freedmen formed mutual aid associations allocating land, seed, farm animals, and credit. "It has been practically demonstrated that the freed-men were able to manage by themselves cane and cotton plantations," cheered a report on the Freedman's Aid Association of New Orleans in the summer of 1865.[27]

[25] Daniel W. Stowell, *Rebuilding Zion: The Religious Reconstruction of the South, 1863–1877* (New York, NY: Oxford University Press, 1998); James T. Campbell, *Songs of Zion: The African Methodist Episcopal Church in the United States* (New York, NY: Oxford University Press, 1995).

[26] Elizabeth Hayes Turner, *Women, Culture, and Community: Religion and Reform in Galveston, 1880–1920* (New York, NY: Oxford University Press, 1997), chap. 8; *The Freedmen's Bureau and Reconstruction: Reconsiderations*, ed. Paul A. Cimbala and Randall M. Miller (New York, NY: Fordham University Press, 1999), introduction.

[27] *New Orleans Tribune*, July 11, 1865, 4.

Freedpeople gathered in places like Edgefield, Tennessee, and Houston, Texas, to meet with leaders of the Freedmen's Bureau, the government's eyes and ears in the defeated Confederacy.

As presidential Reconstruction encouraged conservative reaction in ex-Confederate states, African Americans brought their concerns and reports of violence to the Freedmen's Bureau. John Berry had escaped slavery in northern Virginia and fought for the Union. When he returned home to his wife and six children in August 1865, his former owner hissed that "the war was not over yet – that the niggers were not free." When Berry asked for his family, the man shot back that "he should not have them – that nobody should take them away, and that if anybody came into the yard he would shoot them."[28] Berry sought federal protection, and agents of the Freedmen's Bureau provided security when and where they could.

They intervened in places where lynchings and mobbings might have otherwise occurred more. Federal troops saved several freedpeople from a lynch mob in Lauderdale Springs, near Meridian, Mississippi, in 1865. Planter William B. Wilkinson had sold his cotton in Meridian, cashing out in gold, and prominent local whites formed a vigilante group after a rumor spread that black workers had murdered him and taken his money. The posse broke into the freedmen's quarters searching for evidence, then rounded up and tortured a group of black suspects for several hours, attempting to coerce confessions. Despite beatings, the men denied killing Wilkinson and were saved from being hanged by US soldiers arriving from Meridian. The mystery unraveled the following day when the planter was found in a brothel after days of celebrating his cotton sale.[29] But the Freedmen's Bureau had limited power to counteract a much broader process.

Former enslavers stacked the labor market against freedpeople, insisting that only a system that mimicked slavery could salvage production and lead an economic recovery. And their object won some Northern support. "If the rebellion has exploded the idea that American cotton is the autocrat of the world's policy," a New York newspaper correspondent contended in July 1865, "it has also established the fact that American cotton is [k]ing of the cotton world." That was an overstatement. Indian production had more than doubled during the Civil War. Egypt produced three

---

[28] "Statement by a Discharged Virginia Black Soldier," August 11, 1865, *Freedmen and Southern Society Project*, online: http://www.freedmen.umd.edu/Berry.html, accessed: August 8, 2016.

[29] Dan T. Carter, "The Anatomy of Fear: The Christmas Day Insurrection Scare of 1865," *Journal of Southern History* 42 (August 1976): 349–50.

and a half times more cotton after the war than before. And Brazil's output was nearly four times its prewar total. But the great hope of Southern US recovery was still pinned to the staple. "A well-organized free-labor system may be made in time as efficient and productive as the forced-labor system of the past," the New York writer argued, but the benefits of free labor coupled with black civil rights were secondary to the abiding faith in a cotton-led recovery, however brutal its achievement.[30]

In the Deep South, that was a new twist on an old strategy: for the fifty years before the Civil War, the cotton states had responded to each economic crisis by forcing black people to make more white lint. The economic lifeline of a devastated South seemed to be made of cotton, and that path to recovery gave war-weary Northerners powerful reasons to look the other way when ex-Confederates exploited black workers.

Cotton states dug in their heels further in 1865, passing what were effectively re-enslavement schemes, including Black Codes designed to force African Americans back into servitude on their former owners' terms. The codes banned black landownership in cotton districts, denied black political participation, and criminalized black unemployment. Louisiana's was a revision of the antebellum slave code with "negro" substituted for "slave." Vagrancy and unemployment were criminalized. "Every negro is required to be in the regular service of some white person, or former owner, who shall be responsible for the conduct of said negro," and "impudence, swearing, or indecent language" to white people were crimes.[31] Mississippi's Vagrancy Act punished idleness and vice in African Americans, which it defined so broadly that any misstep could bring a charge. Vagrants included "idle and dissipated persons, beggars, jugglers, or persons practicing unlawful games or plays, runaways, common drunkards, common night-walkers, pilferers, lewd, wanton, or lascivious persons, in speech or behavior, common railers and brawlers, persons who neglect their calling or employment, misspend what they earn, or do not provide for the support of themselves or their families, or dependents, and all other idle and disorderly persons, including all who neglect all lawful business, habitually misspend their time by frequenting houses of ill-fame, gaming-houses, or tippling shops."[32] Fines of up to $100 equated to $20,300 in 2016 income value. Convictions could result in an offender being auctioned off for a term, being forced to work in a chain gang, or suffering the removal and forced labor of their children.[33]

Many African Americans faced the tortured logic of being required to exercise their newly won freedom of contract or else lose their personal freedom and be reduced to forced labor. Vagrancy acts were not unique to the South. The Mississippi Vagrancy Act was very similar to a Massachusetts law on the books for decades. Northern state legislatures thought it a good idea to punish idleness too, but work requirements were most pronounced in the cotton regions of the defeated Confederacy. Most freedpeople did not have the means to move to the North or to seek employment far from home. Northern states made clear that African-descended people were not welcome. Free labor ideology was racially coded in the North and West. In the South, African Americans had little choice.[34]

They received little sympathy. As General Carl Schurz contended after touring the South in 1865, "[a]side from the assumption that the negro will not work without physical compulsion, there appears to be another popular notion prevalent in the [S]outh ... that the negro exists for the special object of raising cotton, rice and sugar for the whites, and that it is illegitimate for him to indulge, like other people, in the pursuit of his own happiness in his own way."[35] Yet there was some internal mobility within the South.

Many freedmen sought job opportunities in cities and flocked there in 1865. Leaving farms or plantations, they moved into tent encampments or shantytowns outside of Southern cities, which drew rebukes from both labor-hungry Southern landowners and Freedmen's Bureau agents wary of rootless black men. Both applied pressure to bring laborers back to the fields and reassert white control over them.[36] Southern states moved to

---

[33] David M. Oshinsky, *"Worse than Slavery": Parchman Farm and the Ordeal of Jim Crow Justice* (New York, NY: Free Press, 1997), chaps. 2–3.

[34] Amy Dru Stanley, *From Bondage to Contract: Wage Labor, Marriage, and the Market in the Era of Slave Emancipation* (New York, NY: Cambridge University Press, 1998), chap. 3; Douglas A. Blackmon, *Slavery by Another Name: The Re-Enslavement of Black Americans from the Civil War to World War II* (New York, NY: Anchor Books, 2008).

[35] Carl Schurz, "Report on the Condition of the South, 1865," in *Reading the American Past: Volume I: To 1877*, 5th edn., ed. Michael P. Johnson (New York, NY: Bedford/St. Martin's, 2012), 310.

[36] Roger L. Ransom and Richard Sutch, *One Kind of Freedom: The Economic Consequences of Emancipation*, 2nd edn. (New York, NY: Cambridge University Press, 2001), 64.

limit black mobility. Mississippi passed the Enticement Act, which forbade luring a worker away from an employer with the promise of higher wages.

Many African Americans found themselves forced to work for hostile employers without even the formality of a conviction. "The bewildered and terrified freedmen know not what to do – to leave is death," reported a Freedmen's Bureau agent in southwestern Alabama in July 1865, "to remain is to suffer the increased burden imposed upon them by the cruel taskmaster, whose only interest is their labor, wrung from them by every device an inhuman ingenuity can devise; hence the lash and murder is resorted to to intimidate those whom fear of an awful death alone cause to remain."[37]

Forced to find employment but blocked from moving in many cases, black workers saw their bargaining power undercut. One labor contract bound a female worker in Louisiana "to labor diligently" for her former owner, and in her words, to "conduct myself as when I was owned by him as a SLAVE."[38] In many cases, cash wages were not on offer. James G. Tait of Wilcox County, Alabama, hired nineteen workers in the summer of 1865 for the balance of the year. All bound themselves to grow cotton and other crops under Tait's direction or that of an overseer and receive as payment "one-eighth part of the present growing crop of corn, fodder, cowpeas & ground peas, and also one half of the potatoes & sorghum syrup . . . & rice, & also to furnish food, clothing, houses, fuel, & medicines – & in bad cases a physician." Tait had discretion over workers' visits or visitors, and "[t]he [f]reedmen, or [l]aborers further bind themselves to account . . . for the value of any property of whatever kind or description that may be wasted, lost, or destroyed by reason of the negligence, or careless conduct," to be decided by Tait. The contract added that "if any of the said [f]reedmen or [l]aborers shall refuse, or fail to work faithfully & diligently," they would be fired.[39] Unpaid wages would be forfeited. Like most landowners broke by the war, the main

---

[37] Carl Schurz, "Report of Carl Schurz on the States of South Carolina, Georgia, Alabama, Mississippi, and Louisiana," in *Index to the Senate Executive Documents for the First Session of the Thirty-Ninth Congress of the United States of America, Vol. 1* (Washington, DC: Government Printing Office, 1866), 19.

[38] Copy of E. W. Reitzell's Contract, Columbia, Louisiana, August 1, 1865, Freedmen and Southern Society Project, online; www.freedmen.umd.edu/Webber.htm, accessed: August 9, 2016.

[39] Freedmen's Contract, July 31, 1865, LPR 35, Box 1, folder 2, Alabama Department of Archives and History, online: www.archives.alabama.gov/teacher/recon.recon1.html, accessed: August 9, 2016.

thing he had to offer workers was a share of what they made by the sweat of their faces. Some owners economized by hiring workers at planting season and casting them off in the summer doldrums when plants needed little attendance, then hiring back workers at harvest when they were most needed. Other employers continued to beat black workers like they were slaves.

By harvest time in the summer and fall of 1865, the Freedmen's Bureau had one arm pulling African Americans into freedom and one pushing them back into slavery.[40] It investigated cases of violence and maltreatment. But it also enforced contracts, even punitive ones. And cotton production rebounded from wartime lows, reaching 2 million bales in 1866. That was only about two-fifths the 1860 total, but seemed to support the course of holding black workers to labor in the fields. Even in the best cases of black workers producing their own cash crop, there were perils. "I particularly warn you against those [c]otton [a]gents, who come honey mouthed unto you, their only intent being to make profit by your inexperience," black leader Martin R. Delany warned a gathering of 500–600 freedpeople outside a brick church in St. Helena Island, South Carolina.[41] Stories abounded of fraudsters cheating farmers and then reselling crops at market price. Delany and other leaders understood that free labor alone was not enough to give the formerly enslaved a chance to earn a decent living.

Without capital or credit, few African Americans could make good on the promise of freedom. Radicals understood that, and when Congress authorized the Freedmen's Bureau in 1865, it also chartered the Freedman's Savings and Trust Company. Also known as the Freedman's Bank, it had thirty-seven branches operating by 1870. The bank accepted $57 million in deposits from 70,000 African Americans and made loans to black customers to start farms and businesses. Frederick Douglass was elected its president in 1874, but it went bankrupt as a result of the larger crisis of confidence and closed in 1874. The demise of the bank encouraged black distrust of banking institutions, and when it went out of business, depositors lost their assets.[42] Most African Americans had little

[40] Susan Eva O'Donovan, *Becoming Free in the Cotton South* (Cambridge, MA: Harvard University Press, 2007).

[41] Martin Delany to S. M. Taylor, July 24, 1865, in *Lift Every Voice: African American Oratory, 1787–1900*, ed. Philip S. Foner and Robert James Branham (Tuscaloosa, AL: University of Alabama Press, 1998), 448.

[42] Carl R. Osthaus, *Freedmen, Philanthropy, and Fraud: A History of the Freedman's Savings Bank* (Urbana, IL: University of Illinois Press, 1976).

access to credit outside face-to-face networks that usually included white landowners willing to advance credit solely if part of an agreement to work their land.

By the time the Thirteenth Amendment was ratified in December, the landscape of opportunity for African Americans already had been severely constricted. After touring the Deep South during the summer of 1865, General Schurz warned, "it is of the highest importance that the people lately in rebellion be not permitted to build up another 'peculiar institution' whose spirit is in conflict with the fundamental principles of our political system."[43] But by winter it seemed too late. Organized white Southern terrorist organizations like the Ku Klux Klan were already becoming an ugly appendage to state coercion.[44] Freedpeople protested. And when the 39th Congress met in December, Republicans faced the monumental task of arresting the process. It was time for repudiating the failed strategy of relying on moderates to temper the reactionary forces of slavery's resurgence. It was a time for a radicalism not contemplated during the war that did the seemingly impossible work of making former slaves into full citizens.

By the end of 1865, congressional Republicans were realizing that African Americans in the South were the sole available political allies, and an important opportunity to enfranchise them had been missed. The year had seen a tumultuous process of Union victory and emancipation in the spring followed by a swift and bitter reaction in the summer and fall, abetted by President Johnson and led by resurgent ex-Confederates. Confederate armies disbanded only to regroup at statehouses, commemorating the Confederate Lost Cause by pledging allegiance to a version of white supremacy that kept African Americans in slave-like conditions. To stem that tide of postwar reaction, congressional Republicans went to war with their own president. They refused to seat congressional delegations from ex-Confederate states and seized control of Reconstruction from the president early in 1866, passing the Civil Rights Act of 1866 and reauthorizing the Freedmen's Bureau over Johnson's vetoes. The Civil Rights Act invalidated state Black Codes, but many Southern states ignored it based on their assertion that the Thirteenth Amendment left civil rights to states. To make up for the lack of civil rights protections in

---

[43] Schurz, "Report of Carl Schurz," 46.
[44] Elaine Frantz Parsons, *Ku-Klux: The Birth of the Klan during Reconstruction* (Chapel Hill, NC: University of North Carolina Press, 2016).

the Thirteenth Amendment, Congress passed the Fourteenth Amendment in June 1866.

The Fourteenth Amendment contained the most sweeping civil rights provisions of any constitutional amendment to date. It guaranteed both US and state citizenship to "[a]ll persons born or naturalized in the United States, and subject to the jurisdiction thereof." It nationalized the Bill of Rights, extending to the states what had been restricted to the federal government. "No State shall make or enforce any law which shall abridge the privileges or immunities of citizens of the United States; nor shall any State deprive any person of life, liberty, or property, without due process of law; nor deny to any person within its jurisdiction the equal protection of the laws." This, combined with the Civil Rights Act, cut the legal heart out of Black Codes. Or so Radicals hoped.

Congress packed solutions to many festering postwar problems into the Fourteenth Amendment. It disqualified ex-Confederates from elective office and settled the issue of Confederate debt, denying any scheme to repay investors in the defunct Confederacy. Yet the Fourteenth Amendment stopped short of explicitly granting the right to vote to African Americans. It merely gave Congress the power to deny states that refused to extend the franchise to black men the corresponding proportion of their congressional delegation. If, for example, a state that was half African American barred African Americans from voting, then that state would lose half of its congressional representation. Even though the amendment swept away the Supreme Court's *Dred Scott* decision and boldly asserted equal protection of the laws, it too was a compromise among Radicals who insisted that the ballot box was the surest way to ensure equality and moderates who persisted in efforts to recruit white supremacists into the Republican Party. Legislators sent the Fourteenth Amendment to states for ratification, and President Johnson urged states not to approve the measure. To Republicans there was political benefit in this kind of aggressive legislating: African Americans made up the largest bloc of Union-loyal Southerners during the war and were potential Republican voters. But even before the ink was dry on the 1866 Civil Rights Act, violence broke out in Tennessee.

The Memphis Massacre of May 1866 showed both the tentative accomplishments and gruesome limitations of Reconstruction. Three days of anti-black violence left forty-six dead and scores more injured. More than ninety buildings were burned and wrecked, whole African American neighborhoods were gutted, and black residents were terrified. Many scattered. Violence started with a rumor of black-on-white crime:

black soldiers stationed at Fort Pickering on the city's south bluffs had allegedly killed white policemen attempting to arrest an African American soldier. The Civil Rights Act of 1866 ostensibly guaranteed citizens equal protection under the law and outlawed race-based discrimination. But in Memphis there was a lack of federal oversight. Murder, arson, rape, and assault were all state crimes, and even the presence of federal soldiers could not bring to heel determined ex-Confederates. Lack of federal oversight and enforcement can made a mockery of even the most robust civil rights laws.[45] The Memphis Massacre showed that progress did not prevent violence.

In many ways, Tennessee was a model of moderate reunification. The state had a Republican majority assembly and governor. Ulysses S. Grant would carry Memphis's Shelby County in two presidential elections – 1868 and 1872 – aided by African American men, to whom the state extended voting rights in 1867, three years before the Fifteenth Amendment guaranteeing the right to vote for all male citizens. During the Civil War, Memphis was a beacon to freedpeople. Union forces had captured it in June 1862, and the city on the Mississippi River attracted thousands of formerly enslaved people. It was diverse, too: by 1866, Memphis was home to Yankees, Jews, and Germans. The city was roughly one-fifth Irish, including 90 percent of its police and 87 percent of its fire department.

But as in so many corners of the Confederacy, the camps where former slaves lived swelled with the hungry, the sick, and those seeking opportunity and family. The Memphis refugee or contraband camps bred suspicion and hatred among local whites. Black Memphians competed with the Irish for low-paying jobs. Following the war's end – in Memphis as elsewhere in the former Confederacy – politicians prioritized peace with ex-Confederates over justice for African Americans.

Terror had become an instrument of politics. In the aftermath of the Memphis Massacre, neither state nor federal authorities arrested the attackers nor attempted prosecution. There was no Justice Department, and the attorney general's office was not prepared to prosecute federal civil rights cases. Despite the Civil Rights Act of 1866, federal civil rights

---

[45] Stephen V. Ash, *A Massacre in Memphis: The Race Riot That Shook the Nation One Year after the Civil War* (New York, NY: Hill and Wang, 2013); Calvin Schermerhorn, "Civil-Rights Laws Don't Always Stop Racism," *The Atlantic*, May 8, 2016, online: www .theatlantic.com/politics/archive/2016/05/the-memphis-massacre-of-1866-and-black -voter-suppression-today/481737/, accessed: August 1, 2016.

enforcement was lacking. Congress could make the law, but it was up to President Johnson to enforce it. The local army commander, General Stoneman, refused to intervene, the army not having a mandate to hold civilians accountable in military tribunals. Mayor John Park washed his hands of the matter. Congress investigated, producing a detailed report. But there were no arrests, no trials, and no convictions. Even if the Fourteenth Amendment seemed to solve some of the legal problems of Reconstruction, there was no political will to bring the perpetrators to justice. Down the Mississippi River, in New Orleans, racist violence broke out over the question of black political participation.

A civil war that supposedly settled the question of states' rights versus federal supremacy was reviving in the summer of 1866. In Louisiana, the overwhelmingly ex-Confederate legislature clashed with Republican Governor James Madison Wells, a Unionist and former sugar planter. Wells was no Radical but decided that enfranchising black men was the best antidote to the conservative ascendancy. The right to vote was becoming a matter of life and death as white citizens' clubs became the nucleus for an armed white supremacist insurgency. Wells joined Radicals in reconvening the constitutional convention in New Orleans, delegates exploiting a loophole in the 1864 convention, which adjourned with a provision that it might reconvene at a future date to finish unfinished work.

In New Orleans, just ten weeks after the Memphis Massacre, one of Reconstruction's deadliest days started over the refusal to accept civil rights as a verdict of the Civil War and, more broadly, how whites left behind tried to turn back the clock with violence. The New Orleans Massacre left forty-eight men dead and more than 200 injured, nearly all African Americans.[46] The massacre was naked political violence, organized beforehand, and directed at black delegates to the Louisiana constitutional convention of 1866. Attackers included policemen led by ex-Confederate Mayor John T. Monroe. It started on July 30, a hot summer day, after a gathering of more than 200 African American New Orleanians marched to drumbeats, beneath an American flag, on Burgundy Street to the Mechanic's Institute (now the Roosevelt Hotel on Canal Street and Roosevelt Way). "This was a procession of friends of the convention," a congressional investigation reported. "Many of them had canes and walking-sticks, but were otherwise unarmed." Many were

---

[46] James G. Hollandsworth Jr., *An Absolute Massacre: The New Orleans Race Riot of July 30, 1866* (Baton Rouge, LA: Louisiana State University Press, 2001).

Union war veterans, and thirty black delegates planned to take part in drafting a new state constitution that included the right to vote for all men.[47]

Police opened fire on the proceedings. "They fired at every colored man in sight," a witness testified.[48] Some black delegates took refuge inside, and the mob surrounded the building. Some shot through windows, seemingly indiscriminately. "We returned no shots from the Mechanic's Institute at all," New Orleans coroner (and assistant sergeant-at-arms for the convention) R. F. Daunoy told a congressional investigator, "all the shooting came from them."[49] Attackers reloaded and reorganized, battering down doors and gunning down African Americans. Black passersby were attacked, stabbed, clubbed, and shot. The city erupted in racial violence. Late in the afternoon federal troops arrived to restore order.

None of the attackers was charged, but the massacre sent another shockwave to Washington, DC, putting a gruesome head on a tortuous process of reunion. Congress soon discovered what most New Orleanians already knew, that the force attacking African Americans was composed of many ex-Confederates whose main qualification for police work was being a Confederate veteran. African American New Orleanian Albert Pitman put it more bluntly. The metropolitan police "were organized as 'thugs,'" he told investigators.[50] Others reported seeing badges of white supremacist organizations worn by attackers. In New Orleans as in Memphis there seemed to be a powerful interlocking force of state legislators, courts, political party organizations, and local officials terrorizing freedpeople.

African American reformers like William Wells Brown argued that without black civil rights, Reconstruction was in eminent danger of failing. A civil war fought for a new birth of freedom had not brought about the death of slavery. "The negro must be placed in a position to protect himself," Brown argued in 1867. "The Civil Rights Bill passed by Congress is almost a dead letter, and many of the rebel judges declare it unconstitutional." Massacres at Memphis and New Orleans underscored the necessity of a political solution, Brown contended, and "the only thing

---

[47] Thomas D. Eliot and Samuel Shellabarger, et al., *Report of the Select Committee on the New Orleans Riots* (Washington, DC: Government Printing Office, 1867), 5.

[48] *Report of the Select Committee on the New Orleans Riots*, 188.

[49] *Report of the Select Committee on the New Orleans Riots*, 136 (quotation); Frank J. Wetta, *The Louisiana Scalawags: Politics, Race, and Terrorism during the Civil War* (Baton Rouge, LA: Louisiana State University Press, 2013).

[50] *Report of the Select Committee on the New Orleans Riots*, 208.

to save him is the ballot. Liberty without equality is no boon." "Talk not of civil without political emancipation!"[51]

The violence in Memphis and New Orleans forced Congress to militarize Reconstruction. Gone was any moderate solution. In March 1867, congressional Republicans passed the Reconstruction Acts over President Johnson's vetoes dividing the old Confederacy into five military districts and requiring each state to ratify the Fourteenth Amendment before readmission. Johnson dug in, vetoing the Reconstruction Acts, which Congress overrode. To keep the president from appointing ex-Confederates to oversee the military phase of Reconstruction, Congress passed the Tenure of Office Act in March 1867, requiring the US Senate's approval before the president dismissed a cabinet officer. Johnson defied it, firing Secretary of War Edwin Stanton, and the House impeached him for it. That summer, the nation watched as the Senate held the first presidential impeachment trial, Johnson narrowly escaping removal from office by a single vote.

Military oversight provided security for civil rights reforms, but it remained difficult to administer states of the former Confederacy from Washington, DC. There was progress, however. Louisiana's 1868 constitution enfranchised black men, disenfranchised ex-Confederates, and laid the groundwork for readmission with black civil rights – four years after Lincoln's experiment. Freedman Oscar J. Dunne became Louisiana's first African American lieutenant governor in 1868, a position he held until his death in 1871. P. B. S. Pinchback was the first African American governor of Louisiana and the first black governor of any state, serving a thirty-five-day appointment from 1872 to 1873 after a bitterly contested election. Under the auspices of military Reconstruction, African Americans were elected to serve in influential government posts from local sheriffs and justices to state representatives and senators to the US Congress. Robert Smalls of South Carolina, former pilot and Rebel code stealer, became a US congressman. Reverend Hiram Rhodes Revels of Mississippi was elected in 1870 to fill the US Senate seat last held by Jefferson Davis.[52]

And yet while African Americans cast ballots and made up a loyal contingent of the Republican Party in the South, white supremacist forces continued to gather, organize, and dig in. Georgia Republican state

---

[51] William Wells Brown, *The Negro in the American Rebellion: His Heroism and His Fidelity* (Boston, MA: Lee and Shepard, 1867), 355–56.

[52] Philip Dray, *Capitol Men: The Epic Story of Reconstruction through the Lives of the First Black Congressmen* (New York, NY: Houghton Mifflin, 2008).

senator Benjamin F. Conley reported in 1870 "that, in many portions of Georgia, there has been no justice, no enforcement of law, no maintenance of order; that juries have been prejudiced and overawed by bands of prowling assassins; that magistrates have refused to do their duty, or done wrong in cases where the rights of certain classes of our citizens have been involved. In fact, that while some have cried 'peace, peace,' there has been no peace."[53]

The overture provided by Andrew Johnson's immediate postwar policies had emboldened the forces of reaction. A *Harper's Weekly* writer summed up Reconstruction's failures in 1868. Confederates lost the war, he wrote. "But defeat never converts. It is to the defeated what persecution is to the persecuted. The cause becomes even more precious, and fidelity to it a more sacred duty. The history of the Southern States since the surrender shows this plainly." Ex-Confederate intransigence proved more tenacious than any civil rights protections that followed, "the old spirit stealthily reveal[ed] its old character wholly alert and unchanged. The Black [C]odes; the reluctant legislation upon secession and emancipation; the denunciation and hatred of Union soldiers and loyal citizens; the massacres at Memphis and New Orleans; the refusals of the [Fourteenth] [A]mendment; the terrorism at elections, were signs of the old vigor."[54]

The "old vigor" flared in white supremacist violence in Pulaski, Tennessee, in the summer of 1867, and in Opelousas, Louisiana, in 1868, amid widespread lynching, arson, and terrorism against African Americans. The Opelousas Massacre was carried out by a chapter of the Knights of the White Camellia, a white Democratic paramilitary group not unlike the Ku Klux Klan. It started in a clash of black Republican and white Democratic political clubs. African Americans protesting the apparent murder of a Republican journalist were ambushed and taken prisoner by the heavily armed Democratic partisans. At least thirty were killed, many after being captured, in the weeks before the 1868 presidential election. Reconstruction violence needed a political solution and firm federal enforcement.

General Ulysses Grant had won the Union war, and he was elected president in 1868 to win the peace. He was a reluctant candidate, but Grant was coming around to the Radicals' insistence that African

---

[53] Benjamin F. Conley to Georgia State Senate, January 8, 1870, *Journal of the Senate of the State of Georgia January 10, 1870* (Atlanta, GA: Public Printer, 1870), 27.

[54] [Anon.] "What! Old Mole!" *Harpers Weekly: A Journal of Civilization*, August 22, 1868, 530.

Americans' voting rights were critical to the future of the Republican Party in the South and the salvation of Reconstruction. All understood that black voters needed to be allowed to elect representatives that would protect and not attack and terrorize them. Grant was popular among African Americans in the South and rank-and-file voters in the North. He won a decisive electoral victory in the 1868 presidential election against an overtly white supremacist opponent, Democrat Horatio Seymour of New York. And he won on the margin of African American votes in Southern states.

Between Ulysses S. Grant's election and inauguration, Congress again used a lame duck session to pass the third and last Reconstruction amendment to the Constitution. The Fifteenth Amendment was supposed to finish the work left undone by the Thirteenth and Fourteenth Amendments. "The right of citizens of the United States to vote shall not be denied or abridged by the United States or by any State on account of race, color, or previous condition of servitude," it declared, and Congress would have the power to enforce it. "Never was a revolution more complete," Frederick Douglass cheered in April 1870, after the Fifteenth Amendment was ratified. "The black man is free, the black man is a citizen, the black man is enfranchised, and this by the organic law of the land.... Today we are free citizens."[55] Yet constitutional amendments did not by themselves turn back the massive resistance among ex-Confederates.

African American political participation needed to be protected against the kinds of violence that characterized the Memphis and New Orleans massacres. And so the Grant administration put teeth in federal civil rights measures. Grant was not a believer in racial equality, but sided with African American veterans and against those he deemed to be violating the Civil War's verdict. And yet Grant's administration faced new perils, some of its own making.

The reform momentum of the 1868 election was blunted as ex-Confederate states rejoined the Union. And domestic corruption, including the New York Gold Conspiracy of 1869, the Crédit Mobilier scandal of 1872, the Whiskey Ring scandal of 1875, and ongoing railroad chicanery, exposed corruption in Congress and the Grant administration. Voters rebelled and diluted Republican majorities. Congressional Republican supermajorities that had overridden Johnson's vetoes declined into

---

[55] Frederick Douglass, "At Last, At Last, The Black Man Has a Future," April 22, 1870, *The Frederick Douglass Papers, Series 1, Vol. 4*, 266–67.

a simple majority. Leading radicals like Thaddeus Stevens had died. Radicals like Charles Sumner ran afoul of Grant. Nevertheless, Congress passed key legislation outlawing both state and private violence against African Americans, including the Enforcement Acts of 1870 and 1871, also known as the Ku Klux Klan Act, reenacting the 1866 Civil Rights Act under the auspices of the Fourteenth Amendment. The 1871 Klan Act further penalized private and organizational violence under the authority of the Fifteenth Amendment.

The Grant administration's enforcement was valiant but uneven. In 1871, the federal government placed nine South Carolina counties under martial law, and federal courts convicted more than 100 defendants charged under these acts. In 1872 and 1873, courts made close to 900 total convictions in the South. But dismissals outnumbered convictions in 1873. The Panic of 1873 betokened a wider crisis of confidence, some born of suspicion that government was corrupt. Economic hard times set in, Northern voters lost interest in Reconstruction, and the political will to protect African American civil rights dissipated. Nearly 90 percent of cases brought under the enforcement acts in 1874 were dismissed. And as states of the old Confederacy ratified the Fourteenth and Fifteenth Amendments, federal troops were removed.

And as federal troops retreated, political violence against African Americans increased. And even though soldiers remained in Louisiana, camps of federal troops could not prevent the 1873 Colfax Massacre of more than eighty African Americans – perhaps many more – in Grant Parish, Louisiana. The massacre brought to a head a political crisis in the state. In 1872 Louisiana elected two rival administrations, one a Republican government recognized by the Grant administration and Congress and a Democratic government rival that was openly collaborating with white supremacist paramilitaries. By then the Louisiana Republican party was in turmoil with radical and moderate factions stabbing each other in the back. Republican William Pitt Kellogg won the governorship. Democrats united in opposition, overthrowing the Kellogg government for most of 1873. Dual appointments of law enforcement and court officials in Grant Parish led to the conflicts that erupted in the Colfax Massacre. Scores of African American citizens took refuge in the Colfax courthouse while white militiamen attacked and burned it, executing any black man who surrendered while hunting down those suspected of supporting the Republicans. Scores were executed in cold blood, shot in the back of the head. Federal officials investigated and charged several of the perpetrators under the civil rights and enforcement acts.[56] But by then it was becoming clear that public support in the North had waned. Reconstruction foundered on Grant administration scandals, economic hard times, and even outright enmity for African Americans whom many considered the recipients of undeserved welfare.[57]

By 1876, Reconstruction was in full retreat and, with it, federal civil rights protections. That year, the number of federal civil rights convictions plummeted to nearly zero, and the US Supreme Court retreated on civil rights. *United States* v. *Cruikshank* was a case involving three men convicted in the Colfax Massacre who appealed their federal civil rights convictions to the high court. The unanimous decision, handed down by Chief Justice R. Morrison Waite – who had been nominated by President Grant – held the perpetrators of the 1873 Colfax Massacre in Louisiana could not be convicted for federal civil rights violations because the Fourteenth Amendment's Equal Protection Clause did not extend to individuals' crimes, just state actions. The justices ignored the fact that perpetrators of the Colfax Massacre targeted politically active African Americans. And later that year, the presidential election of 1876 sealed the fate of militarized Reconstruction.[58]

It was a tragic end to what might have been a "glorious second American Revolution."[59] The Republican nominee, Rutherford B. Hayes, lost the popular vote to Democrat Samuel Tilden, and election results were disputed in three Southern states, Florida, Louisiana, and South Carolina. Congress convened an electoral commission early in 1877, which through a series of contingent events selected Hayes. Civil unrest spread in many corners of the country. Outraged Democrats threatened secession, and Republicans promised another civil war should their side lose. In a conference in February 1877, Republicans reached a corrupt bargain with Democrats, allowing Hayes to ascend to the presidency in exchange for the end of military Reconstruction in the former Confederate states and a federal blessing on the rule of white insurgents.

---

[56] Charles Lane, *The Day Freedom Died: The Colfax Massacre, the Supreme Court, and the Betrayal of Reconstruction* (New York, NY: Henry Holt, 2008).

[57] Heather Cox Richardson, *The Death of Reconstruction: Race, Labor, and Politics in the Post–Civil War North, 1865–1901* (Cambridge, MA: Harvard University Press, 2001).

[58] David W. Blight, *Frederick Douglass' Civil War: Keeping Faith in Jubilee* (Baton Rouge, LA: Louisiana State University Press, 1989), 221 (quotations); Richard M. Valelly, *The Two Reconstructions: The Struggle for Black Enfranchisement* (Chicago, IL: University of Chicago Press, 2004), chap. 3.

[59] *Principia*, May 4, 1861, cited in James McPherson, *Battle Cry of Freedom: The Civil War Era* (New York, NY: Oxford University Press, 1988), 358.

African American civil rights eroded further as white supremacists retook statehouses and disenfranchised African Americans. Pockets of black political activism and voting remained, and some representatives in heavily African American districts in states like South Carolina and Texas continued to serve. But the 1880s saw the rise of Jim Crow. "The future historian will turn to the year 1883," Frederick Douglass mourned, "to find the most flagrant example of this national deterioration." That year the US Supreme Court ruled 8–1 in *United States v. Stanley* – in a decision called collectively the Civil Rights Cases – on gutting the Civil Rights Act of 1875 and abandoning civil rights for African Americans. The majority held that the Fourteenth Amendment did not prevent discrimination in public accommodations such as railroads, restaurants, theaters, and hotels because those were not state-owned properties. It also held that the Thirteenth Amendment did not extend any civil rights protections to African Americans. Douglass framed the decision as part of a betrayal of the Civil War and African American sacrifices for the cause of Union. "From the hour that the loyal North began to fraternize with the disloyal and South, from the hour they began to 'shake hands over the bloody chasm,' from that hour the cause of justice to the black man began to decline and lose its hold on the public mind, and it has lost ground ever since."[60] Lynchings of black men rose dramatically after the 1870s, peaking in the 1890s.[61]

In giving up the cause of civil rights, Republicans sacrificed justice for reconciliation. The white South, having lost the war, had won the peace. The fragile gains African-descended people made in the eight years between 1866 and 1872 were reversed in a retreat from Reconstruction after 1873.[62] During those hopeful years, the political victories African Americans were able to achieve were not enough to change the economic calculations in which they lived their lives. Political participation held out a fleeting hope of gaining an economic footing that would support social advancement.

---

[60] Douglass, *Life and Times of Frederick Douglass*, 652–53 (quotations).

[61] Christopher J. Waldrep, *Rough Justice: Lynching and American Society, 1874–1947* (Urbana, IL: University of Illinois Press, 2004).

[62] A. J. Langguth, *After Lincoln: How the North Won the Civil War and Lost the Peace* (New York, NY: Simon and Schuster, 2014).

Conclusion

Reconstruction was in a profound way a second American Revolution. Like the Revolution, the Civil War brought sweeping changes as it brought terrible destruction, but the political landscape that took shape after the Civil War held the promise of a revolution that extended freedom's promise to those who had been deprived of the rights and liberties of citizenship. The Thirteenth Amendment abolished chattel slavery, ending enslavers' constitutional protections for property in people. The Fourteenth Amendment guaranteed equal protection of the laws, birthright citizenship, and extended the federal Bill of Rights to the states. And the Fifteenth Amendment enshrined the right to vote, at least for adult males, regardless of race or heritage of slavery. Millions who had been enslaved were eligible for citizenship, and the principle of individual rights for all Americans was reestablished while it was expanded. In districts and counties in which African Americans constituted an overwhelming majority, black political participation and leadership remained palpable even after 1873. That was the result of massive black political mobilization, as spontaneous as it was savvy. Its leaders and supporters accomplished a stunning set of achievements in building schools, places of worship, and political hubs.[1] Many African American and Radical leaders rose into local, state, and national leadership positions as sheriffs, justices, mayors, delegates, congressmen, and senators. Virginia native Blanche K. Bruce was born in slavery in 1841, yet served in the US Senate representing Mississippi from 1875 to 1881. Thousands more became teachers,

---

[1] Stephen Hahn, *A Nation under Our Feet: Black Political Struggles in the Rural South from Slavery to the Great Migration* (Cambridge, MA: Harvard University Press, 2005).

pastors and ministers, lawyers, and doctors. Schooling and mutual assistance gave the next generation chances those born enslaved had not seen. And black landownership rose dramatically. One in four Southern black farmers owned their own farms by 1900, just thirty-five years after slavery ended. In South Carolina in 1900, nearly 30 percent of farm owners were African-descended. Large estates tended to be held by whites, and black farmers owned fewer lands in cotton areas than in the upper South, but that advance is remarkable by any measure.[2] Yet the rearguard actions of valiant African American activists could not roll back a gathering storm of reaction as the states of the vanquished Confederacy returned to white supremacist rule.

America's second revolution still fell far short of its goals. Reconstruction's failures stand in relief precisely because of its successes and accomplishments. As W. E. B. Du Bois explained, "[t]he attempt to make black men American citizens was in a certain sense all a failure, but a splendid failure."[3] Congressional Reconstruction failed to achieve civil equality or widespread opportunity. What made it splendid was the audacity of the project as it took shape after 1865. "Its very comprehensiveness exposed many flanks," argues a historian.[4] And like the Civil War, the push for justice for African Americans required victory. The push back toward slavery was like a war of attrition. "The slave went free; stood a brief moment in the sun; then moved back again toward slavery."[5]

White conservatives in the South rallied around a banner of redemption, a euphemism for reversing Reconstruction's accomplishments. In some ways, the radical vision involved an impossible task. Slavery's two-and-a-half-centuries-long legacy of racism excluded African Americans from the possibility of citizenship in the minds of most whites, no matter what the laws or the Constitution held. In 1870, Frederick Douglass argued that "slavery has left its poison behind ... both in the veins of the slaves and those of the enslaver." The "settled habits of a nation," he contended, are "mightier than statute." Reconstruction foundered on ex-Confederate intransigence and Northern antipathy

---

[2] Edward L. Ayers, *The Promise of the New South: Life after Reconstruction*, 2nd edn. (New York, NY: Oxford University Press, 2007), 208, 519–20, n. 60.

[3] W. E. B. Du Bois, *Black Reconstruction in America, 1860–1880* (New York, NY: Free Press, [1935] 1998), 708.

[4] Edward L. Ayers, *The Thin Light of Freedom: The Civil War and Emancipation in the Heart of America* (New York, NY: W. W. Norton, 2017), 460.

[5] Du Bois, *Black Reconstruction*, 30.

toward African-descended people.[6] Freedom without civil rights was no true freedom. Liberty without opportunity was no real liberty.

In many areas of the cotton South, the afterlife of slavery was a grinding cycle of toil and debt. Forced labor crept back into the structure of African American life. In the sugar parishes of southern Louisiana, formerly enslaved people's working lives suffered setbacks after a brief postwar boost. Sugarcane cutters toiled in gangs, lived in repurposed slave quarters, ate at the pleasure of growers, and earned starvation wages in scrip redeemable solely at plantation stores for overpriced items.[7] In cotton regions, immediate postwar labor contracts gave way to tenancy and sharecropping in which a farmer rented land from the owner by promising to pay a percentage of the harvest. Usually, sharecroppers also had to borrow against a further portion to buy seeds, farm animals, food, clothing, medical care, transportation, and other necessities. Owners heaped interest on top of what were often high prices and exorbitant rents. Most croppers or tenants had no other option.

But at least sharecropping preserved family togetherness under a rented roof. Families lived together without an enslaver carrying off a spouse, sibling, or child. There were no prohibitions on reading, even if schooling was hard to come by. Still, social relations remained strained as sharecropping families struggled to stay afloat. Many pledged more than 100 percent of their annual crops, and even those who were fortunate or exceptionally diligent faced other hurdles. Those who did so faced a choiceless choice of debt bondage or starvation. Landowners supervised contracts and did the accounting. Some cheated sharecroppers. Freedpeople who had been deprived of an education were at the mercy of former enslavers when it came to settling accounts. Retreat from Reconstruction put many courts and legal protections off limits to African Americans, and sharecropping did not end until the 1930s when a combination of New Deal policies and mechanical harvesters drove them off the land. By then African Americans were leaving the South in the Great Migration north and west, seeking opportunities in places where Jim Crow's grasp was not so pernicious.[8]

---

[6] Douglass quoted in *Slavery's Ghost: The Problem of Freedom in the Age of Emancipation*, ed. Richard Follett, Eric Foner, and Walter Johnson (Baltimore, MD: Johns Hopkins University Press, 2011), 7; Michael W. Fitzgerald, *Splendid Failure: Postwar Reconstruction in the American South* (Chicago, IL: Ivan R. Dee Publishers, 2007).

[7] John DeSantis, *The Thibodaux Massacre: Racial Violence and the 1887 Sugar Cane Labor Strike* (Charleston, SC: The History Press, 2016).

[8] Isabel Wilkerson, *The Warmth of Other Suns: The Epic Story of America's Great Migration* (New York, NY: Random House, 2010).

At the same time, the promise of the New South lay in shifts from cotton and corn to extractive and processing industries such as timber, meat production, factories, and processing facilities. But that promise largely excluded African Americans. Southern cities like Atlanta rebuilt, rising along with new cities like Birmingham, Alabama. White Southerners embraced new technologies even as they channeled racist violence into a new Jim Crow order of legal segregation, including a wave of new state constitutions writing black and white inequality into the fundamental law beginning in 1890. African Americans fought back. There were middle-class African American enclaves in cities like Memphis, where Ida B. Wells launched her anti-lynching campaign in 1892 that found allies in a far-flung Atlantic network. Many migrated within the South, finding opportunities to own land in places like northwestern Mississippi.[9] The forces of white reaction were in tension with those of black freedom. After segregation became law, it would take ninety years for the state-built edifice of Jim Crow to be compromised by the Civil Rights Acts of 1957, 1960, and 1964. It took ninety-five years between the Fifteenth and final Reconstruction Amendment and the Voting Rights Act of 1965 to sweep away disenfranchisement for most African Americans. But after the Civil Rights Era, the forces of reaction regrouped. Half a century after the Voting Rights Act, black voting rights were under assault again through voter identification laws targeting minorities. The US Supreme Court gutted the Voting Rights Act when it struck down key provisions in *Shelby County v. Holder* (2013). The rollback of civil rights in the twenty-first century is redolent of the way attempts to fulfill the promises of Reconstruction were undermined in the years after it ended.

Labor was supposed to be a path to uplift. But as civil rights protections eroded and opportunities closed after Reconstruction, African Americans faced many obstacles to getting paid fairly for their work. Race trumped class when it came to worker organizing. African-descended sugar workers in Louisiana organized under the Knights of Labor and struck over punishing working conditions in 1887. The swift and brutal white response to black sugar strikers was known as the Thibodaux Massacre. Some sixty African American strikers and their family members were murdered in November 1887. Perpetrators were never brought to justice,

---

[9] Sarah L. Silkey, *Black Woman Reformer: Ida B. Wells, Lynching, and Transatlantic Activism* (Athens, GA: University of Georgia Press, 2015).

and workers returned to the fields on owners' terms.[10] Labor solidarity between black and white workers foundered on racist divisions, which drove down all workers' wages, and black farm workers would not organize again in the South until the 1930s. New South boosters made Jim Crow's evils a virtue when they invited in businesses seeking low pay and a nonunion workforce divided by race.[11] And even in the twenty-first century, the Southeast has the lowest wages of any region of the United States, and the seven least-unionized states are all members of the former Confederacy.

Convict leasing in the Jim Crow South brought industries seeking cheap prison labor as the criminal justice system shifted from punishing whites in the prewar South to punishing blacks with a vengeance after slavery. Some 800,000 African Americans in the South were subject to a corrupt judicial system that sent them to unpaid work in mines, factories, farms, and swamps between the end of the Civil War and the beginning of World War II. Twenty-two-year-old Green Cottenham was arrested for vagrancy in 1908 in Shelby County, Alabama. Sentenced to thirty days' hard labor for being unable to prove he was employed, the term was extended to a year when he could not pay court fees. "Cottenham's offense was blackness," argues Douglas A. Blackmon. And he paid with his life after being leased to the U.S. Steel Corporation to work unloading eight tons of coal from a mine car each day under an overseer's whip.[12] John Henry, the famous Steel Drivin' Man of folk music legend, was Prisoner 497 in the Richmond Penitentiary, hired out to the C&O Railroad to dig a tunnel through Virginia's Blue Ridge Mountains. He died of silicosis as a result of poor job safety. But the only requirement from the prison was that his body be returned to be buried in the sandlot adjacent to the prison, a death penalty for which his family received no apology or compensation.[13] Often local law enforcement entrapped promising young workers since companies paid wages to the county for bound workers like Cottenham or Henry. Convict leasing kept

[10] DeSantis, *The Thibodaux Massacre;* John C. Rodrigue, *Reconstruction in the Cane Fields: From Slavery to Free Labor in Louisiana's Sugar Parishes, 1862–1880* (Baton Rouge, LA: Louisiana State University Press, 2001).

[11] James C. Cobb, *Selling the South: The Southern Crusade for Industrial Development, 1936–1990,* 2nd edn. (Urbana and Chicago, IL: University of Illinois Press, 1993).

[12] Douglas A. Blackmon, *Slavery by Another Name: The Re-Enslavement of Black Americans from the Civil War to World War II* (New York, NY: Anchor Books, 2008).

[13] Scott Reynolds Nelson, *Steel Drivin' Man: John Henry, the Untold Story of an American Legend* (New York, NY: Oxford University Press, 2006).

taxes low so long as revenues were paid by companies economizing with judicially forced laborers. In many cases, all a white witness had to do was point a finger and say a black person owed a debt. Women and children were swept up in the system too.[14] And the constellation of re-enslavement schemes, debt peonage, and civic exclusion impoverished generations of nominally free people of African descent.

The historical momentum of slavery that stole the wages and hampered the transmission of wealth down generations of enslaved Americans continues. "The sins of slavery did not stop with slavery," argues Ta-Nehisi Coates. Making the case for reparations for slavery, he contends, "[o]n the contrary, slavery was but the initial crime in a long tradition of crimes, of plunder even, that could be traced into the present day."[15] Freedpeople received no pensions or reparations for slavery. Civil rights were supposed to provide the basis of economic uplift, but that progress was mired in slavery's legacy. Even after 1865, wealth had trouble sticking to African Americans because they owned precious little capital and because freedpeople began the contest of upward social mobility 250 years behind other Americans. Whites who emigrated to the United States got a head start since they were not subject to civic exclusions and predatory social and legal circumstances.

As in slavery, Jim Crow–era theft of wages limited the accumulation and transmission of capital down the generations. Convict leasing attenuated during World War II, but its sequel is mass incarceration of African Americans, a practice that increased dramatically in the late twentieth and early twenty-first centuries. Black men are several times more likely to be sent to prison as white men. And Mississippian Jarvious Cotton is an example of how slavery's poison still runs in the national veins. "Cotton's great-great-grandfather could not vote as a slave," argues Michelle Alexander. "His great-grandfather was beaten to death by the Klu Klux Klan for attempting to vote. His grandfather was prevented from voting by Klan intimidation; his father was barred by poll taxes and literacy tests. Today, Cotton cannot vote because he, like many black men

---

[14] Sarah Haley, *No Mercy Here: Gender, Punishment, and the Making of Jim Crow Modernity* (Chapel Hill, NC: University of North Carolina Press, 2016); Talitha L. LeFlouria, *Chained in Silence: Black Women and Convict Labor in the New South* (Chapel Hill, NC: University of North Carolina Press, 2016).

[15] Ta-Nehisi Coates, *We Were Eight Years in Power: An American Tragedy* (New York, NY: One World, 2017), 158 (quotations); Ana Lucia Araujo, *Reparations for Slavery and the Slave Trade: A Transnational and Comparative History* (London and New York, NY: Bloomsbury, 2017).

in the United States, has been labeled a felon and is currently on parole."
Mississippi forbids felons from casting a vote, and Cotton is among them.
In 2015, it was estimated that 1.5 million African American men are
missing from America's homes and streets as a result of early deaths and
mass incarceration. Cities with the widest gaps include North Charleston,
South Carolina, and Ferguson, Missouri, sites of high-profile killings of
unarmed black men by police in the 2010s.[16] That is not coincidental.

Federal housing policies foreclosed on opportunities to live and work in
prosperous areas for African Americans during the New Deal and in the
post–World War II housing boom. When the federal government built
public housing in non-segregated urban areas, it segregated units, which
led to separate neighborhoods, schools, and consequent opportunities.
When homebuilders lured workers to suburbs, the federal government
provided loan guarantees and other protections so long as dwellings were
owned and occupied by whites. Rising home values, well-funded schools,
and other related advantages accrued disproportionately to whites as
a consequence of government programs that segregated cities and suburbs. Public housing, once a respectable option for urban workers regardless of race, became associated with poor, black, and broken families.
As American urban centers deindustrialized, the once-high-paying jobs
disappeared. They did so at exactly the time union strength began to
weaken and wages fell for workers. A terrible irony of the Civil Rights
Era of the 1960s and 1970s was that civic gains in voting and legal rights
such as antidiscrimination in housing came at exactly the moment worker
wages declined and inequalities of income began to divide rich and poor
Americans as never before. And black people largely missed out on the
wealth accumulation of whites' rising home values and consequently
better-funded schools and more abundant social services. Pollution and
poor public health exacerbated income inequalities. Environmental
racism became a consequence of polluters' moving into where African-
descended people were forced to live, harming children who drank water
poisoned with lead and breathed air choked with industrial contaminants.
The mutually reinforcing legacies of slavery are visible in other stark
measures. By the twenty-first century, African Americans earned sixty

---

[16] Michelle Alexander, *The New Jim Crow: Mass Incarceration in the Age of
Colorblindness* (New York, NY: New Press, 2010), 1 (quotations); Justin Wolfers,
David Leonhardt, and Kevin Quealy, "1.5 Million Missing Black Men," *New York
Times*, April 20, 2015, www.nytimes.com/interactive/2015/04/20/upshot/missing-black
-men.html, accessed: April 30, 2017.

cents on the dollar compared to whites while white Americans owned ten times the wealth of black Americans per capita.[17] It is difficult to dismiss the legacy of forced labor and an institution of racial control over African Americans for the lasting legacy of US slavery. And in many profound ways Americans are still paying slavery's costs.

---

[17] Richard Rothstein, *The Color of Law: A Forgotten History of How Our Government Segregated America* (New York, NY: Liveright, 2017); Dorceta E. Taylor, *Toxic Communities: Environmental Racism, Industrial Pollution, and Residential Mobility* (New York, NY: New York University Press, 2014).

Index